KAPLAN

Other Kaplan Books to Help You Succeed After Graduating from College

The Buck Starts Here: The Beginner's Guide to Smart Financial Choices
Business School Admissions Adviser
Going Indie: Self-Employment, Freelance, and Temping Opportunities
John Douglas's Guide to Careers in the FBI
Law School Admissions Adviser
Medical School Admissions Adviser
Reality 101
Résumé Builder with Career Counselor
Student's Guide to On-Campus Job Recruitment
Yale Daily News *Guide to Internships 1999*

OLDEST COLLEGE DAILY — FOUNDED JANUARY 28, 1878

Yale Daily News Guide to Fellowships and Grants 1999

By Ali Mohamadi

Simon & Schuster

Kaplan Books
Published by Kaplan Educational Centers and Simon & Schuster
1230 Avenue of the Americas
New York, NY 10020

For bulk sales to schools, colleges, and universities, please contact Vice President for Special Markets, Simon & Schuster Special Markets, 1633 Broadway, 8th Floor, New York, NY 10019.

Project Editor: Julie Schmidt
Cover Design: Cheung Tai
Database Administrator: Enid Burns
Production Editor: Maude Spekes
Desktop Publishing Manager: Michael Shevlin
Managing Editor: Brent Gallenberger
Executive Editor: Del Franz

Special thanks to Amy Arner Sgarro, Jude Bond, McElroy Consulting Associates, Kiernan McGuire, and Sara Pearl.

Manufactured in the United States of America
Published simultaneously in Canada

August 1998
10 9 8 7 6 5 4 3 2 1

ISBN: 0-684-85240-3
ISSN: 1096-813X

About the Author

Ali Mohamadi hails from Washington, D.C. and is a 1998 graduate of Yale University. At Yale, Ali majored in biology and served as sports editor of the *Yale Daily News*. A victim of the medical school application process, he plans to enjoy life after college by subjecting himself to over a decade of servitude as a medical student.

About the Contributors

Jake Sullivan majored in political science and international studies at Yale, where he was the 1997–97 editor in chief of the *Yale Daily News*. After graduating in 1998, he will spend a year as a Rhodes scholar at Oxford University and obtain a master's degree in international relations. Jake, who was also a recipient of the Marshall Scholarship and the Truman Scholarship, plans to attend law school and pursue a career in diplomatic and international law.

Special thanks are due to the following people: Karen Abrecht, Herbert Allen, Mackenzie Baris, Christopher Deutsch, Daniel Fleschner, Erik Johnson, Katie Lindgren, James McGuire, Milan Milenkovic, Sung Il Moon, Matthew Obernauer, Zachary Pines, Asher Price, Letitia Stein, Alexander Taylor, and Benjamin Trachtenberg. This book would not have been possible without their assistance.

Yale Daily News

OLDEST COLLEGE DAILY | FOUNDED JANUARY 28, 1878

Founded on January 28, 1878, the *Yale Daily News* is the oldest college daily paper in the United States. The all-student staff publishes a 10- to 16-page newspaper five nights a week, reporting stories related to the Yale and New Haven communities. Financially independent from the university, the *Yale Daily News* supports its own production through student-sold advertising.

Boasting an alumni list that includes Henry Luce, Sargent Shriver, Potter Stewart, William F. Buckley Jr., Garry Trudeau, Calvin Trillin, and Shelley Fisher Fishkin, the *Yale Daily News* has been called the best unofficial undergraduate school of journalism. Today's *Yale Daily News* remains committed to the mission of teaching journalism, conducting skills workshops, and hosting alumni speakers.

In addition to the daily newspaper, the *Yale Daily News* publishes a weekly news magazine, a monthly compilation of stories, and the *Insider's Guide to the Colleges*—a guidebook to the nation's colleges created by interviewing current undergraduates.

Most recently, the *Yale Daily News* has entered a joint venture with Kaplan Books and Simon & Schuster to produce a series of guide books to assist and advise students throughout their college careers. Titles include *Yale Daily News Guide to Succeeding in College*, *Yale Daily News Guide to Internships*, and this publication, *Yale Daily News Guide to Fellowships and Grants.* Authored by staff members of the *Yale Daily News*, all the books offer valuable tips for college success drawn from the experiences of actual students.

Foreword

by Jake Sullivan

Applying for a fellowship is like playing a high stakes game of craps. You need a certain level of achievement, preparation, and dedication to get a seat at the table, and then it's just a roll of the dice. I say this not to imply that fellowship selection is random, but rather to acknowledge the extremely stiff competition, flexible selection criteria (interpreted differently by each panelist), and large number of variables that play a role in the selection process. My approach to the competitions was to recognize the long odds I faced, and then do everything in my power to shorten them. Just as you can't will the dice to come up seven each time, you can't punch in a formula that guarantees selection. But there are clear steps you can take to at least somewhat load the dice. That's where this book comes in.

Above all, I realized that applying for a fellowship is not something to do on a lark—it takes intense thinking, planning, and execution. For example, in writing my personal statements, I needed to condense my past achievements, present activities, and future plans into 1,000 words or less. The first draft I wrote required 3,000. After four months of rewriting based on consultations with my mentors and parents, I finally turned a certain recipe for rejection into an image on paper that accurately reflected me as a person. From that first draft to the final product, a grand total of fifteen or twenty words remained the same.

The mechanics of condensing my life into 1,000 words was not as daunting a task as answering the all-important questions of which fellowships were right for me and what opportunities they would provide. Before I got into the "how" of applying, I needed to address the "why." Applying for fellowships and grants is a heck of an investment, and I wanted to be sure the ones I had selected would lead me down the right path before I set out to win them. I spent days thinking about my goals and aspirations before jumping into the fray. Ultimately, I came to view the fellowships I was seeking as a chance to broaden both my intellectual and cultural horizons in order to become a more effective scholar or policymaker.

Finally, a word about the interviews. A lot of fellowship competitions have them, and they are the single biggest turn-off to prospective applicants. Let's face it, how many of us relish the prospect of squaring off against experienced experts as they grill us on a range of esoteric subjects? In the abstract, it's about as appealing as 8:00 A.M. classes. But I came to realize through my experiences that the interviews are the most effective way for committees to make final selections. The panels learn most about you by making you think and articulate on your feet. This in its turn offers you great preparation for all sorts of situations in both the academic and professional worlds. Remember, the committees are not there to humiliate you. They are there to give you a chance to prove yourself. I went in with this perspective in mind, and I seized my opportunity.

There is no one way to win a fellowship, no one reason to apply, and no one type to chase after. There are, however, hundreds of cliches that apply to the fellowship process: be prepared, plan ahead, stay focused, and so on. So read this book, get a sense of the steps you must take and the type of fellowship you want, and keep in mind the most important cliche of all: Be yourself.

Editor's Note: Jake Sullivan applied for, and won, three of the most prestigious fellowships available to graduate students: the Rhodes Scholarship, the Marshall Scholarship, and the Truman Scholarship. In his capacity as editor in chief of the Yale Daily News, *he formulated the proposal for this book and served as an adviser to the author during its writing.*

Preface

by Ali Mohamadi

What on Earth are fellowships and grants? And why apply for them? Those were the questions I asked myself in the summer of 1997 as I prepared for my senior year in college and for the unknown future that lay directly ahead. In the process of researching and writing the *Yale Daily News Guide to Fellowships and Grants*, I've discovered the answers.

This book is both a manual on how to apply for fellowships and grants and a guide to over 500 of the world's best opportunities. Your first step should be to look through the first four chapters, which detail the intricacies of the application process. These early chapters will provide you with the background you need to make an informed decision about whether or not you should apply for a fellowship or grant. They will also guide you through the task of narrowing down your list of awards. The rest of the book offers data on 11 categories of awards, including key contact addresses, phone numbers, and selection criteria, with short pieces of advice on how to apply for these different types of awards. These listings will be a useful resource for you once you've decided what type of fellowship or grant you want.

The content of this book was drawn in part from surveys sent out to award-issuing organizations and undergraduate career/fellowship advisors. You will also find tips, pointers, and personal anecdotes from the real experts in the fellowship and grant field: those who have applied for them. The *Yale Daily News Guide to Fellowships and Grants* is packed with unique perspectives on what worked—and didn't work—for these applicants.

What made the experience of writing this book enjoyable and worthwhile for me was that by the time I had completed my work, I had come to the conclusion that applying for a fellowship or grant was something that would greatly augment my ability to reach my ultimate goals in life. If you've already decided likewise, I hope this book helps you make the right choices along the way. And if you've never before given much thought to what makes these awards special, I hope that this book opens a few new windows of opportunity for you.

Good luck, and here's to the future!

Yale Daily News
OLDEST COLLEGE DAILY FOUNDED JANUARY 28, 1878

The Application Process

An Introduction to Fellowships and Grants

1

The Real World. It's more than just a hot show on MTV. It's the place where fun-loving college kids often go to die. Unfortunately, it isn't all fun and games once you get shoved out of your dorm and onto the mean streets of life after college. It's tough to make it out there. But it's anything but impossible—all you've got to do is figure out how!

Any way you slice it, the real world definitely isn't the same one your parents entered not so long ago. But you have one key advantage over Mom and Dad that could end up making all the difference: an abundance of postgraduate fellowships and grants. Never before have there been more opportunities for students to earn funds for advanced study than there are today. The money is out there and ripe for the taking. Now it's up to you to decide whether you're up for the challenge.

Maybe you're a junior in college with concrete plans on what to do after graduation. Maybe you still don't know what to do once you leave the ivory tower and the pampered lifestyle you've led there. Maybe you've already graduated and are trying to find your niche in a competitive job market. If any of the above sounds like you, maybe you're ready for a fellowship or grant.

What Are Fellowships and Grants?

Whether you call them fellowships or grants, the general principle is one and the same: to provide money toward study, research, and other academic projects. Both are awarded by foundations and individuals and pay for a wide variety of endeavors.

A Wide Variety of Endeavors

Fellowships may support:

- Study in a given field, either as part of an organized program or as independent research
- Study in a particular location (in the United States or abroad) or research facility
- Student-conducted research
- Dissertation research
- Professional development

Unlike most U.S. colleges and universities, which offer aid based on need, fellowship committees select recipients without regard for financial need—their awards are given out on a competitive basis. Winners are selected based on a number of key benchmarks, including grades, standardized test scores, letters of recommendation, and personal characteristics.

Just as the selection criteria for fellowships and grants are varied, so too are the kinds of organizations that offer these awards. From small, locally based companies to sprawling, nationally renowned corporations, fellowship-issuing organizations represent the gamut of academic fields and champion their causes in idiosyncratic manners.

Ever heard of the Rhodes Scholarship? Probably. Its list of alums is a veritable who's who of American history, and for good reason. The award is peerless in terms of its visibility, which in large part is due to the organization that sponsors it. The Rhodes Scholarship Trust—one of the wealthiest and most influential fellowship-issuing organizations in the country—sponsors an annual competition for the United States' best and brightest undergraduate students, culminating in the selection of 32 elite individuals as Rhodes Scholars. And the committee is generous to the winners, offering them full tuition to Oxford University, as well as travel expenses, board, lodging, incidental college expenses, and an allowance for personal needs.

Ever heard of the Interchange Fellowship? Probably not. Its sponsor is the Garden Club of America, a New York City–based institution that (it is safe to say) isn't very well known outside of the botany crowd. But the Interchange Fellowship does just as much for students of horticulture and landscape design as the Rhodes Scholarship does for students interested in learning at Oxford, offering them full tuition at a designated botany school in the United Kingdom, as well as travel expenses, board, lodging, incidental college expenses, and an allowance for personal needs.

Undoubtedly, the awards we all recognize by name are sponsored by large groups that have the type of prestige and money that engenders respect. But this is not to say that the only good fellowships are the ones that we hear about on the evening news. Just about anyone interested in pursuing a fellowship should be able to find at least one award that is perfect for him. There is no limitation on either the types of organizations that can offer fellowships or the types of prizes that these thousands of organizations can award.

Regardless of what type of organization issues them, fellowships generally fall under one of two categories: *academic* or *working*. Academic fellowships include prizes that are used toward education at postgraduate institutions, while working fellowships consist of awards that pay for study or research independent of an academic institution. Your future plans will determine which one is better for you.

Should You Apply?

Since the fellowship application process is often both highly competitive and time-consuming, you should consider two key elements of the application process before you embark upon it. First, you should figure out why you are interested in receiving an award. Second, you should look at your overall profile as an applicant and decide whether it meets the competitiveness level of the given award.

Why Apply?

For some students, applying for fellowships or grants is a matter of course. This Tulane University senior knew from the get-go that applying for a fellowship was the right thing to do:

> *There didn't seem to be much of a decision process about it. I had good grades, had had some interesting experiences, and had been involved in some interesting activities as an undergrad, so it made sense to aim as high as possible.*

Applying for a fellowship or grant, however, is not always such a simple decision, and your choice should ultimately be based upon what you as a student are looking to gain through such an award. Whatever your goals, you will most likely be able to find at least one fellowship or grant that fits your personal interests as a student and as a future member of the working world.

Although successful fellowship applicants continue on to a wide variety of pursuits, college career advisers agree that the majority of applicants plan to attend graduate school or professional school, study abroad, and/or develop professionally after graduating from college. If your plans include any of these activities, going after a fellowship may well be the right step for you to take.

Sizing Yourself Up

It's one thing to fall in love with particular fellowships or grants. It's another to win their awards. How do you decide whether or not you've got a shot at them?

All fellowships and grants have several basic requirements you need to meet in order to apply. Before you begin, you need to be sure you fulfill these requirements, if only to avoid unnecessary embarrassment. Certain fellowships and grants are targeted for certain people. If you fall under the categories below,

Are You Eligible?

Many fellowships and grants are only available to particular kinds of applicants. You may be eligible for such awards if you:

- Live in a specific region (either within the United States or abroad)
- Are a member of a specific racial, ethnic, cultural, or gender group
- Are a member of a particular group or organization

make sure to take advantage of anything in your background that may increase both your choices and your likelihood of earning an award.

Some fellowships are extremely competitive, while others are less so. However, just like anything else for which you may have applied over the years, grades are definitely a key factor for most committees. If you've got a GPA of 3.5 or higher, great! You've earned a ticket to apply for the more prestigious fellowships available. But if you're not quite there, don't worry. An average academic record won't necessarily keep you from earning dough for your proposal.

Above and beyond what shows up on your transcript, award committees are looking for candidates who have contributed in some way to their particular field of study. One way you can achieve this end is through extracurricular activities at school and at home. Devoting yourself to your cause or field of study will certainly make you a stronger applicant. In addition, even if your grades aren't a strong selling point, the proposal you submit can make a world of difference. If your idea is well planned, relevant to your field of expertise, likely to produce concrete results, and, most important, *feasible*, you will most likely outshine a candidate with superior grades and an inferior proposal.

Once you've earmarked particular fellowships or grants, the best thing you can possibly do to help your chances is to research them thoroughly. Meet with people who have earned these awards in the past, and seek out those who have failed to learn what to do and what not to do. Find out about the selection process. Be sure you're eligible to apply. And above all else, make sure your vision of the award meshes with the award's stated principles. A combination of all these factors can only make you a stronger candidate, and it can save you a great deal of stress during the application process.

Researching Fellowships and Grants

No matter which fellowships and grants you choose, the beginning of the application process is always the same. It involves hours of research and thought, which should culminate in a list of fellowships and grants that best suit your skills, needs, and interests. There are a number of different sources to which you can turn for the information you need.

Sources

Not to sell this fine piece of writing short, but there are a number of (other) great books out there that can help you get started in your search for awards. You can find many of these titles at any public or university library, and if you can't get them there, your undergraduate career services office should have them on file.

Good Books on Fellowship/Grant Hunting

You might want to check out these resources as you embark on your award search:

- *Annual Register of Grant Support* (published by Marquis Academic Media)
- *The Catalog of Federal Domestic Assistance* (U.S. Government)
- *Directory of Research Grants* (Oryx Press)
- *The Foundation Directory* (The Foundation Center)
- *The Foundation 1000* (The Foundation Center)
- *The Grants Register* (St. Martin's Press)
- *Harvard College Guide to Grants* (Harvard University)
- *Scholarships, Fellowships, and Loans* (Bellman Pub. Co.)
- *Worldwide Graduate Scholarship Directory* (Career Press)

For those of you who are Internet fiends, the World Wide Web abounds with sites that list fellowship and grant opportunities and give you advice on how to start your search. Some of the best sites include:

- Cornell University: Fellowships Guide
  http://132.236.180.90/ccs/Graduate_School/Fellowships/entrypage.html
- Council on Foundations
  http://www.cof.org
- University of Virginia: Science and Technology Research Funding Agencies
  http://www.cs.virginia.edu/research/sponsors.html
- Yale University: Fellowship/Grant/Award Information
  http://www.cs.yale.edu/homes/tap/fellowships.html

As useful as the fellowship-grant databases featured at these sites are, it is not advisable to rely upon any particular one of them too heavily. Each database uses different search criteria and lists different awards, so you may miss out on learning about good opportunities if you do not diversify your Web search as much as possible. Check out a range of sites for the widest possible coverage of available fellowships and grants.

The Undergraduate Career Services Office: A Mecca for Applicants

As you proceed further with your search for fellowships and grants, your undergraduate career services office is the best place to go. These offices usually offer an array of fellowship-related services for applicants, including information sessions, workshops, and advising. They may serve as liaisons between universities and major funding agencies and/or screening agencies, and they often administer and coordinate fellowship and grant applications. Their resource libraries should stock directories, past applications, program brochures, student evaluations of fellowships (from both those who were accepted and rejected from the fellowships), and other relevant information for prospective applicants. Many of these resources are also made available on career services office Web sites.

In general, your career services office can assist you most by pointing you in the direction of the people that can help you to ultimately win an award. Among the most qualified to give you guidance are fellowship advisers, committee members, and former applicants.

Fellowship/Grant Advisers

Fellowship/grant advisers are the people you go to when you need advice on the nuts and bolts of the application process. These are the individuals you want to seek out when you're deciding in which fellowships or grants you're interested and how to put together your application materials. Fellowship advisers will help you assemble an attractive file that shows committees not only why you're qualified for the award, but also how you're going to put the award to good use. Any time you have technical questions about your application—whether it be how to phrase a sentence in your personal statement or which activities to put at the top of your résumé—these are the people you should go to first.

Committee Members

While former award committee members are difficult to find on your own, your undergraduate career services office should have a list of them (often alums of your institution) who can answer questions for you. Committee members can provide invaluable advice on how you might consider packaging yourself in your application. One of the most important parts of the fellowship-grant application process is painting a portrait of yourself that is tailor-made for the specific award to which you're applying. Who better to ask about what a committee wants to see and hear than someone who has served on a committee herself?

Former Applicants

Last—but certainly not least—you should seek the advice of former applicants to the fellowships and grants in which you are interested. You'll notice that this book is filled with sidebars that offer comments on the fellowship application process from these valuable sources. Read these sidebars, and find former applicants of your own to interview. Names of such people should also be on file in your career services office.

Perhaps the most important thing a former applicant can help you with is deciding for which fellowships you'd like to apply. They've gone through the process of paring down a list to a select few awards, which is often the most difficult part of the application process. Use the advice they can give you on how to succeed in the fellowships race!

Q&A: How to Avoid Making a Fool of Yourself

There is a right and wrong way to go about gaining information from fellowship advisers, committee members, and former applicants. Of course, much of the etiquette for asking questions is stuff you've heard from your parents when growing up—always be polite, seem interested in what they have to say (even if it's drivel), and look the other person straight in the eye.

But half the battle is just knowing what types of questions you should be asking these invaluable sources of knowledge. If you go into a session with one of them without a plan, they're going to think you're wasting their precious time. So below is a list of questions you can start out with. Where you go from there is entirely up to you.

Questions to Ask Fellowship/Grant Advisers:

- Where do I begin?
- What types of awards should I be looking for?
- How many awards should I consider applying for?
- How should I frame my personal statement?
- Who else should I look to for help in the process?

Questions to Ask Former Committee Members:

- What are committees looking for in an applicant with my interests?
- How should I package myself for committees?
- What do you think is the most important part of the application?
- Am I cut out for these particular awards?
- What makes a successful applicant?

Questions for Former Applicants:

- So tell me: how in the world did you do it?
- Do you think applying for your award was worth it?
- How did you prepare for interviews?
- If you could apply again, what would you change about your application process?

- Out of these fellowships and grants, which do you think I should choose?

Narrowing Your Search

The enormous range of fellowships and grants available reflect the varying styles and purposes of the funding sources. The application process, however, varies little among the majority of awards (the exceptions being several of the more competitive prizes). The first step toward earning an award is always the same: narrowing your search.

While conducting your search, it helps to focus on what you would actually do with your fellowship or grant if you landed it. It's extremely important to search for programs that fit your project, rather than to choose a fellowship or grant first and then conjure up an idea that falls within its general bounds. If you

A Basic Analysis

"When you're trying to pick the fellowships that best fit your academic needs, you need only apply a basic analysis:

1) *Who:* Is there a particular professor or group of professors you want to study with?
2) *What:* Which field or course of study do you plan to pursue, and what school offers the best such program?
3) *When:* Do you want to go directly to postgraduate academic work, and how many years do you want to spend?
4) *Where:* Choosing the right city or country in which to study is extraordinarily important.
5) *How:* How much money do you need, and which fellowships provide the best deal?

If you go through these simple steps and critically appraise your needs and desires, it will become clear which of the hundreds of fellowships you should pursue."

—Yale University Senior

manage to pull this off, you will have hurdled one of the toughest obstacles of the process: matching yourself with the best possible fellowship or grant.

But because there are so many interesting fellowships out there—and because many of us aren't that picky when selecting ones that sound "really good"—an applicant could literally find herself swamped in attractive opportunities. Ultimately, your goal should be to whittle your final list to a number that will allow you to explore varied options without forcing you to spend all your time at a computer working on your application materials.

Working or Academic?

One of the first steps you must make in order to narrow down your list is to decide whether you're looking for an academic or a working fellowship. For many applicants—especially those who are not yet sure whether they intend to ever set foot in a classroom again—working fellowships are the way to go. They serve as an easy way to obtain the funding necessary to gain the type of experience in your area of interest that will translate into job offers upon completion of your project.

With working fellowships, where you end up after you've completed your fellowship is completely up to you. This makes them both scary and exciting at the same time. Scary because if you don't enter with a good idea of your ultimate destination, you may end up stuck in Nowheresville. Exciting because if you know where you're headed, your fellowship will open all the doors to getting there.

Conversely, anyone who has settled on graduate school for their immediate future should take the time to consider an academic fellowship. Whether it be in the form of tuition money, a stipend, or both, these prizes help thousands of recipients survive the financially taxing nature of postgraduate education.

But while this may be the way to go if you're ready for graduate study, potential applicants should realize that the commitment you make if you accept the award is binding. In other words, once you've taken an academic fellowship, you've committed yourself to spending at least one year in graduate school, and usually more. For many, this is a daunting proposition.

What many students do not realize is that academic fellowships are not the only way to finance a graduate education. Chances are, your college may offer scholarships for undergraduates to stay on as graduate students. In addition, a number of need-based programs are available to graduate students. Unlike the scholarships that many of you undoubtedly used toward your college education, the majority of these graduate financial aid packages are loan-based programs. If the prospect of having to reimburse your graduate school for a number of years after graduation seems unpalatable, you'll do the right thing in choosing a fellowship or grant.

Show Me the Money!

Applying for fellowships and grants can yield a pot of gold for those lucky enough to have made it to the end of the rainbow. And depending upon which award you choose, it can be a really big pot.

Fellowship money serves primarily to cover the expenses you accrue in both studying and living independently. Fellowships may be awarded for only one year or for multiple years, and, depending on the competitiveness of the fellowship, they range anywhere from about $1,000 to $30,000. Some fellowships pay for students' tuition and expenses in graduate school. Others cover the costs of research or travel. All of these factors make for a great range in terms of the amount each committee designates for its students.

Keep in mind that the amount you will receive depends upon factors over which you have only marginal control after you've graduated (or once you've chosen your major, if you're still in college). Make sure that the awards you pursue will compensate you adequately for the effort you put into them.

Your Field's Role

As you will see later on in this book, some areas of study simply have more opportunities and more money to dole out than others. A student who studies the sciences, for example, has hundreds of fellowships at his fingertips; a communications major has fewer than ten. This certainly doesn't mean that certain fields have higher quality fellowship opportunities than others. But it definitely means that certain individuals will have a better shot at getting a fellowship than others, based solely upon their field of study.

Your School's Role

Keep in mind that whether or not you have already graduated, your affiliation to your alma mater can play a large role in determining to which fellowships you may choose to apply. While the majority of fellowships or grants available to postgraduates are awarded through national competitions, many universities hold competitions of their own whose prizes are given only to current students or alumni of their particular school.

Furthermore, candidates for certain fellowships must be selected and endorsed by their academic institutions. The majority of these fellowships require current undergraduates or recent graduates to compete first with other candidates at their school. After students have sent their applications to a committee at their undergraduate institutions, it is at this committee's discretion to choose an allotted number of candidates from the applicant pool. The candidates endorsed by their schools then go on to the national competition, and their fate becomes at the discretion of the organization's own committee.

Trying for Both

"Applying for both the Rhodes and Marshall may have seemed daunting at first, but after a closer look, it was the only option that made sense. The two applications were so similar that I only had to put in a few more hours to complete two applications instead of one. My personal statements were nearly identical, my recommenders simply sent in another copy of their letter, and all I had to add for the Marshall application was a 500-word study plan that I had previously worked out in developing my Rhodes application. I would recommend tossing your hat into the ring of both competitions, because they both involve a significant element of luck, and they both offer the same opportunity."

—Yale University Senior

For How Many Should You Apply?

Many applicants narrow their list to between three to six fellowships, and the process isn't much different from the days when they were applying to college. It helps to rank these fellowships in terms of your likelihood of acceptance and your interest in them, ending up with a range of opportunities that includes at least one "likely" acceptance, a couple of middle-rangers (for which your chances of getting in are around fifty-fifty), and at least one "stretch." This way, you can still shoot for the stars and be pretty sure if you don't get your first choice, you'll have something to bank on anyway.

Maybe you think you're too lazy or don't have the time to apply for as many as six fellowships. Nonsense. A common myth is that the more applications you fill out, the more time you'll spend losing your eyesight from staring at your screen. This isn't the case (unless, of course, you apply for hundreds). Since the application process is similar for most fellowships, applying for one takes about as much time as applying for a handful.

Why not go for the glory and give several fellowships or grants a shot? If you end up getting one you didn't think you had a shot at, it'll just give you more money with which to play in the end.

Winning Multiple Fellowships

It is, however, important to note that just because you end up winning multiple fellowships doesn't mean that you can keep all the loot. If you apply for a number of opportunities that fund different aspects of your project, you will

Deferring One to Land Another

"After receiving the Truman, and before applying for the Rhodes, I spoke with the chairman of the Truman Foundation and was assured I would be able to defer my Truman Scholarship without compromising my standing. I then went forward with the Rhodes process."

—University of Michigan Senior

generally be able to use all the money you win. But many fellowships whose fields of study fall under the same general category—the Rhodes and Marshall, for example—require recipients to decline or defer all other offers until they have fulfilled the terms of the award.

It is possible to make use of multiple fellowship opportunities, but it can be tricky. For this reason, it is crucial to make sure you will actually be able to use the prizes you may receive before starting the application process.

The Chance of a Lifetime

Despite all the hurdles you must overcome in the application process, there is no question that the benefits of applying far outweigh the negatives. The bottom line is that those who take the time to map out their application plans well in advance and choose the awards for which they plan on applying wisely often end up sitting pretty in their first few years out of college.

Take Your Application Seriously

"The judges are not fools. They know the difference between the applicant who is sitting around eating Doritos and musing about how awesome it would be to get ten grand to hang out in Australia, versus the one who has researched exactly how and why she will establish a women's health clinic in India. (Guess which one got the grant?) Applying for an award is a lot of work, especially in the midst of finishing your senior thesis or worrying about post-graduation career plans. Don't bother writing the essay and embarking on the process if you are not in it one hundred percent—you'll be wasting your time. I regret my lax attitude, because I know that if I had actually put in the effort, it could have really paid off, and I could have had the experience of a lifetime."

—Harvard University Senior

Don't underestimate the effect that winning the right fellowship or award can have on your life. Just listen to one Yale University senior whose award will send him to England next year: "The fellowship will help me attain any goal I set for myself."

2 Applying Successfully

It's one thing to decide you want a fellowship or grant. It's another to survive the application process. Many a brave soul has started the fellowships race only to have his engine stall once the daunting task of filling out forms, writing proposal essays, and speaking in front of an intimidating committee rears its ugly head. Often, what separates successful applicants apart from the crowd has little to do with what they plan on doing with their fellowship or grant. Instead, it has a great deal to do with whether or not they actually have the courage and time to place their hopes and aspirations on paper or elaborate on them in front of others.

But fear not, potential applicants, there is good news on the way: The application process isn't as scary as it may look from the outside. Certainly, there is a great deal you have to do if you want to get your fellowship or grant. And those of you who have trouble with a typewriter or speaking in public may have to take some lessons on the side. But just like anything else, submitting a successful application and scoring well on your interview are more than feasible if you handle them the right way.

Requesting the Forms

Once you've generated a list of awards to which you would consider applying, you need to send away for the pertinent documentation packets and application materials issued by the fellowship and grant committees.

Most of the fellowships and grants listed in this book will gladly send you the relevant information and forms if you send away for them by mail. All you need to do is find out the address (either from the listings in the relevant chapters of this book or at your career services office) and send a postcard to the organization asking for the award's application materials. Alternatively, you might want to send a cover letter together with a stamped, self-addressed envelope—this will only improve your chances of being sent the materials you need.

In this era of modern technology, there are other avenues you can use to request an application form. Many of the fellowships listed in this book have e-mail addresses or even web sites you can use to request information. And then there's the telephone, for those of you who hate writing and computers, and just need to hear a (hopefully) friendly voice from time to time.

Deadlines

Ultimately, the difference between winning the race or crashing in the first turn is a matter of how you choose to spend your time. If you map out your plan early on in the process and set goals for when and how you plan on completing each step of the process, the checkered flag is just a few turns away.

Start Early

"The reason I won my fellowships was because I started early. If you wait until the early fall, you are fried. This is an important law of fellowships that too many students who want a carefree summer conveniently ignore. I wrote the first draft of my personal statements in late May, and continually revised it until the October due date. By starting early, I gained the additional benefit of having professors and other people edit it for me and provide suggestions for improvement. In the end, a grand total of six sentences stayed the same. Also, I asked my professors to write letters of recommendation during the late spring so that they would have ample time to do a good job. A well-planned, thoughtful letter can go a long way."

—Yale University Senior

Whatever your preferred mode of communication may be, it is always a good idea to send away for information packets well in advance. Make sure you send away for application forms early enough to meet all the different deadlines for each fellowship or grant in which you are interested. Monitor your responses closely, and follow up by contacting the organizations a second time if you have not received materials by a certain date. You need time to pore over the materials and figure out how you want to present yourself to fellowship committees before you actually sit down at the typewriter and fill out your forms. So send away for any fellowship or grant applications that you might even remotely consider using a good two or three months before the deadline. If you end up using the forms, you won't regret it!

Unlike college, where professors hand out extensions like Santa Claus, fellowship and grant committees are serious about considering only those applications that meet their deadline. In many cases, the date requested by committees is a postmark date. This means that you must hand your materials to the post office by the given deadline, and as long as the postmark comes on or before the application's due date, you will be fine (even if the package arrives at the fellowship office after the deadline).

Other organizations require that your application arrive at their office by the deadline, which means you must allow enough time for the package to get from your home to its final destination. If you are applying for this type of award, make sure you send your materials at least a week before the deadline. As we all know, the U.S. Postal Service isn't exactly the world's most efficient organization!

Because not all fellowships and grants follow the same deadline policy, it is crucial that you contact the organizations to which you plan to apply at the beginning of the application process and find out what they mean by their deadlines. Most organizations will specify it on their actual application form, which makes life easier for you. But if they don't, be sure to use the addresses, telephone numbers, e-mail addresses, or Web sites listed in the following chapters to get the scoop. Remember, the penalty for not meeting an organization's deadline—no matter what its definition of a deadline may be—is having your application thrown in the trash.

Once you've settled on which fellowships interest you and taken the all-important step of mailing the organizations for information and applications, you'll need to face the task of completing the various components of the application form. Before you do that, you'll need to take a moment to think about how to package yourself.

Packaging Yourself

At first, many applicants believe that once they've finally chosen their target fellowships, the rest of the process is smooth sailing. Then they actually look at the applications and panic sets in. If and when this happens to you, it's important to take a step back from the form and ask yourself what you want to jump out from the paper when the committee looks at your application. In other words, what you need to do first—in fact, preferably before you've actually received your forms—is decide how you want to sell yourself.

Many applicants fall into the trap of using individual parts of the application as their key selling points. For example, an individual with outstanding credentials outside the classroom may (whether or not he realizes it) concentrate most on the extracurricular activities section of the application. A terrific writer may put his heart and soul into the personal statement. If those sections best demonstrate the qualities you wish to make the committee aware of, that's

A Single, Large Knot

"I think it is essential to paint a coherent portrait for the selection committee. I tied all of my activities and coursework and jobs together into a single, large knot. I outlined my worldview and my diverse pursuits, and then drew the links between all of my work in the personal statement. I also had each of my recommenders articulate a different aspect of my character or achievements. It is suicide to ignore the need to stress broader themes and focus independently on several different features of your work and beliefs."

—Yale University Senior

wonderful. The problem is, no application can be completely successful unless the applicant finds a way to tightly mesh all its components together.

What most committees are really looking for in a candidate is personal character. A key step in crafting your application, then, is to offer committees a complimentary, yet *realistic* look into your record as a student and professional. It is the rare candidate who can combine outstanding grades with significant contributions outside the classroom, an amazing essay, and stellar recommendations. Among those of us who are not from Krypton, it is even more rare to find a candidate who can use his weaknesses to his advantage.

Committees are bound to notice if your grades are poor or you lack extracurricular experiences. The best approach to take if you are in this position is to explain in your personal statement that you recognize your own shortcomings. You should be perceived as both honest and self-aware, and committees might well enjoy the breath of fresh air a humble candidate represents after plowing through hundreds of applications from people who are more than willing to sing their own praises.

Getting Feedback

After going over your materials for the one-millionth time, you will find it difficult to separate what is actually heartfelt and relevant from what is insincere and trivial. It becomes increasingly important, then, to have several new sets of eyes look over your applications as they get closer to being done.

The Importance of Feedback

"My written applications (for both the Truman and Rhodes competitions) were carefully edited and meticulously criticized by skeptical readers. I had friends, professors, and advisers read my essays, and this helped improve the overall quality. I warn, however, against *too much* feedback, because the applicant is prone to frustration when each new reader gives different advice."

—University of Michigan Senior

Be sure to ask others to help you out along the way, but at the same time, don't ask just anybody to do so. There are clearly certain individuals who know you better than others. Parents, siblings, friends, and significant others are especially helpful when it comes to appraising the type of character you have portrayed yourself to be in the personal statement. Equally appropriate are faculty members and career advisers, who can not only help you with your recommendations, but can also provide perspective on what committees are actually looking for in an applicant. Last but not least, be sure to consult former winners of the fellowships to which you are applying. They know what it takes to be accepted, and they can also let you know if you're getting into something with which you'll be uncomfortable.

The Application Form

Although all are different, many fellowship and grant applications forms require the following information:

- Your official undergraduate/graduate transcript(s)
- Graduate Record Examination (GRE) scores
- A list of extracurricular activities
- At least two letters of recommendation
- A personal statement
- A written proposal

Grades and Standardized Test Scores

There's no question that grades and test scores matter when applying for fellowships. Many fellowship committees limit the number of applicants by requiring certain minimum grade-point average requirements. To make things even hairier, many will not accept individuals whose scores on the GRE do not meet certain levels.

The importance of grades and test scores obviously means that you should do everything in your power to make sure you own transcript(s) and test scores are as impressive as possible. It also entails that you make every attempt to get the

> **Help—If You Need It**
>
> Kaplan Educational Centers offers a myriad of courses and test-prep guides to help you get the best score you can on the GRE and other standardized tests that fellowship and grant committees may require. For example, you might want to check out *GRE 1998–1999*, published by Kaplan Books and Simon & Schuster. For more information, call 1-800-KAP-TEST or 1-800-KAP-ITEM, or visit Kaplan's web site at http://www.kaplan.com.

relevant records in to fellowship committees in good time. Schools tend to take a few weeks to process requests for official transcripts; put in your requests early. Sign up for all the required tests well in advance.

In order to qualify for the majority of fellowships that require the test, the best time to take the GRE is while you're still in college. Most students sit for the examination during their senior year, when it is offered numerous times throughout the year. If you take the required tests as early as possible, you'll have a chance to retake them and raise your scores if you don't do as well as you would like.

Don't despair if your grades and scores aren't as impressive as they could be. While low grades and scores may preclude you from applying to certain fellowships, you should view your chances from a much broader perspective. It is important to excel academically, but fellowship committees are not looking for individuals who have locked themselves in their rooms to study without experiencing the world around them.

Beyond merely reporting what you have done inside the classroom, your transcript is an indicator to committees that you have gained a wealth of knowledge in the subject that you have chosen to pursue in your proposed fellowship. Just as much as grades, the classes you have chosen go a long way toward proving to organizations that you have that requisite base of knowledge.

Extracurricular Activities

Many straight-A students have a shoddy track record when it comes to extracurricular activities. When you ask them why excelling in both realms seems impossible, the answer you often receive is that "Extracurriculars take up too much time and don't allow me to study." If you're looking to receive a fellowship or grant and feel the same way, take this attitude, throw it in the trash, and do your best to change. Quickly.

There are few better indicators of a person's character than his extracurricular docket. However, it often proves to be the case that it doesn't really matter to committees what you choose to do, as long as you're doing something. Avoid at all costs coming across as an individual who is so concerned with his own work that he neglects working with others. For this reason, honing your GPA at the expense of spending quality time away from your books is a fatal plan to follow. And those students who claim that there just isn't anything interesting to do out there definitely should not be considering applying for awards.

As much as it may seem like "résumé padding," it definitely doesn't hurt to hold a position of leadership in your activities. If research is your boat, any significant findings or publications to which you can attach your name are a plus. And awards aren't bad either.

The most important thing committees see in applicants who have rich extracurricular backgrounds—in addition to any distinctions they may have received while outside the classroom—is their passion for and commitment to causes they find meaningful to their lives as students. After all, that passion and commitment will go a long way toward determining whether or not these students make the most of their fellowships.

Letters of Recommendation

Before you request letters of recommendation, it is vital to think carefully about the answers to two questions: whom to ask and how to ask them.

Who to Ask

Those of you familiar with the *Indiana Jones* films probably know a little about Harrison Ford's search for the Holy Grail. Remember the advice the old knight gave Indy before he drank from the fabled goblet? "Choose wisely." It probably helps to look at the way you choose your recommenders in the same vein. Without positive input from them, the Holy Grail—a successful fellowship application—may well prove unattainable, so you'd better choose them wisely. If you choose the wrong recommenders, your fate could be the same as that of that guy who drank out of the wrong cup in the movie!

Admittedly, getting good letters of recommendation isn't quite as fateful a situation as the one described above. But there's no doubt that the appraisals you receive from teachers, employers, advisers, and the like weigh heavily in an award committee's mind when it comes to assessing you as an individual. And as a result, just like any other section of your application form, it is important to view the letters you receive as critical pieces needed to complete a puzzle.

Letters of recommendation are of particular importance because they are the only way you can prove to a committee that all the wonderful things you've said about yourself in your application are in fact true. If you've chosen your recommenders wisely, they can paint just as accurate and flattering a portrait of your credentials as a candidate as you can.

There are many reasons certain individuals make better choices than others. It is wise to choose those who:

- Know you well and know how you wish to package yourself as a candidate
- Know you as a person as well as a student
- Know your character from outside the classroom
- Have seen your work in more than one class or situation
- Can give poignant and accurate examples of your best work
- Can weigh your personal achievements against those of others (and, hopefully, place it pretty high on the ladder!)
- Can actually say something substantial about you

An issue that is a perpetual point of contention is deciding which is a more important characteristic in a recommender—fame or familiarity. Applicants often seek out recommenders primarily for who they are or what they have contributed to their field, rather than getting letters from those whom they really know. But it is always better to choose an unknown individual who is familiar with your work and character than to receive a recommendation from a powerful person who has only met you in passing.

Another sticky issue is deciding what types of people you should have represent you. Should you just get recommendations from professors? From employers? Or should you strike a balance? Unfortunately, there isn't a golden rule to picking your recommenders; instead, you should tailor your choices to the fellowships or grants you've chosen. If you're a science major applying for a fellowship in broadcast journalism and you've never taken a journalism or writing course in college, there's probably little one of your physics teachers could do to significantly aid your cause. Of course, he could say nice things about you and rave about your mastery of Bernoulli's Principle, but that won't get your face on the *Today* show. In a case like this, an applicant is much better off getting letters from those who know him both as a person and a journalist.

Recommendations Strategies

"I tried to use the recommendations as an opportunity to demonstrate intellectual breadth. Obviously, I opted for two or three of the recommenders to be in my own discipline (math and economics), but I consciously picked a few in other areas of interest (philosophy, history, and political science) to emphasize the fact that I was well rounded and could think intelligently regardless of the subject matter."

—Tulane University Senior

"I started early. Throughout my freshman and sophomore years, I cultivated strong friendships with several professors. These friendships grew out of conversations about course work during office hours. By the time I finished junior year, I knew enough professors intimately that I was able to secure solid, thoughtful letters of support."

—University of Michigan Senior

Above all, the most important thing is to choose people who can sell you to committees the way you would sell yourself. Before you've chosen your recommenders, make sure you are on the same wavelength by asking them a few key questions. What do they think are your strengths and weaknesses as a candidate? What are their impressions of you as both a student and a person? And most importantly, do they believe you'd make a strong candidate for the position?

In addition, a good recommendation becomes a great one when it specifically concerns the fellowship or grant at hand. Unlike when you applied to college or grad school, when you could just get a stock recommendation from someone and make 101 copies for all those schools to which you applied, it is important to rub committees the right way by adapting everything you send them to their own award.

Committees want to see you made the effort to please them, and this includes getting your recommenders in on the act. For this reason, not only it is a good idea to get them to tailor each recommendation to the individual committees, but also it's a bonus to get them talking about your proposed project on top of your personal characteristics. It certainly doesn't hurt if the people who put in a good word for you also put in a good word for the work you plan on doing.

How to Ask

So you've done your homework and figured out a handful of people you'd like to write letters of recommendation on your behalf. The job's now half done. The tricky part is actually getting them to do it for you.

In a perfect world, all the people you choose to write your recommendations would bend themselves backward just to help you out. They'd declare you to be one of the most fellowship-worthy individuals they'd ever known, and be honored to assist you on your journey. And to top it all off, they'd actually get your recommendations in on time!

But it definitely isn't a perfect world. Chances are, at least one of the people you'd like to ask for a recommendation gets swamped with requests like these all the time. And chances are, your request isn't exactly going to make her do the dance of joy. So how do you get on her good side? Easier said than done. But there are some tricks of the trades you might consider following.

First and foremost, it is imperative that you get a head start on the whole game. Figure out who you're going to ask early on, and ask for their letters well in advance of the due date. For a recommender, there's nothing more frustrating than to be handed a form days in advance of the due date. It's a sure bet that the candidate who cuts it close will end up receiving a substandard letter from a time-pressured recommender. So the easy solution is to leave your recommenders plenty of time to complete the forms. This gives them the chance to sit down, think about your qualifications, and write their absolute best. Handing them the forms a good three to four weeks before the deadline should suffice.

But to truly keep a recommender happy, it isn't enough just to request his assistance at an early date. Throughout the weeks when they're (presumably) toiling away at your recommendation, you should be prepared to serve your recommenders hand and foot. Applicants tend to believe that their recommenders have all the information they need to write the letters in their head. This is not the case. Therefore, it's up to you to provide them with all the information they could possibly need to write you the type of recommendation you deserve.

Once they've agreed to help you out, the first thing you should do is provide your recommenders with a description of the fellowship's purpose and selection criteria. This will both help them frame your recommendation in terms of the

Help Recommenders Help You

"I asked a wide variety of academic and nonacademic figures in the late spring to write me a letter. As part of the request, I offered to sit down with each of them and explain why I wanted the fellowship, what I planned to do with it, and what qualities and achievements I wanted them to stress. That conversation proved crucial in improving the quality of my recommendations."

—Yale University Senior

fellowship and allow them to write with a specificity that the committees will appreciate. Then make sure your recommenders have a copy of your academic and extracurricular records and your personal statement. Even if they've heard about your accomplishments 1,000 times, it never hurts to fill them in again. And when it comes to pleasing your recommenders, spare no expense. Provide them with stamps and envelopes for their letters and give them one less thing to worry about.

The moment your recommenders let you know they've sent off your letters, it's a good idea to send them a thank-you note. Nothing too fancy, just something that serves as a token of your appreciation. This also serves as a way to stay on their good side in case you ever need their help again!

The Personal Statement

The personal statement is a sample of your writing that committees use to gain an understanding of who you are, what your goals are, and how you might plan on accomplishing them. Committees almost always give you free reign over the topic you choose, so this is your chance to let them know something they can't find elsewhere on your application form. Of course, despite the amount of independence the committee gives you, you'd be foolish not to present them with solid arguments for why you want their fellowship, how the opportunity ties in with your future goals, and what makes you a solid candidate. It's not a long piece of writing (usually about one, single-spaced page), your goal should be to be concise without compromising any of the important points you wish to emphasize.

There is a great deal a committee can glean from the personal statement, but if you fail to present your side in a coherent, thoughtful, and well-written manner, all your best efforts will be wasted. Committees receive hundreds of applications and often go over all of the essays in a very short period of time. If your essay doesn't stand out from the crowd, it's not going to help your chances of acceptance much.

Choosing a Topic

The single most important step in crafting your personal statement is coming up with a solid topic. And this is an extremely difficult task, considering all the angles you must cover in such a short amount of space. Of course, there isn't a formula for what makes a good topic, but areas that may provide a good starting point include:

- Issues or courses about which you feel passionately
- Contributions to your community or field of study
- Experiences that have formed your character
- Your strengths and skills
- Personal values
- Personal interests
- Obstacles you have encountered and how you overcame them

In the end, your idea should tie in with your reasons for applying to the fellowship or grant. Particular events in your childhood that have shaped your identity might make a great topic. Nevertheless, if it lacks relevance to your decision to apply or to making you a stronger applicant, it's best if you go back to the drawing board.

When coming up with a topic, always keep in mind the audience for whom you are writing. This applies not only to what subject you ultimately choose for your essay, but also to the way you write it. Remember, committees want a reason to like the character you portray in the essay, but more importantly, they

Go With Your Gut Feeling

"If you have a gut feeling that something in the essay really conveys a sense of who you are in a particularly pithy or innovative way, do not let any one talk you out of including it in the essay. Conventions are ultimately useless (that is, they usually don't award the scholarship to the person that most strictly adheres to conventions), so one should never feel the need to respect them in something like this."

—Tulane University Senior

want a reason to select that character. Nothing solves this problem better than tailoring your personal statement to their particular fellowship.

Writing the Essay

After you've tackled the toughest part of the essay, coming up with a topic, all that's left is the actual writing. If you stick to a few important guidelines, the writing process should be much less intimidating than you might expect!

Organization is the key to any well-crafted piece of writing, and the first thing you should do with your personal statement once you've chosen your topic is to make an outline. Start with the basics—decide how many paragraphs you want and what the gist of each paragraph will be—and then add complexity to your outline. Come up with topic sentences for your paragraphs. Put your best ideas on paper and figure out where they should go in the framework. And work on transition sentences from paragraph to paragraph.

The next step in the process is to create a rough draft. Take your outline and fill in the blanks, turning disjointed thoughts into completed sentences. When this is done, tighten up your syntax and correct your grammar. Make sure you've done all those things your high school English teachers taught you. Write sentences that support your main ideas. Use only strong verbs and change them from passive to active form. Eliminate qualifiers when possible. Rid your essay of extraneous language and make sure every single word in your essay says exactly what it means to say. Keep jargon to a minimum. Place transition sentences at the beginning of each new paragraph. Above all else, spellcheck!

Once you've gone over the technical issues, you need to take a good look at the message in your words. Do your points seem weak and poorly supported? Are you listing achievements you've already included in another section of the application form? Is your writing style sensational? Does it make you seem egotistical? If the answer to any of these questions is yes, then you need to make some changes.

In writing classes, you may have been taught to assume the reader knows nothing about the topic you've chosen. That may work in English 101, but it's a fatal mistake in an application essay. There's nothing worse than to talk down to

Different Takes on the Writing Process

"The essay was not the sysphean effort I'd heard people make it out to be. I simply put a draft together late in the summer (the Rhodes is due in the early fall), and set about systematically revising it over the course of the next 6–8 weeks. I think the mistake is in expecting the first or second draft to get it done, or even that the essay you ultimately submit will look anything like what you started out with. It's just not the case. And you should realize this at the outset."

—1998 Rhodes Scholar

"A vexing matter! I started and restarted my Rhodes personal statement perhaps 20 times. What helped, I think, was visiting Web sites that feature other students' statements (from years past; see, for example, Boston University's Web site on scholarships). This gave me an idea of style. But in the end, I wrote a very original piece that touched on a few important biographical points and explained, without verbosity, my academic experiences and goals. I did not overedit the personal statement; to do so would have stiffened its voice."

—University of Michigan Senior

"Since personal statements are invariably short, they seem appealing—any self-respecting college student can whip out 1,000 words. But the word limit soon goes from being a blessing to being the bane of your existence. It's patently impossible to catalog your life (both past and future) in such a short space, and you find yourself hacking and cutting for days on end. Ultimately, you are forced to abandon crucial aspects of your work and your world view, and you can never be completely satisfied."

—Yale University Senior

a fellowship or grant commitee in your personal statement. Always keep in mind that the people who will read the essay are at least as smart, well-educated, and accomplished in their field as you are.

Once you've corrected all the major problems, the key to going from rough draft to your essay's final incarnation is revision. And this doesn't just mean you personally going over the writing. Take your piece to as many people as it takes to get feedback, and then go back to your computer screen and work out the kinks. The more pairs of eyes that take a look at what you've written, the better.

Throughout the process of putting together your personal statement, keep in mind that the essay you write has the potential to either make or break your chances of acceptance. In the worst case, a poor piece of writing can give a committee the impression that you lack the thoroughness, reflection, and professionalism required for their fellowship. On the other hand, putting your time and effort into the personal statement will indicate that you are a candidate with a demonstrated ability to think about the opportunity presented him and to relate those thoughts on paper.

This is your best chance to put a truly personal spin on your written application; let committees really get to know you as more than just a social security number. Make sure you take full advantage of this opportunity!

The Written Proposal

In a way, the application process is analagous to meeting a person you've had your eye on for some time. You start out with small talk. You know: "How's the weather," "How about them Yankees," "What's your name," and so on. In the application process, everything to this point (from filling out the form to writing your personal statement) has just been small talk.

Of course, once you decide that you like the person enough to go beyond small-talk, you've entered uncharted territory. Now you want to know if you're ready for a relationship. Placed in terms of the fellowship application, that uncharted territory is the written proposal. It will only be taken seriously if the committee likes what it has seen in the rest of your application. And you will get the fellowship only if the committee likes your written proposal.

The written proposal is the crux of the fellowship application; it's your chance to prove to selection committees that you actually know what you're doing with their money. Above all else, the proposal is a conduit through which you must convey what you plan on doing with your fellowship, how you plan on doing it, and what your work will lead to in the future.

How Not to Write Your Proposal

"Personality, good grades, and all the peripheral stuff is important, but your main selling point is your proposal, and the only way it will fly is if you research it thoroughly and pack it with details. If you try to get by with 'I plan to go to a university in Australia and talk to some professors,' you will crash and burn in a big hurry, and I know this because I tried it. I had a grandiose fantasy, but nothing concrete to support it. What I did: thought of a cool place to go (Australia), thought of something I could do there (photojournalism), and winged it on how the two would actually intertwine in real life. What the judges did: laughed heartily and tossed my application in the circular file. What I should have done: talked to professors in the pertinent fields at my own university to seek advice or ask for contacts they might have, looked up different universities in Australia on the web, found some names of professors over there and actually contacted them to discuss the feasibility of my plan, and written down detailed information such as where I would stay, how much things would cost, and what my daily itinerary would look like—down to the most minute detail.

"Remember, although this is only a proposal, you should not treat it such. Rather, you should draw up your plan as if it were real. The more realistic you are, the more easily you will persuade the judges that they should help you take your plan to fruition."

—Harvard University Senior

Parts of the Proposal

Most applications will specifically tell you what you need to include in your written proposal, but the majority don't stray from a general pattern that includes several—if not all—of the following steps:

The Cover Letter

The cover letter is a piece of writing that tells committees who you are, why you're applying for their fellowship or grant, and what qualifies you for the award. The letter should be no longer than a page in length, and, whenever possible, should be addressed to a particular member of the committee (and not to the infamous "Sir or Madam"). In particular, you should use this opportunity to present yourself as someone who is both expert in the award's field of study and who has a history of practice in that field.

The Abstract

A summary of your objectives and procedures, the abstract is a brief (no more than three sentences) explanation of the "what" and "how" of your project. But the fact that the abstract is a summation of your work doesn't make it something you can just jot down before moving on to the meat of your application. Many committees will base their decision on whether or not to continue considering your proposal on the abstract, so make sure you write it after you've completed your full proposal, so that you have a clear understanding of your project's goals and methods.

Summary of Proposal

The summary is basically a lengthened abstract, and is usually not required unless your proposal is more than five pages in length. This portion requires that you establish the blueprint for your project; it is an outline of what you will present the committee in your full proposal. It's not necessary to write more than a page or two for your summary, so keep it concise and discuss only the most important details of your project.

Introduction

The main purpose of the introduction is to give your project some historical perspective and explain how your work will contribute and add to past studies in the same field. Use this space to explain how other studies in your field have influenced your project, specifically addressing the breakthroughs that have made your studies possible. This section helps to establish your credibility as a potential fellow, showing committees that you are aware of the contributions of others to your field and that you are capable applying their knowledge to your own work.

Objectives

This section is self-explanatory. Tell committees what you seek to gain from this project, and if applicable, what hypotheses you have made entering the initial stages of the fellowship.

Methods and Materials

Use this section to elaborate on where you're going to do your work and by what means you plan on collecting the information necessary to successfully complete the project.

Budget

The budget is an honest assessment of how much you will need to complete your project successfully. It should include the total projected expenses of the project, and you should fully detail how you plan on meeting those expenses, especially if you feel they may exceed the amount allotted by the fellowship committee.

Calculate Carefully

Be sure to cover all of your financial bases. Many committees award fellows based on need rather than dole out a fixed sum of money, so you may be able to reap the benefits if you can clearly and accurately project the funding you will need to complete your work.

Appendix

Depending upon what the committees request, you may be asked to include your curriculum vitae, a list of prizes and fellowships already awarded, creative work, or publications written. Some committees do not ask for specific materials, just anything you feel may bolster your cause. If you choose to send additional information, choose it wisely; committees frown upon students who send boxes full of materials, as it takes up their valuable time and space.

Setting Yourself Apart

The main goal of the proposal is to describe at length (usually from five to 20 pages, to be exact) your goals for the fellowship or grant and how you plan on achieving them. And just as in any other part of the application, it is important to convey your thoughts in a manner that is tailored for the specific application you're working on. You must show the committee that you have a grasp of the ideals and aims of the fellowship or grant in question while proving yourself to be a qualified candidate.

The best way to really set your proposal apart for your competitors' is through research. You must prove that you are expert in your particular field of study. What better way to become an expert than to talk to experts? Consult with professors, professionals, and students who have experience in your particular field to get a sense of how you might want to use your fellowship or grant. Then, once you've come up with an idea and written your proposal, show it to these same individuals to make sure your proposal will fly.

Make Copies

Be sure to make photocopies of the forms—before and after you fill out the application. Use the first copy (or copies!) for your early attempts to fill out the form. The copy you make after you're all done is the evidence you'll need if and when someone in the fellowships office misplaces your original form.

Do not, however, turn in a photocopied application form after you've filled it out. Committees want you to follow instructions and send back exactly what they asked of you the way they asked you to do it. If you send them a photocopied form, committees will assume that you simply couldn't do it their way, and as nitpicky as that may sound, it's enough reason for them to quickly and easily reject you.

A Note on Presentation

Another important thing to remember about the various components of your application form is one that students often overlook: Neatness counts! Of course, being overly meticulous about the appearance of your application is a great way to take time away from working on its content (which is always the most important part), but this is not to say that you should not pay attention to the way your form looks. If you think you can get away with misspelling words or leaving white-out on your application sheet, you're in for a rough treatment from fellowship and grant committees. Always type your form unless instructed to do otherwise. It's professional, it's neat, and it makes committees think you put some effort into your form.

Because no two forms are the same, it's important to go over the applications fastidiously as you fill them out; there's nothing more embarrassing than putting a response for one question in the box for a completely different one!

It's inevitable that you will make some seemingly fatal error on at least one of your applications. Make sure that you either request more than one application from each organization to which you apply or make copies of each form.

The neatness rule also applies to the essays you write. After having taken their time to perfect their writing, applicants often forget to worry about one final facet of their essay—its presentation. Aesthetics are important when it comes to writing your personal statement. Use a simple font (Times is always a safe bet) that is no larger than 12 point, and keep your margins reasonable and uniform. It may not be a Monet, but it never hurts to make your essay pretty.

The way you fill out our application—both its content and its appearance—is a reflection on the amount of thought you put into it. In other words, a person who handwrites his application or leaves ink splotches on the page will certainly be considered an applicant who was too lazy to put his full effort into his work.

The Next Step

After you send off your completed application forms, the next step is to wait to hear if you will be called in to participate in the next stage of the application process, the interview. Chapter 3 will provide you with valuable tips on how to ace this part of the process.

Acing Your Interview

3

Ask most people who have applied to college or graduate school or for fellowships and grants about their interviews, and you'll generally get one of two answers: either "It went great!" or "It was terrible!" This reflects the common perception that the ability to interview well is a genetic trait and that those of us who have trouble in the interview setting will never improve. Of course, this notion is completely unfounded. Whether or not you consider yourself good at interviews or not, it always helps to prepare yourself to face the selection committee firing squad. Different fellowship committees often ask the same types of questions. So if you take the time to review your application and hone your speaking skills, you should do just fine in the clutch.

It is important to note that the majority of fellowships and grants do not require an interview. However, the more "prestigious" fellowships almost always require one or more interviews in the course of the application process. Those fellowships that do conduct them usually review your materials before deciding whether to invite you for an interview, usually a month or more after the application deadline. If you receive such an invitation, you should be proud of yourself: You've made the first cut, and you're now competing against a significantly smaller applicant pool.

Preparation Methods

To be at your absolute best, it's a good idea to spend some time preparing in the days preceding the interview.

Know Your Stuff

The toughest questions you will be asked in your interview will revolve around your actual proposal. You've made it this far because the committee has confidence in your ideas and abilities. Now they want to make sure that your conception of the fellowship and your particular project jibe with theirs. The only way you can convince them is to know your proposal like the back of your hand.

Many college career advisors agree that the most important factor in separating a successful interview from a dud is the applicant's confidence level. How do you gain confidence for a task as overwhelming as the interview? Know what you're talking about.

So before you head for your interview, reread every section of your application, especially your personal statement and proposal. Take this advice from a future Rhodes scholar:

> *Each applicant should know his essays inside and out. Because the interview committees will have plenty of written information on the applicant, he should be ready for questions about himself. This doesn't mean, "What's your favorite color?" Rather, be ready for questions about academic and political issues designed to reveal something about the applicant.*

Show Your Sophistication

"There's no substitute for being well read. Start subscribing to an intelligent magazine or two (I read *Foreign Affairs*, the *New Yorker*, and the *New Republic*) and a major newspaper your freshman year, and keep up with it. It gives you a range of issue to be able to talk about in an interview beyond your academic interests. Reading serious literature outside your discipline helps as well."

—Tulane University Senior

Also, make sure you know just as much about their fellowship as they do about your application. Go over the description of the award, and figure out how your personal goals mesh with with the fellowship's purpose and ideals. Don't think you can get away with merely giving your interviewers a bare-bones synopsis of your proposal. They will certainly have looked over your materials in detail, and they will know if you're not getting at the heart of the matter.

Finally, decide on how you want to present yourself to the interview committee. Before the interview, it helps to jot down a list of personal characteristics you want to present to the committee and choose a few anecdotes to support your assertions. During the interview, try your best to incorporate these examples into your answers.

Practice Interviews

One of the last things you should do before embarking on your not-so-perilous journey is to schedule a mock interview. Most colleges hold workshops at the beginning of the academic year in which they both detail the fellowship/grant application process and set up times when you can do a practice interview with a member of their career services staff. If your institution offered workshops that you missed and you're still interested in having a mock interview, just head on over to the career services office and find their fellowships and grants department. You should be able to easily reschedule one.

The best way to avoid sticking your foot in your mouth on the day of the interview is to experience the shame a few days in advance with someone who has no stake in your application. That way, you'll never do it again!

The Benefits of Practice

"I found the practice interviews particularly useful. The more you experience the pressure and the rigor of the interview situation, the more comfortable and the more proficient you become with the process. Several people in my residential college and at career services were instrumental in this regard."

—Yale University Senior

Acing the Interview

Once you're done preparing and practicing, it's on to the actual interview. You're already confident. You're totally loose. And you have an idea of how to answer their toughest questions. So what's left to worry about? Being positive and looking sharp!

Interview Committees

The first thing you'll probably note when you enter the interviewing room is the number of people in there with you. Many of the fellowships that require interviews don't conduct one-on-one sessions as college admissions officers do. Instead, you'll probably be interviewed by a few committee members. And chances are, you might not be the only applicant being interviewed.

Don't let sheer numbers intimidate you. You should not allow the group asking the questions to turn into an inquisition panel. Committees are looking to see which applicants crack when placed among a group. Try to think positively: You're in the room because the committee sees something positive in your application. And if you're in there with a few other applicants, try not to view the situation as a competition. Don't belittle the accomplishments of others, and don't try to speak for the whole group of applicants. Just be yourself, go with the flow, and show your pearly whites from time to time!

Stomach Flip-Flops

"The interview portion of the process is almost universally dreaded, and I went in with my stomach doing flip-flops. The first law of fellowships goes something like this: The committee will, without question, find some way to stump you, no matter how much you have prepared. The key is not to know everything, but to keep your cool and hold steady under fire. The committee does not care how many facts you can toss out; they want to learn how you think and react in a dialogue."

—Yale University Senior

High Stakes Craps Games

"If I did the process over again, I would avoid putting so much pressure on myself during the interview stage. When all is said and done, the fellowships are like a game of high-stakes craps. You get to the table with some established level of academic and extracurricular achievement, and then it's just a roll of the dice. All you can do is go in and be yourself. Though it may sound like hackneyed advice, the fact of the matter is that nervousness causes you to tighten up, and being tight counts decisively against you."

—Yale University Senior

"Softball" Questions

While it's impossible to know exactly what you'll be asked, it's a safe bet that committees will limber you up with a few softballs before throwing their heat at you. These "softballs" are usually questions that don't have any one specific answer. Committees generally don't take too much stock in what you say (as long as you don't go off on a rant advocating slavery or something along those lines). Instead, they are interested in how you say it. The key to responding to these questions is to be cool, calm, and collected.

Some frequently asked questions include:

- Tell us a little about yourself.
- Describe your best friends.
- What is your definition of fun?
- How did your extracurricular activities affect you in college?
- What have you gained most from your college education?
- If you could use three words to describe yourself, what would they be?
- What is your biggest weakness?
- If you could go back and do everything over again, would you?

Make sure you've thought about how you might answer these open-ended questions well before you actually begin your interview. They are key opportunities to explain why you are a qualified candidate without being limited by the necessity to tailor your responses to more pointed questions.

When You Don't Know the Answer . . .

"I think it's very important to stay in control of the interview. By that I mean even if you don't know the specific answer to a question, you can probably may a connection to something you can speak intelligently about. It's absolutely essential that you do this. Otherwise, the interviewers sense your weakness, and they jump all over it, asking more and more specific questions about something you obviously know little about. At this point you've lost control and you're pretty much dead."

—Tulane University Senior

Stress Interviews

A common tactic employed by interviewing panels that often fazes candidates is to conduct what is known as a "stress interview." In stress interviews, interviewers attempt to make applicants feel uncomfortable by asking questions that throw them for a loop. Committees often learn the most about their candidates through these types of situations—they can gauge how the applicant reacts to pressure and hostility. But what candidates often fail to recognize is that these interviews aren't really intended to test personal opinions. Instead, committees want to find out if applicants exhibit grace under fire.

Some questions you might encounter in a stress interview are:

- Explain your poor grades/standardized test score.
- You've taken few classes in (subject). Why are you applying for this fellowship?
- You seem to have spread yourself thin with extracurricular activities. How do you expect to have time for this project?
- Your proposal is vague. Why didn't you take more time to improve it?

As you can see, the questions are often brutal. To make matters worse, interviewers have been known to look away from the candidate, chew on their pens, twitch their legs, and partake in almost any other annoying habit you could imagine during stress interviews. But you can dodge these fireballs by keeping your confidence and your cool.

When you've been asked a question in a stress interview, be certain to take a few seconds to compose your thoughts before blurting out a forced answer. The committee is in no rush, and they appreciate the thought you put into your responses. And never allow the panel to change your opinion of your accomplishments. Just as you should be proud to have gotten this far in the application process, you should always be proud of what got you there. Always be honest with your answers, even if it means disagreeing with the panel.

Under no circumstances should you respond to a question whose answer you don't know. Just say those three simple words, "I don't know," and you'll be fine. Or even better, give the committee something to laugh about. When asked a stumper, one applicant told his interviewers that he would find out the answer and fax it to them. Another simply asked the committee what they thought the answer to the question was. Members told him they had no clue.

Probing Your Personal Ethics

"During my final Rhodes interview, I was asked which qualities in a politician's personality should exclude him from elected office. Adultery? Past drug use? Membership in the KKK? Having cheated on a college exam? Nonpayment of taxes? In discussing each shortcoming of the hypothetical politician, I was revealing something about my own ethics."

—University of Michigan Senior

As a general rule, whether it be in an interview or in a nightclub, one of the best ways to make a great impression is with your sense of humor. Putting a smile on your interviewers' faces will get you on the right track. Be open, enthusiastic, and relaxed. Don't slouch, slur your speech, or jitter. And make sure you look into the interviewers' eyes as much as possible. Self-confidence shows both in your body language and your words, and committees can sense whether you've got what it takes just by taking a quick glance at you.

Ask Your Own Questions

When a panel has exhausted its list of questions, they will almost always give you a chance to add something they haven't yet heard in the interview. Just make sure you don't leave without taking advantage of this opportunity. When you step into the room, you should have a number of questions ready, ones that get to the heart of the fellowship. Ask questions that prove you've done your homework and that will show the committee you've got a vested interest in their program.

After the Interview

You may leave the interview thinking you've conquered the world. Alternatively, you may leave thinking your chances of acceptance are next to nothing. Either way, one of the most important parts of the interview comes afterward, when you write your follow-up letter.

Once you're home (and do this immediately, so you don't forget), sit down and write a short letter thanking the individuals who interviewed you. If there was more than one, write a separate letter to each. In the letter, in addition to saying a simple "thank you," it's a good idea to include something you discussed during your visit, just to let your interviewers know that you actually paid attention and that you are still thinking about what they asked you. Whether you write a typed or handwritten letter is up to you.

The Hardest Part

"Most difficult was the waiting period. With the Rhodes Scholarship, I began working on the written portion of the application in June, submitted it to my University's Senior Scholarship Committee in early September, and did not find out my fate until December. Thus I invested almost six months' worth of emotional and physical energy."

—University of Michigan Senior

After your interview, you will most likely have to wait some time to hear whether or not the committee has decided to award you the fellowship or grant you seek. Most committees will inform candidates within a month of the deadline. However, when interviews are required, the waiting process is much more tiresome. In addition to the month or more it takes to get an interview, you will have to wait another several weeks after the interview for the committee's decision. But hang in there! The end is in sight.

Yale Daily News
OLDEST COLLEGE DAILY | FOUNDED JANUARY 28, 1878

Fellowship and Grant Listings

Prestigious Fellowships and Grants

4

"Prestigious" fellowships. Sounds like an awfully haughty title, doesn't it? But ask any college career advisor whether the title indicates that certain fellowships are better than others, and they'll tell you no way. Ask them if they're harder to get, however, and they'll definitely say yes. The admissions policies for these awards are so stringent because, in general, the fellowships and grants listed in this chapter have more money to dole out over a longer period of time. And with these awards, money is usually the name of the game.

So what does it take to have a shot at one of these privileged few? Generally speaking, it helps to have a GPA of 3.5 or higher, an outstanding extracurricular record that demonstrates your leadership skills, distinction in your field of study (both inside and outside of the classroom), several strong letters of recommendation, and a truly outstanding written proposal.

A Two-Stage Process

What truly differentiates the application process for most of the awards listed in this chapter from other awards is that even if you've got all the wonderful characteristics listed above, you can't even apply unless you're nominated by your school. In other words, the application process is divided into two separate stages. First, you must submit your materials to a committee at your undergraduate institution. The committee takes a look at the credentials of all the students applying for that particular fellowship, then invites a select few to continue on to the national competion.

Don't Get Scared—Work Harder

"Do not be daunted by the odds. My adviser told me flat out, 'Every two years, 33 U.S. senators are elected. At the same time, 32 Rhodes Scholars are elected. So you have the same chance of becoming a senator as you do a Rhodes Scholar.' This humbled me, but I was not frightened off; I simply worked harder to prepare."

—University of Michigan Senior

Because the process is divided into two separate parts, it is crucial that applicants pay close attention to deadlines. Most of the fellowships and grants listed below require that you send in your pertinent materials to the appropriate undergraduate selection committee very early in the school year, and as any college student knows, it is a difficult task to motivate during the first weeks back on campus.

The best way to get around procrastinating is to get most of your application done over the summer, when you have time to do just about anything. Think about your proposal and write an outline. Work on your personal statement. Obtain your updated transcipt. And ask your recommenders to write supporting letters well before the first day of school. This way, you can put together a much more polished application than most of your competitors, who will be struggling to juggle finishing their applications and partying.

If you are lucky enough to make it past the intercollegiate competition, congratulations! But don't get too cocky or complacent—you've got some more work ahead of you. Take another look at your materials and be sure to bolster them with all the new activities, accomplishments, or academic achievements you may have stockpiled in the time between the collegiate and national competition deadlines. Keep an open line of communication with the members of the undergraduate committee that selected you to compete in the national competition and ask their advice on how to win the fellowship. And use your career services office to contact former winners of the fellowship and ask them about the next steps in the process—refining your application and making a solid impression. These resources are right at your fingertips, and they will go a long way toward turning you from a contender into a winner.

Be aware that it's a tall order to go after one of these heavy hitters. But if you feel that you've got the credentials, you should definitely consider applying for them. The rewards you reap if selected far outweigh the trials and tribulations of the application process.

If you choose to accept this mission, good luck!

Fellowship and Grant Listings

A Note on Contact Information: As you will see, not all the fellowships listed in this chapter provide addresses to which students can write in order to request application materials. Many prestigious fellowships require that you first register with your undergraduate career services office before actually beginning the applications process. You will receive the materials from a career counselor only after you have checked in with them.

The Barry M. Goldwater Scholarship Program

Fields of Study:

Science and mathematics

Purpose of Fellowship:

Since 1986, the Goldwater Scholarship has provided funding for undergraduate science and mathematics students who demonstrate the ability, potential, and desire to successfully pursue these fields after graduation. The award covers some of the expenses for up to two years of graduate school. Up to 300 students receive the fellowship annually.

Criteria:

Applicants must be current sophomores or juniors pursuing a baccalaureate degree. They must be U.S. citizens or resident aliens with the intent to obtain U.S. citizenship. To be considered for the award, applicants must have a college GPA of at least 3.0, and their ultimate educational goal should be the Ph.D. Students who plan on attending medical school may apply only if they intend to work as researchers rather than as clinical physicians.

Selection Guidelines:

In order to apply for the Goldwater, students must be chosen to represent their college by the appropriate undergraduate selection committee. Those individuals who pass this initial screening must forward their application to the Goldwater committee. Selection criteria for both the initial screening and the national competition are based upon the student's academic record, field of study and committment to that field, career objectives, and letters of recommendation. Applicants are required to submit three recommendations; at least two must come from faculty members.

Financial Award:

The Goldwater covers up to $7,500 per year for tuition, fees, books, and room and board for the first two years of graduate study in the fields of mathematics, engineering, and the natural sciences.

Application Materials:

Can be obtained from your career services office.

Deadline:

Interested individuals must submit their application materials to their college selection committee by early December.

Beinecke Brothers Memorial Scholarship Program

Field of Study:

Open to students of all fields

Purpose of Fellowship:

The Beinecke provides funding for a student's senior year of college, as well as his first two years of graduate school. The award is available to college juniors who have displayed scholastic achievement, motivation, and potential during their time at college. The committee awards approximately 18 scholarships annually.

Criteria:

The award is available to students with demonstrated financial need. Applicants must be U.S. citizens.

Selection Guidelines:

Students must first submit their applications to the appropriate college advisory committee. Upon reviewing the applications, committees may nominate one student for the award. The application is then forwarded to the Beinecke committee.

Financial Award:

A $2,000 grant for use during the recipient's senior year of college, followed by financial support of up to $15,000 per year for the first two years of graduate school.

Application Materials:

Can be obtained from your career services office.

Deadline:

Application must be turned into the candidate's college advisory committee by early February.

The British Marshall Scholarship

Field of Study:

Open to all fields, but students must study in the United Kingdom

Purpose of Fellowship:

In 1953, the British government founded the British Marshall Scholarship to express its gratitude for economic and military assistance provided by the United States following World War II. The scholarship is named for American General George Marshall, the brains behind the postwar European Recovery Program that began in 1947.

The Marshall funds two or three years of either undergraduate or graduate study at any university in the United Kingdom. Along with the Rhodes Scholarship, the Marshall is probably the most prestigious and most generous award available for American students. As such, competition for the fellowship is always fierce. Forty Marshall Scholarships are awarded annually.

Criteria:

Applicants must be U.S. citizens between the ages of 18 and 26 and must have graduated from an undergraduate institution before accepting the award. Students must possess a GPA of at least 3.7 to be considered. Married students are eligible, but those who intend to remain unmarried will be given preference by the selection committee.

Marshall Versus Rhodes

"I chose the Rhodes over the Marshall because I sought the community of scholars that comes along with the scholarship. While Marshall scholars are spread throughout Great Britain at a number of different universities, every Rhodes Scholar attends Oxford. The Rhodes House is there as a resource, and all of the students can provide support and guidance for one another."

—Yale University Senior

Selection Guidelines:

Students must first send their application to the appropriate undergraduate selection committee for an initial review. Those applicants who receive institutional endorsement are eligible for the national competition. Students who have already graduated from college may either apply through their alma mater's committee or may send their form directly to the Marshall Commission, as long as their application has been endorsed by an employer or comparable advisor.

Those applications that receive endorsement are forwarded to one of six regional committees. The candidate chooses either the region in which they claim permanent residence, or that in which they are studying. Applicants interview with their regional officers in mid-November, and each region may elect a predetermined number of candidates for the award. Regional officers also select individuals for the alternate list.

Final decisions are based upon a number of criteria, including the student's academic record, personal statement, written proposal, two letters of recommendation, and the interview. The Marshall interview has typically been rated as one of the most difficult fellowship interviews. The questions posed in this interview often call upon candidates to delineate their philosophical views and to demonstrate their familiarity with current events. Candidates should also be familiar with the achievements of George Marshall.

Financial Award:

Two years of study at any British university. The Marshall committee may grant certain students special permission for a third year of study. The award covers tuition, educational fees, transportation to and from the U.K., and other expenses. The total award averages approximately 16,000 pounds per year.

Application Materials:

Can be obtained from your career services office.

Deadline:

Applicants must submit their application to their undergraduate committee in early September. Finalists are selected in October, and the regional committees conduct interviews in November. Marshall Scholars are selected shortly thereafter and are announced approximately one to two weeks after the interviews.

Fulbright Grants

Field of Study:

Study abroad

Purpose of Fellowship:

The Fulbright Grants are awarded annually by the U.S. government and the Institute of International Education to fund programs of study or research across the globe. Approximately 900 grants are awarded annually for projects in over 100 countries.

Criteria:

Applicants must be U.S. citizens who hold at least a bachelor's degree before beginning the program (the exception: creative or performing artists, who must instead have completed at least four years of professional study). Most grants are awarded to students who already demonstrate proficiency in the designated country's language. Those students who choose to study in France, Africa, or the Far East must apply through their universities.

Selection Guidelines:

In addition to completing the Fulbright form, applicants are encouraged to submit letters of recommendation from individuals from the designated country.

Financial Award:

The fellowship is awarded either as a full grant, a fixed-sum grant, or a travel-only grant. The application form is the same for all three types. The full grant provides round-trip transportation to the student's designated country, as well as language courses, tuition, books, and health and accident insurance. Fulbright fixed-sum grants furnish a set payment in American dollars to recipients whose designated country lacks a Fulbright Commission or Foundation. Travel-only grants offer round-trip transportation, limited health and accident insurance, and the cost of foreign orientation programs. They are awarded only to students studying in Germany, Hungary, Italy, and Korea.

Application Materials:

Can be obtained from your career services office.

Deadline:

Late September

Harry S. Truman Scholarship Program

Field of Study:

Government or public service

Purpose of Fellowship:

The award is offered to students with demonstrated academic and leadership skills who intend to enter the realm of public service after their schooling. It covers the recipient's senior year of college, as well as three years of graduate school, and it also offers leadership development programs and special opportunities for internships and employment with the federal government. Up to 85 applicants receive the award annually.

Criteria:

In order to qualify for the award, students must have a cumulative GPA of at least 3.7 and must major in a field that leads to a career in government. Financial need is not considered. To be competitive, applicants must support their outstanding academic record with demonstrated leadership skills outside of the classroom (especially in the realm of government and public policy), intellectual depth, and communication skills.

Selection Guidelines:

The committee awards one college junior from each of the fifty states, the District of Columbia, Puerto Rico, and either Guam, the Virgin Islands, American Samoa, or the Commonwealth of the Northern Mariana Islands. Thirty-two other applicants are selected as at-large recipients of the Truman.

Applicants must first submit their forms to their undergraduate committee, which chooses as many as four individuals to participate in the national competition. Selection criteria for both college and national committees include the student's academic record, a solid record of public and community service, leadership skills, and commitment to the fields of government and public policy. In addition, applicants must attach a written proposal indicating which graduate degree they plan to pursue and which schools they would consider attending for graduate school, an essay analyzing a significant public policy issue, and letters of recommendation.

Financial Award:

Recipients receive $3,000 for their senior year of college, then $27,000 over three years of graduate school. In those three years, recipients receive from $9,000 to $13,500 per year, depending on the length of their degree program.

Application Materials:

Can be obtained from your career services office.

Deadline:

In mid-October of their junior year, applicants must submit their application to the applicable college committee, which chooses as many as four individuals to represent the school in the national competion. After the selected individuals' forms have been sent to the Truman admissions committee, members select finalists and invite them for regional interviews beginning in February. Final decisions are announced in April.

Hertz Foundation Fellowships

Fields of Study:

Applied and physical sciences, including mathematics, chemistry, physics, and engineering

Purpose of Fellowship:

The Hertz Fellowship is designed for students who display the potential to become leaders in the world of science and technology. The award provides funding for the graduate-level studies of recipients who plan on attaining an advanced degree in the future.

Criteria:

Applicants must be either seniors in college or graduate students majoring in any of the applied sciences. They must also be U.S. citizens or permanent residents. Competitive candidates have an undergraduate GPA of at least 3.75. Students who plan on applying to medical school or joint degree programs need not apply.

Selection Guidelines:

The Hertz selection committee bases its decisions upon the student's application, transcript, letters of recommendation, and interview. While students decide for which school they would like to use the fellowship, the institution of choice must come from a list provided by the Hertz Foundation in the application materials.

Financial Award:

Recipients earn a $20,000 stipend for a nine-month period of study. In addition, the Hertz Foundation provides an educational allowance to the individual's institution of choice. Students may renew the fellowship for as many as five years.

Application Materials:

Obtain by writing to:

The Fannie and John Hertz Foundation
Box 5032
Livermore, CA 94551-5032

Deadline:

Application is due in mid-October. The Hertz Foundation organizes campus interviews in November.

James Madison Fellowship Program

Fields of Study:

U.S. government and politics, American history

Purpose of Fellowship:

A federally funded program, the Madison Fellowship allows students to teach the U.S. Constitution at the secondary school level before receiving funds for up to two years of graduate school.

Criteria:

The Madison is available to graduating seniors without prior teaching experience. Applicants must intend to teach American history or political science as a career. In addition, candidates must plan on attending graduate school with the goal of attaining a master's degree.

Selection Guidelines:

The application includes a 600-word essay on the future of education. In addition, the committee asks for information about your future studies as a graduate student, including a list of masters programs to which you will apply.

Financial Award:

Funding for as many as two years of master's level graduate study of the U.S. Constitution. This award is not activated until the recipient has taught at least one year at the secondary school level. The recipient will only receive two years of funding from the Madison committee if he has spent two years as a teacher at the designated secondary school.

Application Materials:

Obtain by writing to:

The James Madison Fellowship Program
P.O. Box 4030
Iowa City, IA 52243-4030

Deadline:

Early March

Luce Scholars Program

Field of Study:

Asian studies

Purpose of Fellowship:

The Luce pays for one year of work or study in Asia as part of an internship designed by recipients based on their personal interests and qualifications. The program is specifically geared toward students with little or no experience of Asia. The country of choice is at the applicant's discretion. Eighteen individuals receive the fellowship annually.

Criteria:

Applicants must be U.S. citizens under the age of 30 with at least a college degree. Those students who accept the fellowship will not receive academic credit for their project.

Selection Guidelines:

Candidates must submit their application to the appropriate undergraduate committee for an initial screening. Each school may nominate up to three applicants for the national competition.

Selection criteria are the same for both the collegiate and national competition. Students must demonstrate maturity, leadership skills, and sensitivity toward other individuals. The applicant's academic record, personal statement, and four letters of recommendation are considered. Candidates need not have developed a specific plan for their time in Asia by the time they have applied.

Only a select few applicants receive final-round interviews. Those who do are expected to familiarize themselves with the life of Henry Luce.

Financial Award:

The Luce Foundation pays for the recipient's transportation and insurance. In addition, Luce Scholars receive a monthly stipend to cover their expenses. The committee may also award any additional cost-of-living allowances.

Application Materials:

Can be obtained from your career services office.

Deadline:

Candidates must submit their applications to their undergraduate committee by early November. Those individuals who are selected for the national competition receive primary interviews in December and January. Final-round interviews are conducted in February and March.

The Mellon Fellowships in Humanistic Studies

Fields of Study:

Humanistic studies, including American studies, art history, foreign language, history, literature, philosophy, and religion

Purpose of Fellowship:

The award funds one year of graduate study in a Ph.D. program in the United States or Canada for students interested in pursuing the humanities.

Criteria:

Candidates must be college seniors or recent graduates who have not yet enrolled in graduate school. In order to qualify, individuals must intend to pursue a Ph.D. and a career in humanistic studies, preferably teaching. Applicants must be U.S. citizens or permanent residents. All candidates must have taken the GRE and must fill out a foreign language competence form.

Selection Guidelines:

Aside from completing the application form, students must submit a 1,000-word essay describing their academic and intellectual interests and how they relate to the candidate's future goals. Applicants must also list the graduate schools to which they will apply and state why they are interested in those institutions. Three letters of recommendation are required.

Financial Award:

Costs associated with a year of graduate study at the school of the recipient's choice.

Application Materials:

Obtain by writing to:

The Woodrow Wilson National Fellowships Foundation
Mellon Fellowships
CN 5329
Princeton, NJ 08543-5329

Deadline:

Application must be turned in no later than December 31; the candidate must have taken the GRE by December 1.

The Morris K. Udall Scholarship Program

Fields of Study:

Environmental public policy, Native American tribal public policy, or health care

Purpose of Fellowship:

The Udall Scholarship honors Congressman Morris K. Udall, a champion of public service. It is designed to serve undergraduates with a demonstrated interest in careers in public policy. In addition, the fellowship provides opportunities for Native American and Native Alaskan students who are interested in public policy. The committee selects 70 winners annually.

Criteria:

Students must be undergraduate sophomores or juniors who are U.S. citizens or permanent residents. Competitive applicants have a GPA of at least 3.0 and are in the top quarter of the class. The committee selects recipients from two separate applicant pools: those who intend to pursue careers in environmental public policy, and those who are Native American and Native Alaskan students pursuing careers in health care or tribal public policy.

Selection Guidelines:

Applicants must first submit their forms in early February to their undergraduate selection committee, which can nominate up to six individuals for the national competition. Nominees must submit their final applications to the Udall committee in March.

Selection criteria for both the undergraduate and national competitions include the applicant's academic record, three letters of recommendation, potential to contribute to the field of public policy, and a personal statement. The personal statement requires applicants to discuss the impact of a significant public speech, legislative act, or public policy statement by Congressman Udall upon the candidate's particular field of interest.

Financial Award:

The Udall Scholarship covers up to $5,000 for the recipients' tuition, fees, books, and room and board. Winners are eligible for one year of support; however, sophomore recipients may apply again for the award as juniors.

Application Materials:

Obtain by writing to:

The Morris K. Udall Scholarship Program
2201 North Dodge Street
P.O. Box 4030
Iowa City, IA 52243

Deadline:

Candidates must submit their materials to the undergraduate committee in early February. Those who are nominated must send their final application to the Udall committee by March.

National Science Foundation Graduate and Minority Graduate Fellowships

Fields of Study:

Mathematics, physics, biology, engineering, behavioral sciences, and social sciences

Purpose of Fellowship:

The National Science Foundation (NSF) Fellowships provide support for full-time study or research leading to a master's degree or doctorate in the sciences. The award is meant for students at the beginning of their graduate studies who have demonstrated an aptitude for science or engineering. The fellowship generally covers a three-year span, and minorities are encouraged to apply—approximately 150 of the 1,000 total NSF fellowships awarded annually go to minorities. In addition, the NSF awards 90 Women in Engineering and Computer and Information Science (WECS) fellowships each year.

Criteria:

Applicants must be U.S. citizens, nationals, or permanent residents. Only college seniors and first-year graduate students may apply. In addition, candidates must have taken the GRE prior to applying.

Students applying for the Minority Graduate Fellowship must fall into one of the following ethnic groups: African American, American Indian, Hispanic, Native Alaskan, or Native Pacific Islander. The WECS award is available to women who plan to pursue graduate degrees in engineering or computer/information science and engineering.

NSF awards can be used at any non-profit U.S. or foreign graduate school. Those applicants who choose to study outside the United States must submit a letter stating the scientific benefits of studying at a foreign university.

Selection Guidelines:

After sending their form to the NSF, the applications are assigned to panels based on the applicant's chosen field of study. Criteria for acceptance include the student's academic record, GRE scores, written proposal, previous research experience, and four letters of recommendation.

Financial Award:

Recipients are awarded $15,000 for each 12-month period, plus a cost-of-education allowance of $9,500 paid to the graduate institution.

Application Materials:

Obtain by writing to:

The National Science Foundation Graduate Research Fellowship Program
ORAU
P.O. Box 3010
Oak Ridge, TN 37831-3010

Deadline:

The application form must be sent to the NSF by early November. Academic records, letters of recommendation, and GRE scores are due in mid-December.

The Raoul Wallenberg Scholarships

Field of Study:

Open to all fields, but recipients must study at Hebrew University in Jerusalem

Purpose of Fellowship:

The Wallenberg Scholarship is named after Raoul Wallenberg, a Swedish Christian diplomat who rescued Jews from the Nazi threat during the Holocaust. The award allows recent graduates to study in a specially designed graduate program at Hebrew University for one year. It strives to develop cultural awareness among a diverse group of recipients.

Criteria:

Applicants must be college seniors or recent graduates of a U.S. university. The program is nondenominational, with no religious restrictions. Applications are encouraged from students with varied academic interests and from all backgrounds.

Selection Guidelines:

The application requires a signature of endorsement from your institution's president, vice president, dean, or the department chair of your field of study.

Application Materials:

Obtain by writing to:

Office of Academic Affairs
The Hebrew University of Jerusalem
11 E. 69th Street
New York, NY 10021

Students with further questions should call the Office of Academic Affairs at (212) 472-2288.

Financial Award:

The Wallenberg commitee pays for a full year of study at Hebrew University, including transportation to and from Jerusalem.

The Rhodes Scholarship

Field of Study:

Open to all fields, but recipients must study at Oxford University in Oxford, England

Purpose of Fellowship:

One of the oldest and certainly one of the most prestigious fellowships available to American students, the Rhodes Scholarship funds two years of graduate study at Oxford University. It was established through an endowment by Cecil J. Rhodes in 1902. The Rhodes committee aims to reward applicants who have demonstrated leadership, intellect, originality, and the potential to better society in whatever field they choose to pursue after graduate school. Many consider the Rhodes to be the crème de la crème of fellowships, and the list of recipients is a virtual who's who of American celebrity. Thirty-two scholarships are awarded in the United States annually.

Criteria:

Applicants must be U.S. citizens between the ages of 18 and 24 who will have graduated with a bachelor's degree before taking the scholarship. Citizens of Canada, Australia, South Africa, Germany, New Zealand, Commonwealth Carribean, Zimbabwe, Bermuda, Hong Kong, Jamaica, Kenya, Malaysia, Malta, Pakistan, Singapore, Uganda, and Zambia may apply through their own countries. Since 1995, the committee has not restricted married candidates from applying. While there is no basement GPA for consideration, applicants must have a GPA of at least 3.5 to be competitive. Neither field of study nor financial need are considered by the Rhodes Committees.

Selection Guidelines:

Applicants must first submit their application to their undergraduate selection committee, which then nominates candidates for the national competition. Candidates apply as residents of one of the 50 states. They may choose their state of legal residence, or a state in which they have received at least two years of undergraduate schooling.

The national competition begins at the state level. Candidates interview first in their home state, after which each of the 50 committees selects two candidates to move on to the next step in the competition, the district level interviews. Both the state and district interviews take place in the same week. Students learn their fate from state officials after their first interviews, then either continue on to the state competition or head back home. There are a total of eight District Committees, each of which selects four Rhodes Scholars. Unlike with the Marshall Scholarship, the District Committees do not make an alternate list.

Both the state and district interviews are gala events that bring together some of the best and brightest from the regions in which they are held. Candidates initially meet as a group and attend a formal reception and dinner with members of the pertinent committee. On the following day of the competition, applicants are individually interviewed by the committee for approximately 30 minutes, and many are called back for a second, shorter interview. A student that receives a call-back interview does not necessarily stand a better chance of acceptance than one who does not. Once the committee has made its decisions, it calls all of the applicants together and announces the names of the state nominees or, at the district interviews, the two indivuals who have been selected as Rhodes Scholars.

In all three levels of competition—the undergraduate, state, and district levels—committees examine applications. Among the key criteria for selection include the student's academic record, list of activities and honors, five to eight letters of recommendation, and personal statement. The personal statement should be an essay of no longer than 1,000 words and should detail which degree program the candidate would pursue at Oxford and why. Students should be able to tie in their future goals with their time at Oxford, specifically detailing how they might use the specific courses, faculty, and facilities in the pursuit of their ultimate career choices.

The Rhodes interviews are considered extremely challenging, and they play huge roles in determining a candidate's fate. Students should be ready for open-ended questions that often do not have single answers (see chapter 3 of this book for details on how to ace your interview). It is also highly recommended that applicants conduct mock interviews and study the life of Cecil Rhodes before they head for the state and district competitions.

Those individuals lucky enough to earn a Rhodes Scholarship are placed in the Scholar's College of Oxford University, where they live with all the other

Rhodes Opens Doors

"I think it will open many doors for me: some in academia, many elsewhere. Because what matters most is that I will be receiving excellent intellectual training at Oxford University. Such rigorous scholarship will prepare me to work anywhere."

—University of Michigan Senior

"My strongest interest is probably in political journalism, and there's no doubt the Rhodes will probably open some doors there, though I think it's still going to require no shortage of effort on my part. I'm also interested in working in politics at some point, and, again, the Rhodes certainly doesn't hurt in terms of giving you access to a network that can open up opportunities. In both cases, though, I feel like I've already made some of my own opportunities happen. So the Rhodes is both a vindication of that and a way of building on what I've already done. That is, I don't think you come out of nowhere, having not done much with your life, then win a Rhodes and suddenly get elected president. It's a process that the Rhodes certainly complements, but the process must continue one way or another."

—Tulane University Senior

recipients of the award. Scholars may study anything ranging from undergraduate courses to those that qualify the student for the B.Phil., M.Phil., M.Litt., M.Sc., M.St., B.C.L., or D.Phil.

Financial Award:

The Rhodes Scholarship provides direct payment to the Scholar's College at Oxford of all approved fees, which includes matriculation, tuition, laboratory, and other set charges. In addition, recipients are given an annual maintenance allowance, as well as travel expenses to and from Oxford. Students may receive a third year's tuition if their plans of study warrant the award.

Application Materials:

Can be obtained from your career services office.

Deadline:

Candidates must submit their application materials to their undergraduate committees by early September. Once the student is nominated, her final application is due in October. State interviews are held in early December and are immediately followed by district interviews.

The Winston Churchill Foundation Scholarship

Fields of Study:

Engineering, mathematics, or science; subjects include biology, biochemistry, chemistry, computer science, mathematics, metallurgy, pharmacology, physics, plant breeding, and statistics

Purpose of Fellowship:

Established in 1959, the Churchill provides for a year of graduate study in engineering, mathematics, or science at the University of Cambridge in England. Ten recipients are awarded the fellowship annually. Recipients generally enroll in either the Master of Philosophy, Certificate of Postgraduate Study in natural science or chemical engineering, Certificate of Advanced Study in mathematics, or the Diploma in computer science or mathematical statistics programs.

Criteria:

Applicants must be U.S. citizens between the ages of 19 and 26. Their educational background may go as high as having attained an M.A., but students with a doctorate may not apply. To be competitive, applicants should have a GPA of at least 3.5. In addition, candidates must have taken the GRE before applying for the award.

Selection Guidelines:

Candidates must first submit their applications to their undergraduate selection committees, which may nominate up to two students for the national competition. Selection criteria at both the undergraduate and national levels include the student's academic record, GRE scores, and written proposal. Financial need is not a criterion for selection.

Financial Award:

The Churchill committee pays for the recipient's tuition and fees at Cambridge, as well as a maintenance allowance of either $7,200, if the individual enrolls in a nine-month academic program, or $9,000 for a 12-month program. Students are also provided with a $500 travel allowance. Additional funds are available for married students.

Application Materials:

Can be obtained from your career services office.

Deadlines:

Applicants must submit their materials to their undergraduate committee in early November. Those individuals nominated for the national competition must turn in their final materials by the end of November to be considered by the Churchill Committee.

5 The Arts

It has been said that the best route to a career in the arts—especially the performing arts—isn't as much through education as it is through God-given talent. The fact that there aren't nearly as many fellowships available in the arts as there are in other fields would seem at first glance to validate this argument. This is not to say, however, that the opportunities that do exist for postgraduates interested in pursuing an arts fellowship are any less valuable than those in other areas of study.

The fellowships listed in this chapter can generally be grouped into two categories: art history and the performing arts.

Art History Fellowships

The opportunities available to students in art history include the study of:

- History of art, architecture, and music
- Film and literary criticism
- Art conservation

So where do most recipients of these types of fellowships do most of their work? Usually in museums, where fellows generally spend most of their time studying in one or two specific departments within the institution. The educational payoff: Students gain access to their host institution's research collections and the chance to use its resources for projects relating to their field of interest. The financial payoff is not always as clear, however. Prizes vary widely, and are often unspecified until the host institution decides what it considers to be a fair stipend for its fellows. But many fellowships are much more generous than this. The Metropolitan Museum of Art in New York City, for example, pays close to $30,000 per year to some of its fellows.

Applications for fellowships specializing in art history often ask students to attach separate lists of art or art history courses they have taken, in addition to their transcripts. It is important to consider the type of museum or other institution to which you are applying when filling out your forms. Modern art museums might be interested in learning about your interest in the classics, but a better strategy would probably be to highlight your experience with modern art in your application.

Performing Arts Fellowships

If you're accepted to a performing arts fellowship, you should give yourself a standing ovation. Opportunities of this type are few and far between, reflecting the fact that arts organizations in the United States are notoriously underfunded. To make matters all the more difficult, those arts fellowships that currently exist are among the most competitive in the nation. But there's a reason they're so competitive: Performing arts fellowships are generally considered among the best available.

Most performing arts fellowships cover at least one of the following subjects:

- Filmmaking
- Fine art
- Music
- Creative writing

Filmmaking, Fine Art, and Creative Writing

Those applicants interested in writing, fine art, or filmmaking are usually spared having to actually do a song and dance in front of committee members.

Instead, they must submit their films or portfolios in addition to the application form. Most fellowships that require such supporting materials are very specific about what they would like to see, and they often limit both the number and type of pieces you can submit. The first step toward winning one of these awards is making sure you give committees what they actually want. As good as your work may be, your judges will not give you the benefit of the doubt if you submit six watercolor drawings when they asked for six samples drawn in pencil.

As any artist knows, putting together a compilation of work can be a long and arduous process, which means that the fellowship process begins long before you actually send away for the application form. So if you are truly serious about applying, start putting together your materials before you worry about the nitty-gritty details of the form. This will give you the time to package yourself accurately and keep deadline issues at an arm's length.

Performing Arts

The application process for a performing arts fellowship often involves two stages: the application form and the audition. When you're dealing with a field as competitive as the performing arts, it's always a good idea to score as many brownie points as possible with fellowship committees. So in order to win over committees with your application, you must do some background research on the fellowships to which you've chosen to apply. Know what you want from the award as well as as much as possible about the organization that is offering it.

If you've made it to the audition stage of the application, you're definitely in good shape. And if you're a performer, you've probably overcome stage fright at some point in your career as an artist. So don't let it get the best of you now! Practice your performance until you think you've got it down pat, then show it to teachers, parents, and friends. They're the type of audience that can provide you with feedback you can use to make the necessary adjustments for your final performance in front of the fellowship committee.

Once you've made it that far, all that's left for you to do is to break a leg!

Academy of Motion Picture Arts and Sciences—Student Academy Awards

Barbara Scharres
Columbus Drive at Jackson Boulevard
Chicago, IL 60603
Phone: (312) 443-3735

Field of Study: Filmmaking

Purpose of Fellowship: To support and encourage filmmakers with no previous professional experience. Awards are given in four categories—dramatic, documentary, animation, and experimental.

Criteria: Applicants must be enrolled in accredited colleges and universities and must submit films up to 60 minutes long, produced under the academic supervision of a faculty member. Films may be submitted in black-and-white or color and sound or silent.

Financial Award: Up to $2,000

Deadline: Early April

Broadcast Music, Inc. Awards to Student Composers

Barbara Petersen, Director
320 West 57th Street
New York, NY 10019
Phone: (212) 586-2000

Field of Study: Music

Purpose of Fellowship: To encourage young composers in the creation of concert music.

Criteria: Citizens or permanent residents of the Western Hemisphere (North, Central and South American and Caribbean nations).

Financial Award: $500 to $2,500

Deadline: Early February

Edward F. Albee Foundation, Inc.: William Flanagan Memorial Creative Persons Center—Fellowship for Artists/Writers/Composers

The Edward F. Albee
Foundation, Inc.
14 Harrison Street
New York, NY 10013
Phone: (212) 226-2020

Field of Study: Fine arts

Purpose of Fellowship: To provide a supportive atmosphere for one month for writers, painters, sculptors, and composers at the William Flanagan Memorial Creative Persons Center in Montauk, Long Island.

Criteria: Applicants must submit samples of their work. Standards of admission are based on talent and need.

Financial Award: Support for one month at the Center from June 1 to October 1.

Deadline: Early April

Elizabeth Greenshields Foundation Award

1814 Sherbrooke Street W.
Montreal, Quebec
Canada H3H IE4

Field of Study: Fine art, including painting, drawing, and printmaking

Purpose of Fellowship: To aid talented young artists in the early stages of their careers.

Criteria: Artists who are under 31 years of age and have started or completed training in an established school of art, and/or demonstrate a commitment to making art a lifetime career.

Financial Award: $10,000 Canadian

Deadline: Unspecified

Esther Boyer College of Music Doctoral Fellowships in Composition, Music Education, and Performance

Boyer College of Music
Temple University
Box GB
Philadelphia, PA 19122
Phone: (215) 204-7609
Fax: (215) 204-4957
Web site:
http://www.temple.edu/departments/music/index.html

Field of Study: Music

Purpose of Fellowship: To support dissertation work at Temple University in composition, music education, and performance.

Criteria: Awards are contingent upon the candidate's admission to the Graduate School of Temple University, experience, an interview, and departmental recommendation.

Financial Award: Up to $16,000 plus full tuition remission

Deadline: Early February

Getty Center for the History of Art and the Humanities—Research Support Grants

Donald Anderle, Assistant Director for Resource Collections
401 Wilshire Blvd
Santa Monica, CA 90401

Field of Study: Humanities

Purpose of Fellowship: To assist scholars and advanced students who are unaffiliated with the Getty Center to pursue short-term research projects using the resources of the Center's resource collections.

Criteria: Ability to demonstrate a compelling need to use Center materials that are not available to them in other libraries and archives. Limited number of grants to cover a part of travel and per diem expenses; research costs available on competitive basis.

Financial Award: Depends upon distance traveled and length of stay

Deadline: Unspecified

Getty Center for the History of Art and the Humanities—Predoctoral Fellowships

The Scholars and Seminars Program
401 Wilshire Blvd., Suite 700
Santa Monica, CA 90401-1455
Phone: (310) 458-9811
Fax: (310) 395-1515
E-mail: fellowships@getty.edu

Field of Study: Humanities and social sciences

Purpose of Fellowship: To encourage research on Los Angeles and Southern California.

Criteria: Candidates for a doctorate in the humanities or social sciences who expect to complete their dissertations during the fellowship year, and whose research relates to the subject of the nature and the idea of collecting. Residency at the Getty Center is required during the award year.

Financial Award: $18,000 for a nine-month term, plus up to $4,000 for relocation costs

Deadline: Early December

Hagley/Winterthur—Fellowships in Arts and Industries

Dr. Philip B. Scranton
Hagley Museum and Library
P.O. Box 3630
Wilmington, DE 19807-0630
Phone: (302) 658-2400
E-mail: crl.strauss@udel.edu

Field of Study: All fields

Purpose of Fellowship: A cooperative program of short- to medium-term research fellowships for scholars interested in the historical and cultural relationships between economic life and the arts, including design, architecture, crafts, and the fine arts.

Criteria: Available to both degree candidates and senior scholars, as well as applicants without advanced degrees.

Financial Award: No more than $1,000 per month for up to six months

Deadline: Early December

Henry Luce Foundation/ACLS Dissertation Fellowship Program in American Art

Office of Fellowships & Grants
228 East 45th Street
New York, NY 10017-3398
Fax: (212) 949-8058
E-mail: grants@acls.org
Web site: http://www.acls.org

Field of Study: Art history

Purpose of Fellowship: To assist graduate students in any stage of Ph.D. dissertation research/writing focusing on any period of U.S. art history.

Criteria: U.S. citizens or permanent residents. Applicants must be Ph.D. candidates in a department of art history with a dissertation focused on the above topic. Applicants should have completed all requirements for the Ph.D. except the dissertation before beginning tenure.

Financial Award: $18,500 for a one-year term

Deadline: Mid-November

Internship Program at the Solomon R. Guggenheim Museum

Solomon R. Guggenheim
Museum Internship Program
1071 Fifth Avenue
New York, NY 10128-0173
Phone: (212) 423-3526
Fax: (212) 423-3650

Field of Study: Art history

Purpose of Fellowship: To enable graduate students to supplement their course work with practical museum training.

Criteria: Students enrolled in graduate programs in art history. Knowledge of a foreign language required.

Financial Award: Unspecified museum stipend, plus opportunity to work at the Guggenheim Museum

Deadline: Mid-July; call for details

J. Clawson Mills Art History Scholarships

The Metropolitan Museum of Art
1000 Fifth Avenue
New York, NY 10028-0198

Field of Study: Fine arts

Purpose of Fellowship: Awarded for one year's study or research at the Museum in any branch of the fine arts relating to the Metropolitan Museum's collections.

Criteria: Reserved for mature scholars of demonstrated ability.

Financial Award: $26,000 for senior fellows and $18,000 for predoctoral fellows, with an additional $3,000 for travel

Deadline: Early November

James Renwick Fellowship in American Crafts

Renwick Gallery
Smithsonian Institution
MRC-107
Washington, DC 20560
Phone: (202) 357-2331

Field of Study: History of 20th century American art, crafts, or design

Purpose of Fellowship: To promote scholarly research in the modern American craft movement.

Criteria: Master's, predoctoral, or postdoctoral graduate students.

Financial Award: Unspecified

Deadline: Call committee

Jane and Morgan Whitney Art History Fellowships

The Metropolitan Museum of Art
1000 Fifth Avenue
New York, NY 10028-0198

Field of Study: History of art, classics, archaeology, textiles, fine arts

Purpose of Fellowship: Awarded for study, work, or research to students of the fine arts whose fields are related to the Museum's collections.

Criteria: Students of the fine arts whose fields are related to the Museum's collections; preference given to students in the decorative arts who are under 40 years of age.

Financial Award: $26,000 for senior fellows and $18,000 for predoctoral fellows, with an additional $3,000 for travel

Deadline: Early November

Kate Neal Kinley Memorial Fellowship

608 E. Lorado Taft Drive, #117
Champaign, IL 61820
Phone: (217) 333-1661

Field of Study: Fine art, architecture, or music

Purpose of Fellowship: To defray expenses of advanced study of fine arts in America or abroad.

Criteria: Graduates of University of Illinois/Urbana-Champaign or similar institutions of equal educational standing who have studied art, architecture, or music; preference will be given to applicants under 25 years of age.

Financial Award: Up to $7,000

Deadline: Early February

L. W. Frohlich Charitable Trust Fellowship in Conservation

The Metropolitan Museum of Art
1000 Fifth Avenue
New York, NY 10028-1098

Field of Study: Art history, conservation

Purpose of Fellowship: To provide a two-year fellowship in the Department of Objects Conservation.

Criteria: Conservators, art historians, or scientists who are at an advanced level in their training and who have demonstrated a commitment to the physical examination of art objects.

Financial Award: $20,000 for one year with an additional $2,500 for travel

Deadline: Early January

Mary Roberts Rinehart Awards

Mary Roberts Rinehart Fund
Mail Stop Number 3E4
English Department
George Mason University
Fairfax, VA 22030-4444
Phone: (703) 993-1185

Field of Study: All fields

Purpose of Fellowship: The fund awards grants to unpublished creative writers who need financial assistance to complete works of fiction, poetry, drama, biography, autobiography, or history with a strong narrative quality.

Criteria: Unpublished creative writers (unpublished is defined as having no book publications). Awards are made for drama and nonfiction in odd years and for fiction and poetry in even years. Applicants must be nominated by a writing program faculty member, a sponsoring writer, an agent, or an editor. Submit writing samples up to 30 pages.

Financial Award: Approximately $900

Deadline: Late November

Metropolitan Museum of Art—Andrew W. Mellon Art History Fellowships

Pia Quintano
Metropolitan Museum of Art
1000 Fifth Avenue
New York, NY 10028-0198

Field of Study: Art history

Purpose of Fellowship: Provided for promising young scholars with research projects related to the Museum's collections, as well as for visiting scholars from this country and abroad who can serve as advisers and make their expertise available to catalogue and refine the collections.

Criteria: Applicants should have received the doctorate or have completed substantial work toward it.

Financial Award: $26,000 for senior fellows and $18,000 for predoctoral fellows, plus $3,000 for travel

Deadline: Early November

Metropolitan Museum of Art—Andrew W. Mellon Foundation Fellowships in Conservation

The Metropolitan Museum of Art
1000 Fifth Avenue
New York, NY 10028-0198

Field of Study: Art conservation

Purpose of Fellowship: To provide training in one or more of the following departments: paintings, objects, paper, textile, and Asian art conservation; arms and armor; and the Costume Institute.

Criteria: Applicants should have reached an advanced level of experience or training. Previous training and experience is not required for applicants in Asian art conservation.

Financial Award: $20,000 for one year for senior scholars with an additional $2,500 for travel

Deadline: Early January

Metropolitan Museum of Art—Chester Dale Art History Fellowships

Pia Quintano
Metropolitan Museum of Art
1000 Fifth Avenue
New York, NY 10028-0198

Field of Study: Related to the fine arts of the Western world

Purpose of Fellowship: To help support research at the Metropolitan Museum.

Criteria: Preferably U.S. citizens under the age of 40.

Financial Award: Varies, depending on length of program (from three months to one year)

Deadline: Early November

Metropolitan Museum of Art—The Classical Art History Fellowships

The Metropolitan Museum of Art
1000 Fifth Avenue
New York, NY 10028-0198

Field of Study: History of art (classical)

Purpose of Fellowship: To help support an outstanding graduate student who has been admitted to the doctoral program of a university in the United States, and who has submitted an outline of a thesis dealing with either Greek or Roman art.

Criteria: The thesis outline must already have been accepted by the applicant's advisor at the time of application for the fellowship.

Financial Award: $18,000 stipend, with an additional $3,000 for travel

Deadline: Early November

Metropolitan Museum of Art—Norbert Schimmel Fellowship for Mediterranean Art and Archaeology

The Metropolitan Museum of Art
1000 Fifth Avenue
New York, NY 10028-0198

Field of Study: History of art, classics, and archaeology

Purpose of Fellowship: Awarded to an outstanding graduate student who has been admitted to the doctoral program of a university in the United States and who has submitted an outline of a thesis dealing with ancient Near Eastern art and archaeology or with Greek or Roman art.

Criteria: Preference will be given to a candidate who, in the opinion of the Grants Committee, would profit most from utilizing the resources of the Ancient Near Eastern Art or Greek and Roman Art Departments.

Financial Award: $18,000 stipend for predoctoral fellows, with an additional $3,000 for travel

Deadline: Early November

Metropolitan Museum of Art—Polaire Weissman Fund Art History and Conservation Fellowships

The Metropolitan Museum of Art
1000 Fifth Avenue
New York, NY 10028-0198

Field of Study: History of art, art conservation, fine arts, textiles

Purpose of Fellowship: To support qualified graduate students who are interested in pursuing costume history in a museum or teaching career, or other career related to the field of costume.

Criteria: Graduate students who will have completed graduate studies in the fine arts or costume and who are interested in pursuing a career in costume history are preferred.

Financial Award: Conservation fellowships: $20,000 for nine months plus $2,500 travel; Art history fellowships: $18,000 predoctoral plus $3,000 travel

Deadline: Varies

Metropolitan Museum of Art—Starr Fellowship in Asian Paintings Conservation

The Metropolitan Museum of Art
1000 Fifth Avenue
New York, NY 10028-0198

Field of Study: Asian art conservation

Purpose of Fellowship: To provide training in the conservation and mounting of Asian paintings. The department is concerned with the complete mounting, remounting, and conservation of hanging scrolls, handscrolls, folding screens, prints, albums, and books in the museum's collection.

Criteria: No prior experience is expected or required. However, this program is intended for someone who might pursue this field as a lifetime career.

Financial Award: Varies

Deadline: Rolling

Metropolitan Museum of Art—Theodore Rousseau Fellowships

The Metropolitan Museum of Art
1000 Fifth Avenue
New York, NY 10028-0198

Field of Study: Art history

Purpose of Fellowship: To train students whose goal is to enter museums as curators of painting. This award is intended to develop the skills of connoisseurship by supporting first-hand examination of paintings in major European collections, rather than by supporting library research.

Criteria: Applicants must have completed at least one year of an advanced degree program.

Financial Award: $18,000 stipend for one year and $3,000 for travel

Deadline: Early November

Millay Colony for the Arts Fellowship in Conjunction with the Pollock-Krasner Foundation

Steepletop, P.O. Box 3
Austerlitz, NY 12017-0003
Phone: (518) 392-3103

Field of Study: Creative writing, art, music

Purpose of Fellowship: To give one-month residencies to writers, composers, and visual artists.

Criteria: Open

Financial Award: One month free room and board at Millay Colony for the Arts in Austerlitz, N.Y.

Deadline: Call committee

National Gallery of Art Center for Advanced Study in the Visual Arts—Predoctoral Fellowship Program

Center for Advanced Study in the Visual Arts
National Gallery of Art
Washington, DC 20565
Phone: (202) 842-6482
Fax: (202) 842-6733

Field of Study: Art history, theory, and criticism; architecture

Purpose of Fellowship: To support doctoral dissertation research.

Criteria: Candidates must be nominated by their university department. Must be U.S. citizens or enrolled in a university in the United States. All predissertation requirements must be met before the date of application. Candidates must know two foreign languages related to dissertation topic.

Financial Award: $13,000 annual stipend

Deadline: Mid November

Social Sciences 6

What distinguishes the fellowships available in the social sciences from many others is the incredible amount of latitude most organizations give their fellows. Just about any topic of interest is fair game to most committees, and as such, students can truly put their own personal stamp upon their project.

Of course, nothing's perfect—including the fellowships listed in this chapter. In general, social science fellowships do not offer as much cash as most other types. Although there are exceptions (the Woodrow Wilson Fellowship in the Humanities and Social Sciences awards recipients up to $61,000 a year), the vast majority of these opportunities offer less than $10,000 per year. And this often means that potential candidates forego applying for many of the lesser-known fellowships in order to try their hand at some of the more "prestigious"—and, therefore, better endowed—fellowships.

Because the social sciences encompass such a wide variety of academic subjects, it is impossible to list all the fields covered in the listings. Some of the more popular areas include:

- Education
- Archaeology
- Anthropology
- Comparative religion
- History
- Philosophy
- Language
- Literature

The Application Process

Because most organizations do not discriminate based upon the applicant's field of study, it is especially important for the student to make a solid argument for why his particular concentration would prove especially relevant to the fellowship committee. In other words, be specific.

Most successful applicants for social science fellowships tailor their application toward their particular area of study in two ways. First, they demonstrate their mastery of the field. This includes providing evidence of extended study of the subject in the student's transcript. But it is a huge bonus if the applicant has researched or worked in his field outside of the classroom. An example: One particular applicant—a Near Eastern studies and archaeology double major—took a semester off and worked on archaeological excavations in both Abydos and Giza, Egypt to pad his résumé for the Javits and Mellon fellowships. Needless to say, he is not paying a penny for his first year of graduate school.

The second key to gaining a social sciences fellowship is the written proposal. Because applicants for these awards study a variety of subjects, it is often difficult for committees to determine which students are the most worthy fellowship recipients based upon their applications alone. Therefore, the tiebreaker is usually the project proposal. Committees are looking to invest their money in great ideas, and great ideas don't grow on trees. Simply stated, the individual who has most thoughtfully considered his plan will win the award, regardless of his field of study.

Sample Proposal

These excerpts from the written proposal of an applicant for the Jacob K. Javits Fellowship Program should give you an idea of what you should be aiming for with your written proposal. The student in question will attend graduate school in archaeology this fall.

> *I have discovered that there are other topics within the subjects of Egyptian art history and archaeology that need to be more thoroughly researched. Two particular ones have especially stuck in my mind. One*

is the evolution of the Egyptian royal palace during the New Kingdom. Specifically, I want to investigate how the separate palatial components of architecture, sculpture, and painting worked together as an integrated program. Also, where is the primary source of influence for this development: Egyptian temples, or Assyrian and Syro-Palestinian palaces and other royal constructions? Contemporary Egyptian temples and Near Eastern palaces are valid and potentially useful sources of information for reconstructing decorative programs and architectural layouts of Egyptian palaces, whose archaeological remains are virtually non-existent.

The other topic that I want to focus on is the Near Eastern and Libyan influences on Egyptian sculpture during the post-New Kingdom, concentrating on aspects such as proportions, facial characteristics, and statuary genres. In addition, their degree of preservation during succeeding waves of invasion and foreign cultural influx is an important aspect that warrants further study. Previous research into the sculpture of this period has tended to avoid attempting to disentangle the artistic influences of one specific area from another.

The process of writing your proposal shouldn't differ significantly from that of your personal statement. Make your goals specific, relevant, and feasible. Keep your language simple and concise. Cater to your target audience. And be true to your own voice.

American Congress on Surveying and Mapping—American Association for Geodetic Surveying Graduate Fellowship Award

Lilly Matheson
5410 Grosvenor Lane
Suite 100
Bethesda, MD 20814-2122
Phone: (301) 493-0200
Fax: (301) 493-8245

Field of Study: Geodetic surveying, cartography

Purpose of Fellowship: To encourage, recognize, and support exceptional surveying and mapping students.

Criteria: Geodetic surveying focused graduate students; prior employment for at least two years in the surveying profession is desired for some awards.

Financial Award: $250–$2,000

Deadline: Early December

American Numismatic Society

The American Numismatic Society
Broadway at 155th St.
New York, NY 10032
Phone: (212) 234-3130
E-mail: info@amnunsoc.org

Field of Study: Numismatics

Purpose of Fellowship: To support training in numismatics

Criteria: Varies with fellowship

Financial Award: Varies

Deadline: Early March

Bibliographic Society of America

P.O. Box 397
Grand Central Station
New York, NY 10163
Phone: (212) 647-9171
Fax: (212) 647-9171
E-mail: bibsocamer@aol.com

Field of Study: Bibliographical inquiry; history of books

Purpose of Fellowship: To support bibliographical inquiry as well as research in the history of the book trades and in publishing history. Eligible topics may concentrate on books and documents in any field, but should focus on the book or manuscript (the physical object) as historical evidence.

Criteria: Open

Financial Award: $1,000–$2,000

Deadline: Early December

Charles Babbage Institute Center for the History of Information Processing—Adelle and Erwin Tomash Fellowship

117 Pleasant Street, S.E.
University of Minnesota
103 Walter Library
Minneapolis, MN 55455
Phone: (612) 624-5050
Fax: (612) 625-8054
E-mail: cbi@vx.cis.umn.edu
Web site:
http://cbi.itdean.umn.edu/cbi/welcome.htm

Field of Study: History of computers and information processing

Purpose of Fellowship: To promote historical research in the technical and socio-economic aspects of information processing.

Criteria: Priority will be given to students who have completed all requirements for the doctoral degree except the research and writing of the dissertation.

Financial Award: $10,000

Deadline: Mid-January

Dr. George N. Papanicolaou Hellenic Heritage Graduate Research Grant

Hellenic University Club
of New York
P.O. Box 6882
FDR Station
New York, NY 10150-6882
E-mail: vbdd58a@prodigy.com

Field of Study: Hellenic studies

Purpose of Fellowship: To encourage Hellenic studies from the classic period through the eighteenth century.

Criteria: Graduate students of Greek ancestry who are affiliated with an accredited university.

Financial Award: At least $1,000

Deadline: Late December

Fund for the Improvement of Postsecondary Education

Comprehensive Program/U.S.
Department of Education
7th and D St. SW
Washington, DC 20202-4725
Phone: (202) 708-5750
Web site: http://www.ed.gov/prog_info/FIPSE

Field of Study: Open to all fields

Purpose of Fellowship: To support innovative reform projects that promise to be models for the solution of problems in postsecondary education.

Criteria: Open to student groups, institutions, community organizations, and local government agencies, among others.

Financial Award: 1–3 years funding

Deadline: Mid-March

Harriet Pomerance Fellowship

Archaeological Institute of America
656 Beacon Street
Boston, MA 02215-2010
Phone: (617) 353-9361
Fax: (617) 353-6000
E-mail: aia@bu.edu

Field of Study: Archaeology

Purpose of Fellowship: To support a person working on an individual project of a scholarly nature relating to Aegean Bronze Age archaeology.

Criteria: United States or Canada residents only. Preference will be given to candidates whose projects require travel to the Mediterranean for the purpose stated above. Previous fellows are ineligible.

Financial Award: $3,000

Deadline: Mid-November

Health Care Financing Administration—Dissertation Fellowship Grants

Office of Sponsored Programs
120 Day Hall
7500 Security Blvd
Baltimore, MD 21244-1850
Phone: (410) 786-5701

Field of Study: Health care financing and delivery

Purpose of Fellowship: To stimulate involvement of health service researchers in the study of health care financing and delivery issues.

Criteria: Doctoral degree candidates who have completed all requirements for the Ph.D except the dissertation, and are conducting or intending to conduct research on issues related to delivery or financing of health care services, particularly related to Medicare and/or Medicaid.

Financial Award: Direct costs limited to $20,000; indirect costs limited to $1,600

Deadline: Mid-October

Henry A. Murray Dissertation Award Program

Henry A. Murray Research Center
of Radcliffe College
10 Garden Street
Cambridge, MA 02138

Field of Study: Social and behavioral sciences

Purpose of Fellowship: To support research that best embodies Murray's commitment to the in-depth study of individuals in context, over time, and from a variety of perspectives. Priority will be given to projects drawing on the resources of the Center.

Criteria: Applicants must be enrolled in a doctoral program in a relevant field and must have their dissertation proposal approved before the grant application is made. Proposals will be evaluated in terms of potential contribution to the relevant field of study, the adequacy of the research design, and the general academic excellence of the candidate.

Financial Award: Up to $2,500 to cover research costs; up to $1,200 of this award may be used as a stipend

Deadline: Early April

The Herb Society of America—Research and Education Grant

The Herb Society of America, Inc.
9019 Kirtland Chardon Road
Kirtland, OH 44094
Phone: (216) 256-0514
Fax: (216) 256-0541
E-mail: herbsociet@aol.com

Field of Study: Sciences, humanities, social sciences

Purpose of Fellowship: To further the knowledge and use of herbs and contribute the results of the study and research to the records of horticulture, science, literature, history, art, or economics.

Criteria: Persons with a proposed program of scientific, academic, or artistic investigation of herbal plants.

Financial Award: Up to $5,000 for one year

Deadline: Late January

Herman Kahn Fellowships

Hilda Maness
P.O. Box 26-919
Indianapolis, IN 46226

Field of Study: Social sciences

Purpose of Fellowship: To support Ph.D. candidates who have completed their coursework and are willing to conduct policy-oriented dissertation research at the Hudson Institute in Washington or Indianapolis.

Criteria: Ph.D. students who have completed their coursework and are researching their dissertation. Must have an outstanding academic record, strong recommendations by faculty members, and a demonstrated interest in and capability for policy-oriented research and the use of interdisciplinary analysis.

Financial Award: $18,000 stipend plus travel reimbursement

Deadline: Early April

Huntington Library Fellowships

Huntington Library
Director of Research
1151 Oxford Road
San Marino, CA 91108
Phone: (818) 405-2194
Fax: (818) 449-5703

Field of Study: Humanities, floriculture, landscape architecture

Purpose of Fellowship: To support research at the Huntington Library, a research institution devoted to the study of British and American history, literature, art history, the history of science and photography. Fellows apply for one of four awards: Huntington Fellowships, W. M. Keck Foundation Fellowships, Barbara Thom Fellowships, or National Endowment for the Humanities Fellowships.

Criteria: Open to senior and junior scholars.

Financial Award: From $1,800 to $30,000, depending on the award

Deadline: Mid-December

Indiana University/ Bloomington Chancellor's Fellowship

University Graduate School,
Kirkwood Hall
111 Indiana University
Bloomington, IN 47405-3901
Phone: (812) 855-8853
E-mail: hwickers@indiana.edu

Field of Study: Arts, humanities, social sciences, professional studies

Purpose of Fellowship: To provide support for entering graduate students intending to pursue a doctoral degree at I.U.

Criteria: Submit an application for admission and financial aid to the relevant graduate program; students are nominated for the fellowship by the graduate program to which they are applying. Members of groups traditionally underrepresented in graduate education are strongly encouraged to apply.

Financial Award: $14,000 stipend for humanities fellowships; $17,000 for mathematics and science

Deadline: Mid-January

Institute for Advanced Study—Mellon Fellowships for Assistant Professors

Institute for Advanced Study
Olden Lane
Princeton, NJ 08540
Phone: (609) 734-8300
E-mail: mzelazny@ias.edu

Field of Study: Ancient civilization, history of Europe, Islamic culture

Purpose of Fellowship: To support promising young scholars who have embarked on professional careers.

Criteria: By the time of the fellows' arrival, must have served at least two and not more than four years as assistant professors in institutions of higher learning in the United States or Canada.

Financial Award: Unspecified

Deadline: Mid-November

Institute for Humane Studies

4400 University Drive
George Mason University
Fairfax, VA 22030-4444
Phone: (703) 323-1055

Field of Study: Humane sciences dealing with moral and economic studies

Purpose of Fellowship: The Institute offers a variety of awards to promote the advanced study of liberty across a broad range of academic and professional disciplines.

Criteria: Qualifications vary with award.

Financial Award: $500–$27,500

Deadline: Varies

Institute of Living—Predoctoral Internships in Clinical Psychology

Institute of Living
400 Washington Street
Hartford, CT 06106
Phone: (860) 545-7000

Field of Study: Psychology

Purpose of Fellowship: To provide trainees with a diverse, well-supervised, and in-depth training experience that prepares them to assume full responsibility for patient care, and to function as independent practitioners of clinical psychology.

Criteria: Applicants must be enrolled in a clinical psychology program, have completed all academic requirements except the dissertation, and have practicum in psychodiagnostic assessment and psychotherapeutic interventions.

Financial Award: $13,540

Deadline: Call committee

Intercollegiate Studies Institute—Salvatori Fellowship Program

Salvatori Fellowship Awards Program
P.O. Box 4431
Wilmington, DE 19807-0431
Phone: 800-526-7022
Fax: (302) 652-1760
E-mail: isi@isi.org

Field of Study: Liberal arts and social sciences

Purpose of Fellowship: To further an understanding of both the principles of the American founding fathers and the culture that formed their values and views.

Criteria: Students undertaking graduate study in the American founding fathers who plan to pursue college-level teaching careers. Applicants must be U.S. citizens and ISI members who subscribe to the *Intercollegiate Review.* Preprofessional students (medical or law) are ineligible.

Financial Award: $10,000 and a library of works published by the Liberty Fund, Inc.

Deadline: Mid-February

International Research and Exchanges Board—Individual Advanced Research Opportunities

IREX
1616 H St., N.W.
Washington, DC 2006
Phone: (202) 628-8188
Fax: (202) 628-8189
E-mail: irex@info.irex.org
Web site: http://www.irex.org

Field of Study: Humanities and social sciences

Purpose of Fellowship: To support predoctoral and postdoctoral scholars for research at institutions in the host country (Central and Eastern Europe, Eurasia, or Mongolia).

Criteria: U.S. citizen or permanent resident for three years prior to submitting an application; command of the host language; full-time affiliation with college or university. Support proposed for a fellowship tenure of 1–3 or 3–24 months.

Financial Award: Includes round-trip airfare and visa fees, stipend for room and board, local research allowance, excess baggage allowance

Deadline: Early November

International Research and Exchanges Board—Library and Information Service

IREX
1616 H Street, N.W.
Washington, DC
Phone: (202) 628-8188
Fax: (202) 628-8189
E-mail: irex@info.irex.org
Web site: http://www.irex.org

Field of Study: Archival, library, and information sciences

Purpose of Fellowship: To support librarians, archivists, and information specialists pursuing projects relating to Central and Eastern Europe and Eurasia. The objective is to increase access and improve working conditions for American scholars using libraries, archives, and other resources in these regions.

Criteria: U.S. citizen or permanent resident for three years prior to submitting an application; applicants affiliated with U.S. federal institutions should contact IREX regarding eligibility before submitting an application.

Financial Award: Travel, accommodations, facility usage, and other expenses

Deadline: Mid-January

Jacob K. Javits Fellowship

Jacob K. Javitz Fellowship Program
P.O. Box 4129
Iowa City, IA 52244
Phone: (800) 4-FEDAID

Field of Study: Humanities and social sciences

Purpose of Fellowship: To provide financial assistance to students of superior abilities in studies for doctoral-level degrees in selected fields of the arts, humanities, and social sciences.

Criteria: U.S. citizens, permanent residents, people in the process of becoming citizens or residents, and permanent residents of the Pacific Islands or Northern Mariana Islands. Limited to students who have no more than 30 semester hours of graduate credit at the time of application and who are or will be enrolled in doctoral or Master of Fine Arts programs.

Financial Award: $14,400 plus a tuition waiver

Deadline: Mid-May

James Madison Fellowship Program

James Madison Fellowship Program
P.O. Box 4030
Iowa City, IA 52243-4030
Phone: (800) 525-6928
Fax: (319) 337-1204
E-mail: recogprog@act-act4-po.act.org

Field of Study: History, government, or M.A. in teaching

Purpose of Fellowship: To support current and future teachers of American history, American government and social studies for two years of master's level graduate study of the roots, principles, framing, and development of the U.S. Constitution.

Criteria: U.S. citizens who agree to teach full time in a secondary school for no less than one year for each full year of study under the fellowship and who qualify for study toward one of the listed master's degrees.

Financial Award: Unspecified

Deadline: Early March

John Carter Brown Library—Short-Term and Long-Term Research Fellowships

John Carter Brown Library
P.O. Box 1894
Providence, RI 02912
E-mail:
kareen_demaria@brown.edu

Field of Study: Humanities and social sciences

Purpose of Fellowship: To support regular residence and research in colonial American history and culture at the John Carter Brown Library at Brown University.

Criteria: Short program: Open to Americans and foreign nationals engaged in predoctoral, postdoctoral, or independent research. Graduate students must have passed their preliminary or general examinations at the time of application. Long program: American citizens or residents in the United States for three years immediately preceding the term.

Financial Award: Short: $1,000 per month for 2–4 months; Long: $13,375 for five months

Deadline: Mid-January

John F. Kennedy Library Foundation—Hemingway Research Grants

Hemingway Research
Grants/John F. Kennedy Library
Columbia Point
Boston, MA 02125-3313
Phone: (617) 929-4539
Fax: (617) 929-4538

Field of Study: English language and literature

Purpose of Fellowship: To help defray living, travel, and related costs incurred while doing research in the Hemingway Collection.

Criteria: Grant applications are evaluated on the basis of expected utilization of the Hemingway Collection, the degree to which projects address research needs in Hemingway or related studies, and the qualifications of applicants. While preference is given to dissertation research by Ph.D. candidates in newly opened or relatively unused portions of the Collection, all proposals are welcome and will receive careful consideration.

Financial Award: $200 to $1,000

Deadline: Mid-March

Josephine de Karman Fellowships

Josephine de Karman
Fellowship Trust
P.O. Box 3389
San Dimas, CA 91773

Field of Study: All fields

Purpose of Fellowship: To recognize and assist students whose scholastic achievements reflect Professor von Karman's high standards.

Criteria: Graduate students entering the terminal year of a Ph.D. program in the fall of 1998 who have manifested exceptional ability and serious purpose. Special consideration is given to those who have completed their qualifying examinations for the doctoral degree.

Financial Award: $6,000 for one academic year

Deadline: Late January

Kenan T. Erim Award

Archaeological Institute of America
Boston University
656 Beacon Street
Boston, MA 02215-2010
Phone: (617) 353-9361
Fax: (617) 353-6000
E-mail: aia@bu.edu

Field of Study: Archaeology, art history, and related fields

Purpose of Fellowship: Established by the American friends of Aphrodisias to support a research scholar working on Aphrodisias material.

Criteria: Open to American or international research scholars. If the project involves work at Aphrodisias, candidates must submit written approval from the Field Director with their applications.

Financial Award: $4,000

Deadline: Mid-November

Leo Baeck Institute—DAAD Fellowships

Leo Baeck Institute
129 East 73rd Street
New York, NY 10021
Phone: (212) 744-6400

Field of Study: Social, communal, and intellectual history of Germany

Purpose of Fellowship: To assist doctoral students and recent Ph.D.'s in their dissertation and/or academics in the preparation of a scholarly essay or book through the use of the LBI's resources or libraries, archives or research institutions in the Federal Republic of Germany.

Criteria: Candidates must be U.S. citizens, Ph.D. candidates not older than 32, or recent Ph.D.'s not older than 35.

Financial Award: Funds for research at the Leo Baeck Institute or for research in Germany, plus stipend of $2,000

Deadline: Early November

Leo Baeck Institute—David Baumgardt Memorial Fellowship

Leo Baeck Institute
129 East 73rd Street
New York, NY 10021
Phone: (212) 744-6000

Field of Study: Germanic studies, history, Near Eastern studies

Purpose of Fellowship: To assist doctoral students in research connected with writings of Professor David Baumgardt or his scholarly interests (ethics, Wissenschaft des Judentums, and the modern intellectual history of German-speaking Jewry).

Criteria: Doctoral candidate desiring to conduct research at the Leo Baeck Institute in New York.

Financial Award: Unspecified stipend based on demands of project

Deadline: Early November

Leo Baeck Institute—Fritz Halbers Fellowship

Leo Baeck Institute
129 East 73rd Street
New York, NY 10021
Phone: (212) 988-1305

Field of Study: History and Near Eastern studies

Purpose of Fellowship: To assist doctoral students whose projects are connected with the culture and history of German-speaking Jewry.

Criteria: U.S. citizens at the doctoral level.

Financial Award: Up to $3,000

Deadline: Early November

Library Company of Philadelphia—Research Fellowships in American History and Culture

James Green
Associate Librarian
Library Company of Philadelphia
1314 Locust St.
Philadelphia, PA 19107
Phone: (215) 546-5167
E-mail: jgreen@worldlynx.net

Field of Study: American history and culture

Purpose of Fellowship: To support use of the library's collection for both dissertation and postdoctoral research.

Criteria: Scholars possessing Ph.D. degrees or doing dissertation research.

Financial Award: $1,400 for one month

Deadline: Early February

Mellon Fellowships in Humanistic Studies

Mellon Fellowships
CN 5329
Princeton, NJ 08543-5329
Phone: (607) 452-0066
E-mail: jacquie@woodrow.org

Field of Study: Humanities

Purpose of Fellowship: To attract 80 exceptionally promising students annually into preparation for careers of teaching and scholarship in humanistic studies and to contribute thereby to the continuity of teaching and research of the highest order in American colleges and universities.

Criteria: Outstanding college seniors or recent graduates who have not begun graduate work and are U.S. citizens or permanent residents. Applicants must be nominated by a faculty sponsor.

Financial Award: One year of entry-level graduate study in a Ph.D. program in the United States or Canada

Deadline: Call committee

Memorial Foundation for Jewish Culture—International Doctoral Scholarship for Studies Specializing in Jewish Fields

Memorial Foundation for Jewish Culture
15 East 26th Street
Room 1703
New York, NY 10010
Phone: (212) 679-4074

Field of Study: Specialization in a Jewish field

Purpose of Fellowship: To train qualified individuals for careers in Jewish scholarship and research, and to help Jewish educational, religious, and communal workers obtain advanced training for leadership positions.

Criteria: Any graduate student specializing in a Jewish field who is officially enrolled or registered in a doctoral program at a recognized university; priority is given to applicants who are at the dissertation level.

Financial Award:
$1,000–$5,000, based on cost of living in country of choice

Deadline: Late October

Memorial Foundation for Jewish Culture—International Fellowships in Jewish Studies

Memorial Foundation for Jewish Culture
15 East 26th Street
Room 1703
New York, NY 10010
Phone: (212) 679-4074

Field of Study: Any field involving Jewish studies

Purpose of Fellowship: To assist well-qualified individuals in carrying out an independent scholarly, literary, or art project in a field of Jewish specialization that makes a significant contribution to the understanding, preservation, enhancement, or transmission of Jewish culture.

Criteria: Any qualified scholar, researcher, or artist who possesses the knowledge and experience to formulate and implement a project in a field of Jewish specialization can apply for support.

Financial Award:
$1,000–$4,000 for one year depending on cost of living in country of choice

Deadline: Late October

Munson Institute—Paul Cuffe Memorial Fellowship for the Study of Minorities in American Maritime History

P.O. Box 6000
75 Greenmanville Avenue
Munson Institute
Mystic, CT 06355-0990
Phone: (860) 572-5329
E-mail: munson@mystic.org
Web site: http://www.mystic.org

Field of Study: History and related studies

Purpose of Fellowship: To encourage research that considers the participation of Native and African Americans in the maritime activities of New England, primarily its southeastern shores.

Criteria: Open

Financial Award: Up to $2,400

Deadline: Mid-June

National Endowment for the Humanities—Fellowships and Summer Stipends

1100 Pennsylvania Avenue, N.W.
Room 318
Washington, DC 20506
Web site:
http://www.neh.fed.us

Field of Study: Humanities

Purpose of Fellowship: Fellowships: to support six to twelve months of full-time work. Summer: to support two months of full-time work.

Criteria: Applicants need not have advanced degrees, but neither candidates for degrees nor persons seeking support for work toward a degree are eligible.

Financial Award: Up to $30,000 for full-year fellowship; $4,000 for summer stipend

Deadline: Early May/October

National Foundation for Jewish Culture—Doctoral Dissertation Fellowships in Jewish Studies

330 Seventh Avenue, 21st Floor
New York, NY 10001
Phone: (212) 629-0500
Fax: (212) 629-0508

Field of Study: Jewish studies

Purpose of Fellowship: To encourage scholarly research, publication, and teaching in the various disciplines of Jewish studies. Fellowships enable graduate students to complete work on their dissertation.

Criteria: Applicants must be U.S. citizens, have completed all academic requirements, and should be in the advanced stages of writing their dissertations. Preference is given to individuals preparing for academic careers in Jewish studies or who demonstrate a career commitment to Jewish scholarship.

Financial Award: $6,000–$9,000

Deadline: Early January

National Huguenot Society Award

Arthur F. Stocker
Box 3331, University Station
Charlottesville, VA 22903

Field of Study: Humanities

Purpose of Fellowship: To encourage scholarship dealing with any aspect of the Huguenot movement.

Criteria: Award is made on basis of quality scholarship in the form of a thesis, dissertation, article, paper, or book.

Financial Award: $1,000 award offered in spring of every odd-numbered year

Deadline: February

Newberry Library—Herzog August Bibliothek Wolfenbuttel Fellowship

Committee on Awards
The Newberry Library
60 W. Walton Street
Chicago, IL 60610-3380
E-mail: researcch@newberry.org

Field of Study: Open

Purpose of Fellowship: To support related research at the Newberry Library and the Herzog August Bibliothek in Wolfenbuttel, Germany. The award is intended to complement a long-term or short-term Newberry Fellowship.

Criteria: Proposed projects must link the collections of both libraries. Applicants should plan to hold this fellowship sequentially with one at the Newberry in order to ensure continuity of research.

Financial Award: Up to 1,200 DM in travel expenses and a three-month stipend of 2,000 DM per month

Deadline: Call committee

Newberry Library—Short-Term Fellowships in the History of Cartography

Committee on Awards
The Newberry Library
60 W. Walton St.
Chicago, IL 60610-3380
E-mail: research@newberry.org

Field of Study: Social sciences and humanities

Purpose of Fellowship: To support research by scholars whose particular need is to consult the Newberry's cartographic collection for a period of two weeks to two months.

Criteria: Scholars, who hold the Ph.D. or have completed all requirements except the dissertation, researching in any field appropriate to the Newberry's collection.

Financial Award: $800 per month

Deadline: Early March

Newberry Library—Short-Term Resident Fellowships for Individual Research

Committee on Awards
The Newberry Library
60 W. Walton St.
Chicago, IL 60610-3380
Phone: (312) 943-9090
E-mail: u30373@uicvm.uic.edu

Field of Study: Open

Purpose of Fellowship: To help provide access to Newberry Library facilities for scholars who live beyond commuting distance.

Criteria: Appllicants must have completed a Ph.D. or all requirements except the dissertation. Designed primarily to provide access to the Newberry for people who live beyond commuting distance.

Financial Award: $800 per month for periods of two weeks to two months

Deadline: Early March

Richard C. Maguire Scholarship for Postgraduate Study in History

Richard C. Maguire Scholarship Committee
Rock Island Arsenal Museum
Attn: SMCRI-PCA-M
Rock Island Arsenal
Rock Island, IL 61299-5000
Phone: (309) 782-5021

Field of Study: History or related fields

Purpose of Fellowship: To provide one year of support to a student doing postgraduate study in history or related fields.

Criteria: Applicants must be U.S. citizens, be accepted into an accredited college or university postgraduate course of study in history, and intend to complete and earn a master's degree or higher.

Financial Award: $1,000 for one year

Deadline: Mid-April

Richard M. Weaver Fellowships

Richard M. Weaver Fellowships Program
Intercollegiate Studies Institute
P.O. Box 4431
Wilmington, DE 19807-0431
Fax: (302) 652-1760
E-mail: isi@isi.org

Field of Study: Humanities and social sciences

Purpose of Fellowship: To support graduate students planning to teach at the college level.

Criteria: U.S. citizens who are graduate students and members of the Intercollegiate Studies Institute who subscribe to the *Intercollegiate Review.*

Financial Award: $3,000 plus tuition for one year at institution of fellows choice; selection of books from the Library Fund, Inc.

Deadline: Mid-January

Social Science Research Council—Berlin Program for Advanced German and European Studies

Social Science Research Council
810 Seventh Avenue
New York, NY 10019
Phone: (212) 377-2700

Field of Study: German and European studies

Purpose of Fellowship: To encourage the comparative and interdisciplinary study of the economic, political, and social aspects of modern and contemporary German and European affairs. Fellows are expected to produce a research monograph dealing with some aspect(s) of German or European affairs.

Criteria: U.S. citizens and permanent residents. Dissertation level: must have completed all requirements (except the dissertation) for the Ph.D. at the time fellowship begins. Postdoctoral level: open to scholars who have received the Ph.D. degree or its equivalent in the last two years.

Financial Award: Unspecified

Deadline: Early February

Spencer Foundation Dissertation Fellowships for Research Related to Education

Catherine Lacey
900 North Michigan Avenue, Suite 2800
Chicago, IL 60611-1542
Phone: (312) 337-7000

Field of Study: All fields; research pertaining to education.

Purpose of Fellowship: To encourage a new generation of scholars from a variety of fields to undertake research relevant to the improvement of education.

Criteria: Candidates for the doctoral degree, in any field, at a U.S. graduate school.

Financial Award: $17,000 (must be used within a two-year period)

Deadline: Late October

U.S. Army Center of Military History—Dissertation Fellowships

Dissertation Fellowship Committee
1099 14th St, N.W.
Washington, DC 20005-3402
Phone: (202) 701-5402

Field of Study: Humanities and social sciences; preference given to topics on the history of the U.S. Army

Purpose of Fellowship: To support scholarly research and writing among qualified civilian graduate students preparing dissertations in the history of war on land (including biography, military campaigns, organization and administration, policy, strategy, tactics, weaponry, technology, training and civil-military relations).

Criteria: Civilian citizens of the United States. Applicants must have completed all requirements for the Ph.D. by September, except for the dissertation.

Financial Award: $8,000 stipend

Deadline: Early February

University of Louisville—Grawemeyer Award in Education

Dean's Office
School of Education
University of Louisville
Louisville, KY 40292-0001
Phone: (502) 852-6411
Fax: (502) 852-1464
E-mail: edgaward01@ulkyvm.louisville.edu

Field of Study: Education

Purpose of Fellowship: To stimulate the dissemination, public scrutiny, and implementation of ideas that have potential to bring about significant improvement in educational practice and advances in educational attainment.

Criteria: Ideas eligible for nomination may have an individual author or may be the product of an institution or agency, and the ideas may come from anywhere in the world.

Financial Award: $150,000 paid in five annual installments of $30,000

Deadline: Early December

Warren W. Willingham Graduate Research Assistantships in Psychometrics Program

GRE Program, Mail Stop 32-V
Educational Testing Service
Princeton, NJ 08541
Phone: (609) 951-1561
Fax: (609) 951-1090
E-mail: price@ets.org

Field of Study: Psychometric programs

Purpose of Fellowship: To serve as onsite data coordinators for a variety of research studies related to the development of a new, modular, computerized GRE General Test and other new GRE testing initiatives. Specific responsibilities may vary from campus to campus.

Criteria: Applicants must be nominated by the chair of their program, be full-time students, have completed at least one year of graduate study, and should have some research experience.

Financial Award: $12,000 for 10 months, plus $7,500 cost-of-education allowance to the institution

Deadline: Early February

Whitney Museum of American Art Independent Study Program—Curatorial and Critical Studies Program

c/o Ron Clark
384 Broadway, 4th floor
New York, NY 10013
Phone: (212) 431-1737
Fax: (212) 431-1783

Field of Study: Art, history of art, and archaeology

Purpose of Fellowship: To provide a setting within which students engage in ongoing discussions and debates that examine the historical, social, and intellectual conditions of artistic production.

Criteria: Graduate students, candidates for postgraduate degrees, and undergraduates with a demonstrated capacity for advanced scholarship. Although current affiliation with a university is preferred, those working independently in the areas of art history and criticism are encouraged to apply.

Financial Award: $3,500 for curatorial studies fellows

Deadline: Early April

William Schallek Memorial Graduate Fellowship Awards

Nancy Northcott
1915 Euclid Ave.
Charlotte, NC 28203-4707

Field of Study: History, medieval studies

Purpose of Fellowship: To support research on late medieval English history and culture, particularly during the Wars of the Roses (ca. 1450–1487).

Criteria: U.S. citizens, applicants for first citizenship papers, or permanent resident aliens. Must be making normal progress in a degree program at a recognized institution.

Financial Award: $500–$2,000

Deadline: Late February

Woodrow Wilson International Center for Scholars—Fellowships in the Humanities and Social Sciences

The Fellowships Office
The Woodrow Wilson Center
1000 Jefferson Drive S.W.
SI MRC 022
Washington, DC 20560
Phone: (202) 357-2841
Fax: (202) 357-4439
E-mail: wcfellow@sivm.si.edu
Web site: http://wwics.si.edu

Field of Study: All fields, especially the humanities

Purpose of Fellowship: To support project proposals of postdoctoral and professional scholars doing research across the entire range of scholarship, especially projects transcending narrow specialties.

Criteria: Candidates with outstanding capabilities and experiences from a wide variety of backgrounds are eligible. Academic participants must be at the postdoctoral level. International competition.

Financial Award: Stipends of no more than $61,000; travel expenses for fellows, their spouses, and their children

Deadline: Early October

Woodrow Wilson National Fellowship Foundation—Charlotte W. Newcombe Doctoral Dissertation Fellowships

The Woodrow Wilson National Fellowship Foundation
CN 5281
Princeton, NJ 08543-5281
Phone: (609) 452-7007
Fax: (609) 452-0066
E-mail: charlotte@woodrow.org

Field of Study: Social sciences and humanities

Purpose of Fellowship: To encourage the study of ethical/religious values in all areas. In addition to topics in philosophy and religion, these might consider ethical implications of foreign policy, values determining political decisions, moral modes of other cultures, and religious and ethical values as reflected in literature and history.

Criteria: Candidates for Ph.D. or Th.D., who expect to complete all predissertation requirements by late November.

Financial Award: $14,000 for one year

Deadline: Mid-December

Woodrow Wilson National Fellowship Foundation—The Woodrow Wilson Dissertation Grants in Women's Studies

The Woodrow Wilson National
Fellowship Foundation
Dept. WS
CN 5281
Princeton, NJ 08543-5281
E-mail: charlotte@woodrow.org

Field of Study: Open

Purpose of Fellowship: To encourage original and significant research about women, including women's role in society, women in history, the psychology of women, and women as seen in literature and art.

Criteria: Students in doctoral programs who have completed all predissertation requirements at a graduate school in the United States by late October.

Financial Award: $1,500 for research expenses

Deadline: Early November

Public Policy and Politics 7

Politician. Lawyer. Lobbyist. Maybe the thought of these three professions make your skin crawl. But if that's the case, you're becoming part of an increasingly small minority among college graduates. In the 1990s, fellowships in advocacy and politics have become among the most competitive, drawing tens of thousands of applicants each year.

And you don't have to be James Carville to realize why these fellowships are always hotly contested. They pay well, offer the opportunity to travel across the country, and perhaps most importantly, often lead to law school, Ph.D. programs, or even (if you're lucky enough) the campaign trail.

Public Policy Fellowships

When you think of advocacy or public policy organizations, the first thing that probably comes to your mind is impact. From the NAACP to PETA, these groups fight to make an impact upon the general public, thereby making an impact upon government.

So how do you make an impact upon the fellowship committees of these organizations? The best thing you can do to make yourself shine should happen way before you actually put your application form in the typewriter. To secure a public policy fellowship, it's a good idea to establish a record of service that would impress any fellowship-issuing organization. This record is perfect material for your cover letter. Use the letter—and your extracurricular service activities—as your gateway to a fellowship by pegging yourself (albeit in a humble fashion) as a motivated citizen who feels proud and thankful to serve his community.

All this means nothing, however, if you don't know a lick about the organization's goals and policies. So before you fill out that form, take some time to do a little research. Use the Internet and programs such as LEXIS-NEXIS to dig into the issues that make the organization tick. And then apply that knowledge to your application. Proving yourself a worthy salesman of the organization's mission will go a long way toward earning you some fellowship money.

Political Fellowships

Fellowships in politics and government involve a variety of duties, from serving as a library archivist to working for the New York State Assembly. Any way you slice it, however, most fellowships that fall under this category are looking for the same thing—students with a clear career path.

Whether your intended career is law, politics, teaching, or anything else, take some time to explain two things in your essay. First, let the committee know where you're going in life. And second, let it know how you could use its fellowship to achieve your ultimate goals. Because future lawyers and politicians make up a significant percentage of the applicant pool (and because you may very well fall into this category as well), you truly have to stand out from the crowd to secure a political fellowship. Letting committees know you have a future—and that their fellowship is a large part of that future—is a good way to get yourself on their good sides.

Air & Waste Management Association—Scholarship Program

Air & Waste Management Association
One Gateway Center, 3rd Floor
Pittsburgh, PA 15222
Phone: (412) 232-3444

Field of Study: Fields related to air pollution control and waste management

Purpose of Fellowship: To assist graduate students working toward and training for careers in areas of air pollution control or waste management.

Criteria: Full time graduate students in appropriate field. Awards made on basis of academic record; career goals; collegiate, professional and community contribution; and letters of recommendation.

Financial Award: $20,000

Deadline: Early December

Albert Einstein Institution—Fellows Program

Ronald M. McCarthy
Fellows Program Director
The Albert Einstein Institution
50 Church St.
Cambridge, MA 02138
Phone: (617) 876-0311
Fax: (617) 876-0837

Field of Study: Regional science, government, sociology

Purpose of Fellowship: To support research, writing, and systematic reflection on nonviolent action. The award's primary aim is to advance the study of conflict and struggle conducted through nonviolent means, particularly under circumstances in which the adversary may choose repressive violence as a response to nonviolent challengers.

Criteria: Those eligible are doctoral candidates undertaking dissertation research or writing, advanced scholars undertaking specific research projects; or practioners preparing documentation, description, and analysis of conflicts.

Financial Award: Unspecified

Deadline: Late December

American Council of Learned Societies (ACLS)—Fellowships for East European Studies

Office of Fellowships & Grants
American Council of Learned Societies
228 E. 45th Street
New York, NY 10017-3398
Fax: (212) 949-8058
E-mail: grants@acls.org
Web site: http://www.acls.org

Field of Study: Social sciences and humanities

Purpose of Fellowship: For postdoctoral or dissertation research relating to Albania, Bulgaria, the Czech Republic, Hungary, Poland, Romania, Slovakia, and the successor states of Yugoslavia. Also for summer language training and predissertation travel.

Criteria: Candidates must be U.S. citizens or permanent residents.

Financial Award: Up to $30,000 for six to 12 months

Deadline: Early November

American Institute of Pakistan Studies—Predoctoral and Postdoctoral Fellowships

P.O. Box 7568
Wake Forest University
Winston-Salem, NC 27109
Phone: (910) 759-5449
Fax: (910) 759-6104

Field of Study: All fields of the humanities and social sciences

Purpose of Fellowship: To promote research on Pakistan.

Criteria: Must be American citizens. Predoctoral applicants must have completed all requirements but dissertation, and must be pursuing a topic relevant to Pakistan.

Financial Award: Unspecified

Deadline: Early February

American Jewish Archives Fellowships

Director of the American Jewish Archives
3101 Clifton Avenue
Cincinnati, OH 45220
Phone: (513) 221-1875, ext. 403
Fax: (513) 221-7821

Field of Study: Near Eastern studies, American Jewish studies

Purpose of Fellowship: To support research for one month at the American Jewish Archives in Cincinnati.

Criteria: Graduate and postdoctoral students.

Financial Award: Stipends of $1,000 and $2,000 for one month

Deadline: Early April

American Political Association—Congressional Fellowship Program

1527 New Hampshire Avenue, N.W.
Washington, DC 20036
Phone: (202) 483-2512
Fax: (202) 483-2657

Field of Study: Political science, journalism, telecommunications

Purpose of Fellowship: To support midcareer professionals who already have posteducational experience in their fields and whose careers depend heavily upon a sophisticated knowledge of Congress and the political process.

Criteria: Political scientists: scholars who have completed a Ph.D. in the last 15 years (or are near completion). Journalists: bachelor's degree and an interest in Congress.

Financial Award: $28,000 plus travel allowance

Deadline: Early December

American Political Science Association—Joan Shorenstein Barone Congressional Fellowship

1527 New Hampshire Avenue, N.W.
Washington, DC 20036
Phone: (202) 483-2512
Fax: (202) 483-2657

Field of Study: Journalism, political science

Purpose of Fellowship: For broadcast journalists to learn more about the legislative process through direct participation.

Criteria: Broadcast journalists who have two to ten years of full-time professional experience in radio or television reporting, either on the air or as producers, directors, writers, or researchers at time of application.

Financial Award: $28,000 plus travel allowance

Deadline: Late December

American Water Works Association—Academic Achievement Award

Scholarship Coordinator
6666 W. Quincy Avenue
Denver, CO 80235
Phone: (303) 347-6206
E-mail: lsherry@awwa.org

Field of Study: Any field, provided the work is directly related to the water supply industry

Purpose of Fellowship: Intended to encourage academic excellence by recognizing contributions to the field of public water supply.

Criteria: All students whose master's theses and doctoral dissertations are relevant to the water supply industry are eligible. The manuscript must reflect the work of a single author and may be submitted during the competition year in which it was presented for the degree.

Financial Award: Up to $1,000

Deadline: Early October

American Water Works Association—Thomas R. Camp Scholarship

Scholarship Coordinator
American Water Works Association
6666 W. Quincy Avenue
Denver, CO 80235
Phone: (303) 794-7711

Field of Study: Any field related to the drinking water supply industry

Purpose of Fellowship: To support and encourage outstanding graduate students doing applied research in the drinking water field.

Criteria: Granted to doctoral students in even years and master's students in odd years. Master's students must be pursuing a degree in Canada, Guam, Puerto Rico, Mexico, or the United States.

Financial Award: $5,000

Deadline: Mid-January

Brookings Institution—Research Fellowships in Economic Studies

1775 Massachussetts Avenue, N.W.
Washington, DC 20036-2188
Phone: (202) 797-6000
Fax: (202) 797-6181
Web site:
http://www.brook.edu/

Field of Study: Public policy

Purpose of Fellowship: For doctoral candidates whose dissertation topics are directly related to public policy issues, and whose research will benefit from access to the data, opportunities for interviewing, and consultation with senior staff members afforded by the Institution and by residence in D.C.

Criteria: Students must be nominated by their graduate department by mid-December and must have completed the preliminary examination for the doctorate not later than mid-February.

Financial Award: $15,000 stipend; $600 for research expenses; $500 for research-related travel.

Deadline: Mid-December

Brookings Institution—Research Fellowships in Foreign Policy Studies

1775 Massachussetts Avenue, N.W.
Washington, DC 20036-2188
Phone: (202) 797-6000
Fax: (202) 794-6004
Web site:
http://www.brook.edu/

Field of Study: Foreign policy

Purpose of Fellowship: For doctoral candidates whose dissertation topics are directly related to public policy issues, and whose research will benefit from access to the data, opportunities for interviewing, and consultation with senior staff members afforded by the Institution and by residence in DC.

Criteria: Students must be nominated by their graduate department and must have completed the preliminary examination for the doctorate not later than mid-February.

Financial Award: $15,000 stipend; $600 for research purposes; $500 for research-related travel

Deadline: Mid-December

Brookings Institution—Research Fellowships in Governmental Studies

1775 Massachussetts Avenue, N.W.
Washington, DC 20036-2188
Phone: (202) 797-6000
Fax: (202) 797-6004
Web site:
http://www.brook.edu/

Field of Study: Governmental studies

Purpose of Fellowship: For doctoral candidates whose dissertation topics are directly related to public policy issues, and whose research will benefit from access to the data, opportunities for interviewing, and consultation with senior staff members afforded by the Institution and by residence in DC.

Criteria: Students must be nominated by their graduate department and must have completed the preliminary examination for the doctorate not later than mid-February.

Financial Award: $15,000 stipend; $600 for research purposes; $500 for research-related travel

Deadline: Mid-December

Budget Fellowship Program

Budget Fellowship Program
New York State Division of the Budget
State Capitol
Albany, NY 12224
Phone: (518) 474-8616

Field of Study: Open

Purpose of Fellowship: To create an opportunity for the division to employ persons with unique skills and backgrounds not generally available through traditional civil service mechanisms.

Criteria: Postbaccalaureate. Applications from women, minorities, and Vietnam era veterans and the disabled are encouraged.

Financial Award: Salaries ranging from $25,039 to $33,221, varying with education and appointment level

Deadline: Early April

Byron Hanke Fellowship

CAI Research Foundation
1630 Duke Street
Alexandria, VA 22314
Phone: (703) 548-8600
Fax: (703) 684-1581

Field of Study: All fields

Purpose of Fellowship: To fund graduate students working on topics related to community associations.

Criteria: Enrollment in an accredited master's, doctoral, or law program. Studies must relate to community associations generally, and to the topic of the candidate's proposed community associations research project. Recipients are expected to prepare a research project on community associations.

Financial Award: $2,500

Deadline: Rolling

California Executive Fellows Program

California State University/
Sacramento
6000 J Street
Sacramento, CA 95819-6081

Field of Study: Open; persons from all disciplines are encouraged

Purpose of Fellowship: To provide an opportunity for individuals to participate in the development and implementation of public policy in the Executive Branch. The Program is designed to provide insight into the workings of California govenment and promote career opportunities in the public sector.

Criteria: Anyone who has graduated from a 4-year college or university by August, 1995 may apply. Application review is based on academic background and performance, employment history, demonstrated leadership, community involvement, and the applicant's personal statement.

Financial Award: Monthly stipend of approximately $1,560 plus paid enrollment at CSU/Sacramento

Deadline: Early March

The Eisenhower World Affairs Institute—Dwight Eisenhower/Clifford Roberts Graduate Fellowships Program

Ask your university career services office for applications

Field of Study: History, government, economics, and business administration

Purpose of Fellowship: To support study and education dealing with the role of government in a free society, the relationship between international and domestic issues, and improved understanding of world affairs.

Criteria: Applicants should be at an advanced stage of their doctoral candidacies, preferably at the point of preparing their dissertations. Applications of less advanced graduate students or of persons who have recently earned their doctorates will also be considered.

Financial Award: $7,000–$10,000

Deadline: Early February

Ford Foundation Program Assistantship

The Ford Foundation
320 E. 43rd Street
New York, NY 10017
Phone: (212) 573-5000
E-mail: pgmast@fordfound.org

Field of Study: Urban poverty, rural poverty, and resources

Purpose of Fellowship: To provide a two-year professional opportunity for recent masters or law school graduates to learn about philanthropic and nonprofit sectors.

Criteria: Masters or law degree. Excellent written and oral communication and skills. Must be able to work well under tight deadlines and handle multiple projects. Demonstrated academic or work experience in the Program Areas listed above.

Financial Award: $35,000 annual salary plus medical and dental insurance, vacation, sick leave, and a savings plan

Deadline: Mid-December

Graduate Research Award Program—Public Sector Aviation Issues

2101 Constitution Avenue, N.W.
Room GR-326E
Washington, DC 20418
Phone: (800) 424-9818, ext. 3206

Field of Study: Mathematics, political science, economics, engineering

Purpose of Fellowship: To stimulate thought, discussion and research on public-sector aviation issues by those who may become the future managers and policy makers in aviation.

Criteria: U.S. citizens or permanent residents currently enrolled in a graduate program in an accredited institution of higher learning in a graduate course leading to a master's or doctoral degree.

Financial Award: $6,000 stipend

Deadline: Late October

Harry S. Truman Library Institute—Dissertation Year Fellowships

Assistant Secretary-Treasurer
Harry S. Truman Library Institute
U.S. Highway 24 and Delaware Street
Independence, MO 64050

Field of Study: History, government, and related fields

Purpose of Fellowship: To encourage historical scholarship in the Truman era (history of the Truman administration and the public career of Truman).

Criteria: Doctoral candidates who have completed their research and are ready to begin writing. Candidates are not required to come to the library but are expected to furnish the library with a copy of their dissertation.

Financial Award: $16,000 annual stipend

Deadline: Early February

Harry S. Truman Library Institute—Research Grants

Assistant Secretary-Treasurer
Harry S. Truman Library Institute
U.S. Highway 24 and Delaware Street
Independence, MO 64050

Field of Study: History, government, and related fields

Purpose of Fellowship: To support graduate students and postdoctoral scholars wishing to spend one to three weeks using the library's archival facilities.

Criteria: Applicants must be working on a project pertaining to Truman's public career or to the history of the Truman administration.

Financial Award: Up to $2,500 for up to three weeks to cover airfare, living expenses, supplies and costs of reproducing documents

Deadline: Call committee

Herbert Scoville Jr. Peace Fellowship

110 Maryland Avenue, NE
Suite 201
Washington, DC 20002
Phone: (202) 546-0795
E-mail: scoville@clw.org

Field of Study: Government, international relations, and conflict resolution

Purpose of Fellowship: To provide an opportunity for college graduates to gain practical knowledge and experience by contributing to the efforts of nonprofit, public-interest organizations working on peace and security issues.

Criteria: Demonstrated academic excellence and a strong interest in issues of peace and security; graduate study, a college major, coursework, or substantial independent reading that reflects the substantive focus of the fellowship; prior experience with public-interest activism or advocacy; focus on peace and security issues preferred.

Financial Award: $1,500 per month and health insurance, plus travel expenses to Washington, DC

Deadline: Mid-March

Hubert H. Humphrey Fellowships in Arms Control and Disarmament

320 21st Street, N.W.
Room 5726
Washington, DC 20451

Field of Study: All fields (particularly political science and economics)

Purpose of Fellowship: To encourage specialized training and research in the arms control field; to support graduate students working on research designed to contribute to a better understanding of current and future arms control.

Criteria: U.S. citizens or nationals who have completed all Ph.D. or (J.D.) requirements except the dissertation by the date the fellowship begins.

Financial Award: $8,000 stipend plus a $6,000 educational allowance for one year

Deadline: Mid-March

Institute for the Study of World Politics—Doctoral Dissertation Fellowships/ Dorothy Danforth Compton Fellowships

1775 Massachussetts Avenue, N.W.
Washington, DC 20036

Field of Study: History, economics, political science, international relations

Purpose of Fellowship: To promote scholarly examination of political, economic, and social issues that affect the security, well-being, and dignity of the people of the world. Fellowships support work that will develop knowledge and understanding essential to the resolution of fundamental international issues.

Criteria: Doctoral candidates who have completed course work and are conducting dissertation research. Candidates for the Dorothy Danforth Compton Fellowship must be African American, Hispanic American, or Native American graduate students preparing for careers in world affairs.

Financial Award: Varies

Deadline: Mid-February

Institute for the Study of World Politics—Doctoral Dissertation Fellowships/ Dorothy Danforth Compton Fellowships

1755 Massachussetts Avenue, N.W.
Washington, DC 20036

Field of Study: Social sciences

Purpose of Fellowship: To promote scholarly examination of political, economic, and social issues that affect the security, well-being and dignity of the peoples of the world. Fellowships support work which will develop knowledge and understanding essential to the resolution of fundamental international issues.

Criteria: Doctoral candidates who have completed coursework and are conducting dissertation research (Institute's special Dorothy Danforth Compton Fellowship is awarded to African-American, Hispanic American, and Native American graduate students preparing for careers in world affairs).

Financial Award: Varies according to fellows' needs and resources

Deadline: Mid-February

John F. Kennedy Library Foundation—Archival Internships

Intern Registrar
John F. Kennedy Library
Columbia Point
Boston, MA 02125
Phone: (617) 929-4524

Field of Study: History, government, archival administration

Purpose of Fellowship: To help graduate and undergraduate students gain career-relevant archival experience in a presidential library while contributing constructively to the work of the institution.

Criteria: Candidates may be graduate or undergraduate students.

Financial Award: Unspecified

Deadline: Rolling

John F. Kennedy Library Foundation—Kennedy Research Grants

Chief Archivist
Kennedy Library
Columbia Point
Boston, MA 02125
Phone: (617) 929-4533

Field of Study: Government, history, regional science

Purpose of Fellowship: For research requiring the use of the library's archival collections.

Criteria: Preference will be given to Ph.D. dissertation research, research in recently opened or relatively unused collections and the preparation of recent dissertations for publication, but all proposals are welcome.

Financial Award: $500–$1,500

Deadline: Mid-August

John F. Kennedy School of Government, Harvard University: Center for Science and International Affairs—Fellowships in Science and International Affairs

79 John F. Kennedy Street
Cambridge, MA 02138
Phone: (617) 495-3745
E-mail: csia_2@ksgrsch.harvard.edu
Web site: http://ksgwww.harvard.edu/csia

Field of Study: Government, international relations, natural resources

Purpose of Fellowship: To emphasize the role of science and technology in the analysis and design of public policy, seeking primarily to advance the understanding of international security problems and the international dimensions of resource and environmental issues.

Criteria: Research Fellowships: recent recipients of Ph.D. or equivalent, university faculty members, and employees of the government, military, international and private research. Predoctoral: must have passed general exams prior to appointment. Selection process gives preference to candidates whose expertise and research proposals are compatible with CSIA's research agenda. CSIA encourages applications from women, minorities, and citizens of all countries.

Deadline: Mid-February

Morris K. Udall Scholarship and Excellence in National Environmental Policy Program—Dissertation Fellows Program

2201 North Dodge Street
P.O. Box 4030
Iowa City, IA 52243
Phone: (319) 337-1650

Field of Study: Environmental public policy and conflict resolution

Purpose of Fellowship: To cover both economic and living expenses for dissertation fellows.

Criteria: Candidates must be U.S. citizens or permanent residents, applicants must have completed all coursework, passed all preliminary exams, and had the dissertation research proposal or plan approved by mid-January.

Financial Award: Up to $24,000

Deadline: Mid-January

National Security Education Program—Graduate International Fellowships

Please call for application
Phone: (800) 498-9360

Field of Study: Business, economics, history, political science, public policy

Purpose of Fellowship: To enable graduate students to add an international dimension to their curriculum or to intensify their study of areas, languages, and cultures.

Criteria: U.S. citizens who are either matriculated in a graduate program or students in the process of applying to a graduate program. Applicants should demonstrate the significance of their research to global economic, political, and social issues affecting U.S. national security.

Financial Award: Up to $10,000 per year for overseas work and $2,000 per semester for domestic work

Deadline: Mid-January

New York State—Public Management Internship Program

New York State Department of Civil Service, Staffing Section
W. Averell Harriman State Office Building Campus
Albany, NY 12239
Phone: (518) 457-6684
E-mail: bjs3@cs.state.ny.us

Field of Study: Public administration

Purpose of Fellowship: The program prepares participants with master's degrees in public administration or a related field for full-time management positions of increasing responsibility with civil service agencies. Rockefeller Institute provides training. Forty to 50 internships in different services available.

Criteria: Must hold a master's degree in public administration.

Financial Award: Two-year paid program; annual salary ranges from $32–$36,000

Deadline: Early December

New York City Summer Internship Program

Division of Citywide Personnel Services
2 Washington Street
New York, NY 10004
Phone: (212) 487-6100
Fax: (212) 487-6113

Field of Study: Open, particularly relevant to government and public policy

Purpose of Fellowship: To provide employment opportunities to students through internships that allow them to make important contributions to the city, while participating in a challenging and rewarding experience.

Criteria: Applicants must be currently enrolled or accepted into a graduate program.

Financial Award: Varies

Deadline: Varies

One Thousand Friends of Oregon—Paul Gerhardt Jr. Internship

543 S.W. 3rd Avenue
Suite 300
Portland, OR 97204
Phone: (503) 497-1000

Field of Study: Preference for students in planning

Purpose of Fellowship: To provide an opportunity for on-the-job experience for planning students or those in similar fields, especially those with an interest in public service and without a graduate degreee in the field. Intern will work on short-term and large projects in order to gain a wider acquaintance with Oregon's land use program.

Criteria: Academic excellence, evidence of initiative, the ability to work independently, and demonstrated interest in public service. Preference given to undergraduate planning majors or graduates who have not yet begun graduate school.

Financial Award: $1,500 a month for three months with limited travel expenses to and from Portland

Deadline: Mid-March

U.S. Deparment of Health and Human Services—National Center on Child Abuse and Neglect

Call for application
Phone: (800) 351-2293

Field of Study: Human development and family studies

Purpose of Fellowship: To support child abuse and child neglect research. Specifically, these funds are for research on the causes, prevention, identification, treatment and cultural distinctions of child abuse and neglect; for research on appropriate, effective, and culturally sensitive investigative, administrative, and judicial procedures with respect to cases of child abuse; and for demonstration of service programs and projects designed to prevent, identify, and treat child abuse and neglect.

Criteria: Doctoral or medical students, residents, house officers, or enrolled fellows or faculty members.

Financial Award: Varies

Deadline: Mid-August

United Nations Headquarters Internship Programme

Professional Staffing Service,
Room S-2500
United Nations
New York, NY 10017
Phone: (212) 963-1224

Field of Study: Open

Purpose of Fellowship: To promote among the participants a better understanding of major problems confronting the world and to give them insight into how the United Nations attempts to find solutions to these problems.

Criteria: Applicants should be currently enrolled in graduate school and should not be more than 30 years of age. Applicants with a second-level university degree will be considered.

Financial Award: Two-month internship without reimbursement

Deadline: Rolling

Urban Fellows Program

Department of Personnel
2 Washington Street, 15th Floor
New York, NY 10004
Phone: (212) 487-6100
Fax: (212) 487-6113

Field of Study: Open; particularly relevant to government and public policy

Purpose of Fellowship: A nine-month program that combines work in mayoral offices and city agencies with an intensive seminar component that explores key issues facing New York City government.

Criteria: Applicants must be recent college graduates, no more than two full years out of college; must be prepared to participate in the program on a full-time basis for one academic year; must be interested in pursuing a career in public service.

Financial Award: $18,000 stipend plus choice of paid health insurance plans

Deadline: Unspecified

White House Fellowships

712 Jackson Place, N.W.
Washington, DC 20503
Phone: (202) 395-4522
Fax: (202) 395-6179
Web site:
http://www.whitehouse.gov/wh_fellows

Field of Study: Open

Purpose of Fellowship: To give outstanding, promising Americans the opportunity to receive a first-hand introduction to the workings of government at the highest level. Fellows are assigned to the staff of the executive office of the president and to Cabinet-level departments and agencies.

Criteria: U.S. citizenship; must not be a civilian employee of the federal government. There are no formal age or educational requirements, although candidates called for interviews have tended to range from their mid-twenties to their early forties.

Financial Award: Salary and benefits from the agency where fellows work.

Deadline: Early December

Business and Economics

8

The economic climate in the United States has never been better. With the stock market taking a bull ride to record highs, unemployment hitting all-time lows, and the deficit coming out of the red, there is reason for students interested in entering the business world to be optimistic. And even though there is a relative dearth of fellowship opportunities for these students, those that exist are more than worth a look.

In general, fellowships and grants in the world of business and economics cover the following fields:

- Business administration
- Insurance
- Industrial relations
- Finance
- Management

Business fellowship committees are looking for students who show extraordinary leadership and communication skills. An applicant can do wonders for her chances if she devotes time to applicable extracurricular activities. This is not to say that academic factors such as the GPA are not important as well. But organizations are looking for individuals who understand the philosophies and intricacies of the business world. The interview is the part of the application that gives business fellowship applicants the best opportunity to show off these characteristics.

The Interview: A Pivotal Factor

Anyone who has experienced the trauma of applying for a job as a financial analyst, sales and trading representative, stock broker, or any other position at a large firm knows that the key portion of the application process is the interview. The questions are difficult, the setting is formal, and the pressure level is sky-high. Much the same can be said about the business award interview.

Be prepared for the committee to throw everything, including the kitchen sink, at you during the interview. You'll get the generic, everyday questions for certain ("Tell me about yourself" or "Tell me about your college experience"), but you'll also get some serious curveballs. Questions will be geared toward learning whether you have a business mind, and students who have interviewed for business awards—and survived—said the best way to prepare for the impending onslaught is to practice, practice, practice.

Sample Curveball Questions

How many fire hydrants are there in the United States?

If you were offered $20 million or a magic carpet, which would you choose and why?

How much do you drink?

If you were any inanimate object, what would you be?

When was the last time you cried?

Define happiness.

Who is the most influential person in your life?

Do you think you're cool?

Many universities have counselors for students who intend to go into the business world after graduation. These advisers know exactly what these questions are all about and can help you answer them without cracking under the pressure. Be sure to seek their advice, as well as other students who have been through the process. Finding them is as simple as heading to your undergraduate career services office, which will be glad to match you up with one.

When They Catch You Off-Guard . . .

"I was interviewing for a fellowship in investment banking, expecting questions dealing with my life and interests, when the person asked me to make an estimate of how many manholes there were in the continental United States. I was completely caught off-guard and tried to reason through a coherent answer. I stayed calm and thought it out, but my answer was way off. I was sure I was a goner. But I got the fellowship, and I think I know why: Even though my answer was wrong, I was able to present myself as someone who could think through difficult situations. They didn't care so much about what my answer was. They just wanted to see how I tried to answer it."

—Yale University Senior

If you find yourself struggling, just remember to always be yourself. Remember, many applicants who eventually earned fellowships thought they had failed miserably in their interviews. If you find yourself in a hole, don't dig yourself in any deeper by making snide remarks or trying to buddy up to the interviewers. Just keep on treading water until it's all over, and as long as you've kept your cool, chances are things didn't go as badly as you might have imagined.

County of Sonoma Economic Vitality Fellowship

2300 County Center Drive
#A106
Santa Rosa, CA 95403

Field of Study: Public administration, business, and political science

Purpose of Fellowship: To attract and to assist innovative people to pursue fulfilling career positions in the public, private, and educational sectors.

Criteria: Applicants must have satisfactorily completed all courses for a bachelor's and/or master's degree in the above fields.

Financial Award: $2,607 monthly salary

Deadline: Mid-April

Donald E. Sommer/A. J. Viehman Jr. Industrial Relations Scholarship

Education Trust Fund
1730 N. Lynn Street
Arlington, VA 22209

Field of Study: Industrial relations or human resource management

Purpose of Fellowship: To award a student who demonstrates knowledge and understanding of the open-shop philosophy of employee relations.

Criteria: First- or second-year graduate students pursuing a master's degree.

Financial Award: $5,000

Deadline: Early April

Harry J. Loman Foundation Matching Funds Scholarship Program

720 Providence Road
P.O. Box 3009
Malvern, PA 19355-0709
Phone: (800) 932-2728

Field of Study: Insurance or insurance-related field

Purpose of Fellowship: To provide matching scholarship funds to CPCU Society Chapters that establish scholarship programs to foster insurance education at the college level.

Criteria: Full-time students enrolled in insurance or insurance-related fields of study.

Financial Award: Up to $1,000

Deadline: Call committee

International Foundation of Employee Benefit Plans

18700 West Bluemound Road
P.O. Box 69
Brookfield, WI 53008-0069

Field of Study: Business and finance, industrial labor relations

Purpose of Fellowship: To encourage graduate students to pursue the study of problems having legal, economic, social or political consequences for the employee benefits systems in the United States and Canada.

Criteria: Citizens of the United States who have completed the majority of required coursework toward a graduate degree.

Financial Award: Up to $5,000 for graduate grants and up to $10,000 for postdoctoral grants

Deadline: Rolling

J. Desmond Slattery Marketing Awards

Dr. James Burke
One Lomb Memorial Drive
Box 9887
Rochester, NY 14623
Phone: (716) 475-6061
Fax: (716) 475-5099

Field of Study: Hospitality, travel, and tourism

Purpose of Fellowship: To award student achievement in travel and tourism research and marketing.

Criteria: Students enrolled in degree-granting programs.

Financial Award: $1,000 cash, travel allowance, one-year complimentary student TTRA membership and registration at TTRA Annual Conference

Deadline: Early May

Kappa Omicron Nu Fellowships/Grants

4900 Northwind Drive
Suite 140
East Lansing, MI 48823-5031
Phone: (517) 351-8335
Fax: (517) 351-8336

Field of Study: Home economics

Purpose of Fellowship: To support a Kappa Omicron Nu member who has demonstrated scholarship, research, and leadership potential. Funds are awarded for master's and doctoral fellowships.

Criteria: U.S. citizens or foreign students studying in the United States, enrolled in doctoral programs. Preference will be given to members of Kappa Omicron Nu.

Financial Award: $2,000

Deadline: Call committee

National Association of Broadcasters—Grants for Research in Broadcasting

Dr. Mrak R. Fratik
1771 N Street, N.W.
Washington, DC 20036-2891
Phone: (202) 429-5389

Field of Study: Economics

Purpose of Fellowship: To stimulate interest in broadcast research, especially research on economic, business, social, or policy issues of importance to the U.S. commercial broadcast industry. The goal is to make high quality academic research available to industry practitioners as well as other academics.

Criteria: Open to academic personnel and students.

Financial Award: Up to $5,000 for research

Deadline: Late January

Richard D. Irwin Doctoral Fellowships

Irwin Doctoral Fellowships
1818 Ridge Road
Homewood, IL 60430
Phone: (312) 798-6000

Field of Study: Education, economics, management

Purpose of Fellowship: To help in the development of qualified teachers in the areas of business and economics.

Criteria: Doctoral candidates who have completed the A exam. Preference is usually given to those applicants whose contribution to teaching is to be made in the United States and Canada.

Financial Award: $2,000–$2,500

Deadline: Mid-February

University of Delaware/ Hagley Program—Fellowships in the History of Industrialization

Department of History
University of Delaware
Neward, DE 19716
Phone: (302) 831-8226

Field of Study: Business, economic, and technological history

Purpose of Fellowship: To support M.A. or Ph.D. students interested in academic or professional careers in museums, historical agencies, or archives. Students will use the resources of the Hagley Museum to study the history of science and technology.

Criteria: An interest in museum or historical agency is desirable but not required.

Financial Award: Master's candidates receive $9,500; doctoral candidates receive $10,700

Deadline: Late January

Wharton School of University of Pennsylvania—S.S. Huebner Foundation Fellowships

430 Vance Hall
3733 Spruce St.
Philadelphia, PA 19104-6301
Phone: (215) 898-9631

Field of Study: Insurance and risk management, economics

Purpose of Fellowship: To support students and scholars in managerial science and applied economics at the Wharton School.

Criteria: U.S. or Canadian citizens, with a baccalaureate degree from an accredited college or university, who satisfy requirements for admission to the Wharton doctoral program.

Financial Award: Predoctoral: $14,000 per year plus tuition and fees; postdoctoral: $12,000 stipend

Deadline: Early February

Health Professions and the Sciences

9

If you're planning on applying for a fellowship or grant in either the health professions or the sciences, you're in luck. Whereas your nonscience major buddies may be struggling to find suitable awards, there is no shortage of opportunities for you.

Because of the abundance of fellowships and grants in these categories, one of the most important decisions an applicant must make is which are the right ones for him or her. Although it is a good idea to cover your bases by applying for a number of awards, taking shots at too many is often the kiss of death. By spreading yourself too thin, you end up devoting less time to each application and, often, leaving out essential elements.

So where do you begin? A good first step is to decide which facet of either the health professions or sciences interests you most. Once you've made that essential decision, the rest of the application process should be relatively straightforward.

Health Professions Awards

The first thing you should know about this class of fellowships is that earning one isn't going to immediately turn you into Dr. Carter from *ER*. Many of the awards in the health professions provide little opportunity for interaction with doctors and patients.

The most typical categories of health professions awards include:

- Medical sociology
- Nursing
- Counseling
- Scientific research

Another common fallacy is that in order to earn one of these fellowships or grants, you must either be on your way to or already enrolled in medical school. In fact, many of the awards discourage or even deny medical school students. Either way, service and exposure to the applicable field of study is a must to gain acceptance. It's an added bonus if the student has extensively studied science—as a premed certainly has—but this means nothing if she hasn't experienced the world of medicine first hand.

Science Awards

The world of science and technology is rapidly changing, and a wide variety of fellowships and grants have been created to adapt to this dynamic landscape. For this reason, it is impossible to name all the fields that fall under the category of science fellowships, but some include:

- Scientific and technological research
- Physical sciences
- Biological sciences
- Chemical sciences
- Biomedical/chemical engineering
- Zoology
- Horticulture

When applying for the majority of the awards that fall under the categories listed above, follow the same basic procedure that is outlined in chapter 2. There is an exception to this rule, however: research fellowships.

Research Projects

Opportunities in scientific research differ markedly from any other branch of scientific fellowships, especially as regards the application procedure. Committees place an enormous amount of importance upon two central factors—the student's research experience and written proposal.

Research Experience

Needless to say, the best way for an applicant to endear himself to committees is to have established a long record of experience in a laboratory setting. This is an aspect of an individual's extracurricular and work résumé that does not have to be limited to his time at college. Beginning in high school, many future scientists start working in a laboratory. But for those of you who can't see quite as far into the future, it's not a bad idea to spend your summers doing research and learning the techniques that will serve you in your career as a scientist. Many students stay on campus for summer vacation, both to familiarize themselves with a laboratory and to get to know their research adviser. This serves two purposes: Many students end up as researchers in the same lab during the school year, and they gain the trust of their advisers, who in the future can write fantastic letters of recommendation.

Written Proposal

Once the applicant has proven herself to be experienced enough for a committee's liking, the next step is to unveil her vision for her project. This becomes the main focus of the project proposal, which must be both daring and feasible at the same time. No organization will fund a student whose proposed project has already been carried out, and even if the plan is original, it will not be accepted if it is deemed incapable of providing convincing results. In choosing its fellows, the committee is thinking of itself first. It asks itself, "Which applicants will make breakthroughs that will earn our organization some fame?"

It takes a truly outstanding proposal to gain acceptance. And the way to ensure that your plan is truly extraordinary is to consult with experts. Brainstorm ideas with other researchers (particularly those under whom you work) until you've come up with a working proposal. Then think through all the practical details.

Will the fellowship award cover the project's costs? Is it an original plan? And most importantly, is it possible to come up with positive results? If the answer to all three of these questions is yes, then you're on your way to a winning proposal.

Advanced Thermionics Research Initiative 2000 Fellowship Program

University of California/Davis
Department of Applied Science
228 Walker Hall
Davis, CA 95616-9936
E-mail: atri@gregor.llnl.gov
Web site:
http://tempest.ece.ucdavis.edu/atri/atri.html

Field of Study: Physical sciences

Purpose of Fellowship: To train M.S. and Ph.D. engineers and scientists in the great variety of disciplines that are associated with the design and manufacture of microwave and millimeter wave sources.

Criteria: M.S. and Ph.D. students; those to receive a B.S. or B.A. may also inquire.

Financial Award: Unspecified

Deadline: Unspecified

American Foundation for Aging Research

North Carolina State University
Biochemistry Department
128 Polk Hall
Raleigh, NC 27695-7622
Phone: (919) 515-5679

Field of Study: Molecular and cellular biology, immunobiology, neurobiology

Purpose of Fellowship: To support research in the field of aging.

Criteria: Applicants must be enrolled in undergraduate, graduate, or predoctoral degree programs at colleges or universities in the United States.

Financial Award: Unspecified

Deadline: Rolling

American Iris Society Scholarship

Jean Witt, Director
16516-25th NE
Seattle, WA 98155

Field of Study: Plant sciences

Purpose of Fellowship: To support graduate studies in plant sciences.

Criteria: Candidates must be U.S. or Canadian citizens enrolled in graduate studies in the field of plant sciences. There is no application form; rather, candidates must send their résumés, school transcripts, outlines of research programs or goals, and verification of all the above from their academic advisers.

Financial Award: $2,000

Deadline: Early March

American Museum of Natural History—Collection Study Grants

Central Park West at 79th Street
New York, NY 10024-5192

Field of Study: Vertebrate and invertebrate zoology, paleontology

Purpose of Fellowship: To provide financial assistance to enable predoctoral and recent postdoctoral investigators to study the collections at the American Museum.

Criteria: Not available to investigators within daily commuting range of the Museum. Visits of four days or longer must be arranged through a scientific staff member of the Museum.

Financial Award: Up to $400 for stays of four days or longer

Deadline: Rolling

American Museum of Natural History—Frank M. Chapman Memorial Fund

Central Park West at 79th Street
New York, NY 10024-5192

Field of Study: Ornithology, ecology, wildlife conservation

Purpose of Fellowship: To support ornithological reserach anywhere in the world.

Criteria: Graduates or postgraduates conducting ornithological research.

Financial Award: $200–$1,000 for one year

Deadline: Mid-January

American Museum of Natural History—Lerner-Gray Fund for Marine Research

Central Park West at 79th Street
New York, NY 10024-5192

Field of Study: Marine zoology and ecology

Purpose of Fellowship: To support projects in marine zoology with emphasis on systematics, evolution, ecology, and field-oriented behavioral studies of marine animals.

Criteria: Highly qualified people starting careers in marine zoology.

Financial Award: $200–$1,000 for one year

Deadline: Mid-March

American Museum of Natural History—Theodore Roosevelt Memorial Fund

Central Park West at 79th Street
New York, NY 10024-5192

Field of Study: Wildlife conservation, natural history

Purpose of Fellowship: To support research on North American fauna, excluding birds.

Criteria: Advanced graduate students and postdoctoral researchers who are commencing their careers.

Financial Award: $200–$1,000 per year

Deadline: Mid-February

American Water Works Association—Abel Wolman Fellowship Award

Scholarship Coordinator
American Water Works Association
6666 W. Quincy Avenue
Denver, CO 80235
Phone: (303) 794-7711, ext. 6194
Web site: http://www.awwa.org

Field of Study: Biomedical, chemical, civil, electrical and computer sciences

Purpose of Fellowship: To support promising students in the United States, Canada, and Mexico who are pursuing advanced training and research in the field of water supply and treatment.

Criteria: Ph.D. requirements completed within two years of the award, and citizenship or permanent residence in Canada, Mexico or the United States.

Financial Award: $15,000 stipend plus $1,000 for research supplies and $4,000 for tuition per year; award may be extended for a second year

Deadline: Mid-January

American Water Works Association—LARS (Larson Aquatic Research Support) Scholarship

Scholarship Coordinator
American Water Works Association
6666 W. Quincy Avenue
Denver, CO 80235
Phone: (303) 794-7711, ext. 6194
Web site: http://www.awwa.org

Field of Study: Research relating to water chemistry and industry

Purpose of Fellowship: To provide support and encouragement to outstanding graduate students in science or engineering dedicated to research on improving water quality.

Criteria: M.S. to be completed after August 1; Ph.D. to be completed after December 1.

Financial Award: $3,000 for master's students; $5,000 for Ph.D. students

Deadline: Mid-November

Andrew W. Mellon Student Research Grants

Office for Research
College of Agriculture and Life Sciences
Cornell University
245 Roberts Hall
Ithaca, NY 14853

Field of Study: Fields relating to environmental and natural resources

Purpose of Fellowship: To increase the involvement of students with environmental issues by stimulating original research, especially research embodying synthetic concepts and multidisciplinary approaches.

Criteria: Individuals or groups enrolled in graduate or undergraduate programs with the College of Agriculture and Life Sciences or biological sciences.

Financial Award: Up to $15,000

Deadline: Mid-March

Arthur Boller Apple Research Grants

Office for Research
245 Roberts Hall
Cornell University
Ithaca, NY 14853
Phone: 255-2224

Field of Study: Agriculture and life sciences

Purpose of Fellowship: To support research on apples and cherries and to increase the involvement of students in research.

Criteria: Unspecified

Financial Award: $1,000

Deadline: Mid-March

Associated Western Universities, Inc.—Graduate Fellowships at National Laboratories and Cooperating Facilities

4190 S. Highland Drive
Suite 211
Salt Lake City, UT 84124-2600
Phone: (801) 277-5632
E-mail: info@sl.awu.org
Web site:
http://online.awu.org/

Field of Study: Science and engineering

Purpose of Fellowship: To provide qualified master's and doctoral degree candidates in science and engineering the opportunity to conduct research toward their thesis or dissertation, in whole or in part, at one of over 50 cooperating facilities.

Criteria: This program is open to master's and doctoral degree candidates who have an established thesis research program. Institutional affiliation and citizenship restrictions may apply for some awards or facilities.

Financial Award: Stipends of at least $1,300 per month, tuition assistance, and travel allowance

Deadline: Mid-February

Atlantic Salmon Federation: Olin Fellowships

Atlantic Salmon Federation
P.O. Drawer C
Calais, ME 04619

Field of Study: Salmon biology, management and conservation

Purpose of Fellowship: To encourage individuals seeking to improve their knowledge or skills while looking for solutions to current problems in Atlantic salmon biology, management, and conservation.

Criteria: Candidates must be legal residents of the United States or Canada.

Financial Award:
$1,000–$3,000

Deadline: Mid-March

Center for Plant Conservation—Catherine H. Beattie Fellowship for Conservation Horticulture

Beattie Fellowship for Plant Conservation
P.O. Box 299
St. Louis, MO 63166-0299
Phone: (314) 577-9452
Fax: (314) 577-9465

Field of Study: Biology, horticulture, or a related field

Purpose of Fellowship: To promote conservation of rare and endangered flora in the United States. Fellowship will compensate work done by graduate student fellow at botanical garden jointly serving the program of the Center and the student's curricular studies.

Criteria: Graduate students with academic qualifications and an interest in rare plant conservation. Preference given to students whose projects focus on the endangered flora of the Carolinas and the southeastern United States.

Financial Award:
$1,000–$4,000

Deadline: Late December

Dr. Frederick E. G. Valergakis Graduate Research Grant Program

P.O. Box 6882
FDR Station
New York, NY 10150-6882
E-mail: Vbdd58A@Prodigy.com

Field of Study: Biological, medical, or social sciences

Purpose of Fellowship: To provide research support for graduate students of Hellenic ancestry. Not to be applied to either tuition or living expenses.

Criteria: Graduate students of Greek ancestry engaged in doctoral or postdoctoral research and affiliated with an accredited university in the United States.

Financial Award: Minimum $1,000

Deadline: Late December

Edna Bailey Sussman Environmental Internships

Information and applications available at field offices

Field of Study: Environmental studies

Purpose of Fellowship: To support summer research internships in environment-related fields.

Criteria: Students who have arranged a summer research internship with a host organization involving environmentally based research. The research should be of direct benefit to the environment.

Financial Award: $2,500–$4,000 for three months

Deadline: Early March

Environmental College On-Campus Paid Internship

SEEE Internship
P.O. Box 381874
Cambridge, MA 02238
Phone: (606) 268-4211
E-mail: fine@husc.harvard.edu

Field of Study: Open

Purpose of Fellowship: For students to promote energy-efficient technologies on campus.

Criteria: Unspecified

Financial Award: $1,000 and a trip to Washington, DC

Deadline: Early October

Environmental Protection Agency Fellowships

U.S. Environmental Protection Agency, Region II
290 Broadway
New York, NY 10007
Fax: (212) 637-3591
E-mail: hoang.kim-chi@epamail.epa.gov
Web site: http://www.epa.gov/docs/oer/rfa

Field of Study: Mathematics, natural sciences, engineering, social sciences

Purpose of Fellowship: To support graduate students in environmentally related fields of study.

Criteria: Candidates must be masters or Ph.D. candidates in environmental sciences and technology.

Financial Award: Up to $34,000 per year for a maximum three years

Deadline: February

Garden Club of America—Frances M. Peacock Scholarship for Native Bird Habitat

Scott Sutcliffe
159 Sapsucker Woods Road
Ithaca, NY 14850
Fax: (607) 254-2415
E-mail: lhl7@cornell.edu

Field of Study: Environmental sciences, ornithology

Purpose of Fellowship: To provide financial aid to an advanced student to study areas in the United States that provide winter or summer habitat for threatened and endangered native birds.

Criteria: Senior undergraduate students who study habit-related issues that will benefit threatened or endangered bird species and lend useful information for land management decisions.

Financial Award: Unspecified

Deadline: Mid-January

Howard Hughes Medical Institute—Predoctoral Fellowships in Biological Sciences

2102 Constitution Avenue N.W.
Washington, DC 20418
Phone: (202) 334-2872
Fax: (202) 334-3419
E-mail: infofell@nas.edu

Field of Study: Biological sciences

Purpose of Fellowship: To promote excellence in biomedical research by helping prospective researchers with exceptional promise obtain high-quality graduate education.

Criteria: Fellowships are available for students who have completed less than one year of graduate study toward a Ph.D. or Sc.D. degree in biological sciences at the time of application.

Financial Award: $15,000 annual stipend plus $15,000 annual cost-of-education allowance

Deadline: Mid-November

Howard Hughes Medical Institute—Research Training Fellowships for Medical Students

4000 Jones Bridge Road
Chevy Chase, MD 20815-6789
Phone: (301) 215-8889
Fax: (301) 215-8888

Field of Study: Science

Purpose of Fellowship: To enable selected medical students in the United States with an interest in fundamental research to spend a year of intensive work in a research laboratory at their medical school or another academic or not-for-profit research institution.

Criteria: No citizenship requirements. Medical students currently enrolled M.D. or D.O. degree programs in medical schools in the United States. Applicants in the fourth year of medical school must defer graduation until completion of the fellowship year. Prior research experience is permitted, but not required.

Financial Award: Annual stipend of $15,000 plus $5,500 research allowance and $5,500 institutional allowance

Deadline: Early December

Hudson River Foundation for Science and Environmental Research—Hudson River Research Grants

Hudson River Foundation
40 West 20th Street, 9th Floor
New York, NY 10011
Phone: (212) 924-8290
Fax: (212) 924-8325
E-mail: info@hudsonriver.org

Field of Study: Sciences, environmental studies

Purpose of Fellowship: To support scientific and public policy research, education, and projects to enhance public access to the Hudson River.

Criteria: See information file at your campus fellowship office for details.

Financial Award: Unspecified

Deadline: Mid-September

International Lead Zinc Research Organization, Inc. (ILZRO) Fellowship Opportunities

2525 Meridian Parkway
P.O. Box 12036
Research Triangle Park,
NC 27709-2036

Field of Study: Sciences

Purpose of Fellowship: To support research on subjects relating to the metallurgical, electrochemical, environmental, and chemical aspects of lead and zinc.

Criteria: Graduate researchers, preferably those at the Ph.D. level, are eligible, as are faculty members. Before preparing an unsolicited research proposal, the faculty member or student should first submit a brief outline of the proposed area of investigation to the president of ILZRO.

Financial Award: May cover all project expenses

Deadline: Late May

Kieckhefer Adirondack Fellowships

Office for Research
245 Roberts Hall
Cornell University
Ithaca, NY 14853

Field of Study: Life sciences and biology

Purpose of Fellowship: To stimulate original research specifically focused on the Adirondack region.

Criteria: Graduate students from the College of Agriculture and Life Sciences and the Division of Biological Sciences at Cornell University.

Financial Award: Up to $5,000 for as many as two consecutive years

Deadline: Mid-March

Laboratory-Graduate Research

Argonne Division of Educational Programs
9700 S. Cass Avenue
Argonne, IL 60439-4845
Phone: (708) 252-3371

Field of Study: Physical, life, and computer sciences; mathematics

Purpose of Fellowship: To provide the opportunity for graduate students to carry out their master's or doctoral thesis research at Argonne under the cosponsorship of an Argonne staff member and a university faculty member.

Criteria: Full-time graduate students at U.S. universities are eligible.

Financial Award: Up to $4,000 tuition per year, stipend, and some travel expenses

Deadline: Rolling

Los Alamos National Laboratory—Graduate Research Assistant Program

Los Alamos National Laboratory
Mail Stop P282
Los Alamos, NM 87545
Phone: (505) 667-8622

Field of Study: Sciences and engineering

Purpose of Fellowship: To allow students to gain paid relevant work experience while pursuing a graduate degree.

Criteria: Applicants with a cumulative GPA of at least 2.5 who have completed a bachelor's degree by date-of-hire and who intend to continue with graduate studies.

Financial Award: Salaries awarded based on experience and education

Deadline: Not specified

Miccioli Scholars Program

Manager, Technical Training
Raytheon Company
141 Spring Street
Lexington, MA 02173

Field of Study: Physical sciences and engineering

Purpose of Fellowship: To support and assist full-time graduate studies in science and engineering leading to the master's or doctoral degrees.

Criteria: Recent college graduates in engineering or the physical sciences who are applying for full-time positions with Raytheon Corporation, and Raytheon engineers and scientists. Candidates must meet all admissions requirements of the institutions they wish to attend.

Financial Award: Stipend, tuition, and most fees for one academic year plus work at Raytheon Corporation

Deadline: December

Myasthenia Gravis Foundation Research Fellowship—Viets Fellowship

222 S. Riverside Plaza
Suite 1540
Chicago, IL 60606
Phone: (800) 541-5454
Fax: (312) 258-0461

Field of Study: Neurobiology and behavior

Purpose of Fellowship: To support research related to Myasthenia Gravis (MG).

Criteria: Graduate, premed, or medical students involved in basic or clinical research related to Myasthenia Gravis.

Financial Award: $3,000

Deadline: Mid-March

National Aeronautics and Space Administration (NASA)—Graduate Student Researchers Program (GSRP)

Office of Human Resources and Education, Code FE
NASA Headquarters
Washington, DC 20546
Phone: (202) 358-1517
Fax: (202) 358-3048
E-mail: anurridd@hq.nasa.gov

Field of Study: Astrophysics, solar systems exploration

Purpose of Fellowship: To reach a culturally diverse group of promising U.S. graduate students whose research interests are compatible with NASA's programs in space science and aerospace technology.

Criteria: Students may apply at any time during their graduate career or prior to receiving their baccalaureate degree. Applicants must be sponsored by their graduate department chair or faculty advisor. Other requirements listed in application materials.

Financial Award: Up to $22,000 per year for three years

Deadline: Early February

National Aeronautics and Space Administration (NASA)—Space Grant Fellowships

Sue Chamberlain
NASA New York Space Grant Office
517 Space Sciences Building
Cornell University
Ithaca, NY 14853
Phone: (607) 255-2710

Field of Study: Astronomy and space sciences, electrical engineering

Purpose of Fellowship: To attract highly qualified students in space-related fields.

Criteria: Applicants must be U.S. citizens.

Financial Award: Tuition and stipend for one academic year

Deadline: Call committee

National Air and Space Museum—Guggenheim Fellowships

National Air and Space Museum
MRC 312
Washington, DC 20560

Field of Study: Aviation and space sciences

Purpose of Fellowship: To support research related to technology transfer, planetary exploration, or the history of aviation at the National Air and Space Museum.

Criteria: Predoctoral applicants should be engaged in dissertation research. Postdoctoral applicants should have received Ph.D. within the past 7 years.

Financial Award: $14,000 before fellowship; $25,000 after fellowship

Deadline: Mid-January

National Institutes of Mental Health—Behavioral Sciences Track Award for Rapid Transition

Division of Research Grants
National Institute of Health
Rockledge Two, Suite 1040
670 Rockledge Dr., MSC 7710
Bethesda, MD 20892-7710

Field of Study: Psychology

Purpose of Fellowship: To facilitate the entry of new investigators into the field of behavioral science research. NIMH supports research to develop new knowledge on the basic biological, neuroscience, behavioral, social, and environmental diagnosis, treatment, and prevention of mental illness.

Criteria: Quality of the proposed project as determined by peer review. Awards subject to availability of funds and program balance.

Financial Award: Not to exceed $25,000/year

Deadline: Feburary 1, June 1, October 1

National Pork Producers Council—National Pork Fellowship

Rodney Goodwin, Director
National Pork Producers Council
P.O. Box 10383
Des Moines, IA 50306
Phone: (515) 223-2600
Fax: (515) 223-2646

Field of Study: Animal science, meat science, food science, human nutrition

Purpose of Fellowship: To support research on pork as a food.

Criteria: Master's and Ph.D. candidates who are using pork in research for their theses.

Financial Award: $2,000

Deadline: Late December

National Pork Producers Council—Research Solicitation

Eric Hentges
Director of Research
P.O. Box 10383
Des Moines, IA 50306
Phone: (515) 223-2600
Fax: (515) 223-2646

Field of Study: Animal science, food science, human nutrition

Purpose of Fellowship: To encourage research proposals concerning environment/odor research, swine health, animal welfare, pork safety (preharvest and postharvest), pork quality, human nutrition, and discovery concepts.

Criteria: Candidates must be research personnel.

Financial Award: Varies according to topic

Deadline: Early December

National Pork Producers Council—Targeted Research Solicitation

Rodney Goodwin
Director of Research
P.O. Box 10383
Des Moines, IA 50306
Phone: (515) 223-2600
Fax: (515) 223-2646

Field of Study: Animal science, food science, human nutrition

Purpose of Fellowship: To encourage research proposals for pathogenesis, immunology, diagnostics, transmission, and epidemiology.

Criteria: Candidates must be research personnel.

Financial Award: Up to $25,000 per project

Deadline: Mid-May

National Research Council Twinning Program with Belarus, Kazakstan, Moldova, and Romania

2101 Constitution Avenue, N.W.
Washington, DC 20418
Phone: (202) 334-2644
Fax: (202) 334-2614

Field of Study: Biological sciences, physical sciences

Purpose of Fellowship: To link individual U.S. scientists with their counterparts from the states listed above in fields normally supported by the NSF. Proposals should have the strong support of the scientists' home institution.

Criteria: U.S. citizen; national of a possession of the United States; permanent resident of United States; must be engaged in a research career, affiliated with an educational or research institution in the United States, and have existing contacts with researchers and/or institutions in the countries above.

Financial Award: $12,000–$15,000

Deadline: September

National Research Council Twinning Program with Estonia, Latvia, and Lithuania

2101 Constitution Avenue, N.W.
Washington, DC 20418
Phone: (202) 334-2644
Fax: (202) 334-2614

Field of Study: Biological sciences, physical sciences

Purpose of Fellowship: To link individual U.S. sciences with their counterparts from the states listed above in fields normally supported by the NSF. Proposals should have the strong support of the scientists' home institution.

Criteria: U.S. citizen; national of a possession of the United States; permanent resident of United States; must be engaged in research career, affiliated with an educational or research institution in the United States, and have existing contacts with researchers and/or institutions in the countries above.

Financial Award: $12,000–$15,000

Deadline: Mid-May

National Research Service Awards (NSRA)

6701 Rockledge Drive
Room 1040
National Institutes of Health
Bethesda, MD 20892
Phone: (301) 435-0714

Field of Study: Sciences and engineering

Purpose of Fellowship: To increase the capability of the institutes of the National Institutes of Health (NIH) and the Alcohol, Drug Abuse, and Mental Health Administration (ADAMHA) to carry out their responsibility of maintaining a superior national program of research into physical and mental diseases.

Criteria: Demonstrated interest and relevant background in health services research.

Financial Award: Stipends vary with level of experience

Deadline: Call committee

National Scholarship Trust Fund of the Graphic Arts

4615 Forbes Avenue
Pittsburgh, PA 15213-3796
Phone: (412) 621-6941

Field of Study: Mathematics, chemistry, physics, industrial education

Purpose of Fellowship: To promote the progress of science through awards made by the printing, publishing, and packaging industries.

Criteria: Graduate students who plan to seek employment at the managerial or educational level in the graphic communications industry and who have either been admitted or will have been admitted to their selected institutions by the beginning of their fellowship tenure.

Financial Award: $1,500–$4,000

Deadline: January 10

National Science Foundation Graduate Fellowships

ORAU
P.O. Box 3010
Oak Ridge, TN 37831-3010
Phone: (423) 241-4300
Fax: (423) 241-4513
E-mail: nsfgrfp@orau.gov

Field of Study: Science, mathematics, engineering, history, and philosophy

Purpose of Fellowship: To improve the human resource base of science, mathematics, and engineering in the United States and to reinforce its diversity.

Criteria: U.S. citizens, nationals, or permanent resident aliens who are near the beginning of graduate study.

Financial Award: $14,000 stipend for one year, plus tuition

Deadline: Early November

National Science Foundation Grants for Improving Doctoral Dissertation Research

Data Support Services Section
National Science Foundation
Washington, DC 20550

Field of Study: Biological, physical, and social sciences; engineering

Purpose of Fellowship: To provide funds not normally available from the student's university or other sources for items required by a student who is at the point of initiating dissertation research.

Criteria: Candidates must be graduate students.

Financial Award: Varies

Deadline: Rolling

Natural Sciences and Engineering Research Council of Canada Visiting Fellowships in Canadian Government Laboratories

Natural Sciences and
Engineering Research Council
of Canada
350 Albert St.
Ottawa, Ontario
Canada
Phone: (613) 996-4363
Fax: (613) 992-5337

Field of Study: Biological and physical sciences, engineering, computer science

Purpose of Fellowship: To provide promising young scientists and engineers with the opportunity to work with research groups or leaders in Canadian government laboratories and research institutions.

Criteria: Candidates must have received a doctoral degree in the natural sciences or engineering from a recognized university within the past five years.

Financial Award: $35,184 stipend for one year plus travel expenses for fellow, spouse, and children

Deadline: Call committee

New Focus Research Award

2010 Massachussetts Avenue, N.W.
Washington, DC 20036-1023
Fax: (202) 416-6130
E-mail: kdavis@osa.org

Field of Study: Any field using laser and/or electro-optic applications

Purpose of Fellowship: To support research in lasers and electro-optics or technological advancements in other fields through the applications of lasers and electro-optics.

Criteria: Doctoral candidates who are pursuing thesis research in accordance with the fellowship's purpose and who are enrolled at a university in the United States.

Financial Award: $14,400 stipend to the student and $8,600 for departmental expenses that directly support the student's research

Deadline: Mid-April

New Jersey School of Conservation, Montclair State University—Graduate Fellowships in Environmental Studies

Dr. John Kirk
New Jersey School of Conservation
1 Wapalanne Road
Branchville, NJ 07826
Phone: (201) 948-4646
Fax: (201) 948-5131

Field of Study: Natural sciences, social sciences, humanities

Purpose of Fellowship: To provide field teaching opportunities and course work leading to an M.A. degree in environmental studies with a concentration in environmental education.

Criteria: Applicants should hold a bachelor's degree from an accredited institution with a concentration in elementary or secondary education or any of the disciplines listed above. All applicants must have a GPA of 3.0 or better.

Financial Award: Room and board at New Jersey School of Conservation, $1,500 stipend, and tuition

Deadline: Early January

New York Sea Grant—Coastal Management Fellowship

121 Discovery Hall
State University of New York/
Stony Brook
Stony Brook, NY 11794-5001
Phone: (516) 632-6905
Fax: (516) 632-6917
E-mail:
nyseagrant@ccmail.sunysb.edu

Field of Study: Marine-related fields

Purpose of Fellowship: To provide professional on-the-job education and training opportunities for postgraduate students in coastal resource management and policy and to provide specific project assistance for state coastal resource management programs.

Criteria: Any student who has completed a master's, doctoral, or professional degree program in coastal, marine, or Great Lakes-related studies at any accredited U.S. institution of higher education.

Financial Award: $64,00 over two years

Deadline: Late March

New York Sea Grant—Dean John A. Knauss Marine Policy Fellowship

121 Discovery Hall
State University of New York/
Stony Brook
Stony Brook, NY 11794-5001
Phone: (516) 632-6906
Fax: (516) 632-6917
E-mail:
nyseagran@ccmail.sunysb.edu

Field of Study: Graduate and professional degree programs in marine policy

Purpose of Fellowship: To match highly qualified graduate students with hosts in the legislative or executive branch or appropriate associations/institutions in the Washington, DC area for a one-year paid fellowship.

Criteria: Must be enrolled in a graduate or professional degree program in a marine-related field at an accredited institution; must have an academic interest in marine/ocean/Great Lakes resources and in the national policy decisions affecting those resources.

Financial Award: $30,000 per year, plus travel funds, moving costs, and health insurance

Deadline: Mid-August

New York State Department of Health Primary Care Service Corps Scholarship Program

Empire State Plaza
Corning Tower
Room 1602
Albany, NY 12237-0053
Phone: (518) 473-7019

Field of Study: Physician's assistant, nurse practitioner, midwife

Purpose of Fellowship: Scholarships for individuals studying to become physician's assistants, nurse practitioners, or midwives.

Criteria: Must be New York state resident, enrolled, accepted, or applied for study in approved graduate course of study and be within 24 months of completion of professional full-time training or within 48 months of completing on part-time basis. Upon completion of professional training, must be eligible to practice in New York State.

Financial Award: Up to $15,000 per academic year

Deadline: Early April

Oak Ridge Institute for Science and Education—Applied Health Physics Fellowship

Oak Ridge Institute for Science and Education
P.O. Box 117
Oak Ridge, TN 37831-0117
Phone: (423) 576-2600

Field of Study: Sciences and engineering

Purpose of Fellowship: To support highly capable students interested in pursuing an M.S. in applied health physics and a Ph.D. in health physics at participating universities.

Criteria: U.S. citizens and permanent resident aliens who hold a B.S. degree in physical sciences, engineering, or mathematics and have not completed more than one academic term of graduate studies.

Financial Award: $1,200–$1,400 monthly stipend, tuition and fees, dislocation allowance, and travel allowance

Deadline: Call committee

Oak Ridge Institute for Science and Education—Environmental Management Participation Program

Oak Ridge Institute for Science
and Education
P.O. Box 117
Oak Ridge, TN 37831-0117
Phone: (423) 576-8503

Field of Study: Natural and social sciences

Purpose of Fellowship: To provide paid internship positions in environmentally related research and development.

Criteria: Depends upon positions sought; some require doctoral degrees, others not. Most positions are open to U.S. citizens and permanent residents; a few are limited to U.S. citizens only. Some are open to international students also.

Financial Award: Up to $41,000

Deadline: Rolling

Oak Ridge Institute for Science and Education—Industrial Hygiene Graduate Fellowship

Oak Ridge Institute for Science
and Education
P.O. Box 117
Oak Ridge, TN 37831-0117
Phone: (423) 576-7009

Field of Study: Sciences and engineering

Purpose of Fellowship: To support graduate education and research in industrial hygiene and to strengthen the profession and ties between the academic and nonacademic communities.

Criteria: U.S. citizens who hold a B.S. degree in physical sciences, life or health sciences, environmental sciences, or engineering. Applicants who are entering or are first-year graduate students are preferred.

Financial Award: $1,200–$1,400 monthly stipend, tuition and fees, dislocation allowance, travel allowance

Deadline: Call committee

Oak Ridge Institute for Science and Education—Magnetic Fusion Science and Magnetic Fusion Energy Technology Fellowships

Oak Ridge Institute for Science and Education
P.O. Box 117
Oak Ridge, TN 37831-0117
Phone: (423) 576-2600

Field of Study: Sciences and engineering

Purpose of Fellowship: To support highly capable students interested in pursuing doctoral study in fusion sciences or engineering at participating universities.

Criteria: U.S. citizens and permanent resident aliens who hold a B.S. degree in physical sciences, engineering, or mathematics and are entering or first-year graduate students.

Financial Award: $1,200–$1,400 monthly stipend, tuition and fees, dislocation allowance, travel allowance

Deadline: Call committee

Oak Ridge Institute for Science and Education—Nuclear Engineering Graduate Fellowship

Oak Ridge Institute for Science and Education
P.O. Box 117
Oak Ridge, TN 37831-0117
Phone: (423) 576-2600

Field of Study: Sciences and engineering

Purpose of Fellowship: To support nuclear engineering education.

Criteria: U.S. citizens and permanent resident aliens who hold a B.S. degree in physical sciences, engineering, or mathematics, and have not completed more than one academic term of graduate studies.

Financial Award: $1,200–$1,400 monthly stipend, tuition and fees, dislocation allowance, travel allowance

Deadline: Call committee

Oak Ridge Institute for Science and Education—U.S. Nuclear Regulatory Commission Graduate Fellowship

Oak Ridge Institute for Science and Education
P.O. Box 117
Oak Ridge, TN 37831-0117
Phone: (423) 576-9279
E-mail: coxre@orau.gov

Field of Study: Sciences and engineering

Purpose of Fellowship: To support highly capable students interested in pursuing a career in nuclear power regulation, or master's study in health physics, nuclear engineering, criticality engineering, electrical engineering, or probabilistic risk assessment.

Criteria: U.S. citizens who hold a B.S. degree in life or physical sciences, engineering or mathematics, and are entering or have up to one year of graduate study. A minimum nine-month, paid prefellowship orientation period is required prior to beginning graduate studies.

Financial Award: $1,800 monthly stipend plus full payment of tuition and fees; following completion of master's degree, fellows must return to NRC employment to complete four years of obligatory service

Deadline: Late January

Pharmaceutical Research and Manufacturers of America Foundation Fellowships for Advanced Predoctoral Training in Pharmaceutics and Clinical Pharmacology

1100 15th Street, N.W.
Washington, DC 20005
Phone: (202) 835-3470

Field of Study: Pharmacology or pharmaceutics

Purpose of Fellowship: To support promising students during their thesis research.

Criteria: Full-time, in-residence Ph.D. candidates enrolled in United States schools of medicine, pharmacy, dentistry, or veterinary medicine. Candidates must be U.S. citizens.

Financial Award: $12,500 per year plus $500 for expenses associated with thesis research

Deadline: Call committee

Purina Mills Research Fellowship Awards Program

Purina Mills, Inc.
P.O. Box 66812
St. Louis, MO 63166-6812

Field of Study: Animal, dairy, and poultry sciences

Purpose of Fellowship: To assist in the training of personnel for leadership in the nutritional sciences of food and companion animals.

Criteria: Any individual enrolled for graduate study in an accredited graduate program at a U.S. university or institution who possesses desirable personal qualifications and submits a completed application may be eligible.

Financial Award: $12,500

Deadline: Early February

Semiconductor Research Corporation Education Alliance Graduate Fellowships Program

SRC Education Alliance
P.O. Box 12053
Research Triangle Park, NC 22709

Field of Study: Sciences

Purpose of Fellowship: To improve educational opportunities at the doctoral level and supply a relevantly trained work force for the semiconductor industry.

Criteria: U.S. or Canadian citizens who are pursuing or plan to pursue a Ph.D. degree under the guidance of an SRC-designated faculty member. Students must be willing to provide a copy of Ph.D. thesis to the SRC and are expected to pursue careers at accredited colleges or SRC member institutions.

Financial Award: $1,400 stipend per month

Deadline: Early February

Smithsonian Astrophysical Observatory Predoctoral Fellowships

60 Garden Street
Mail Stop 47
Cambridge, MA 02138

Field of Study: All branches of astronomical and astrophysical research

Purpose of Fellowship: To allow students from other institutions throughout the world to do their thesis research at the Observatory.

Criteria: Unspecified

Financial Award: Unspecified

Deadline: Mid-April

Smithsonian Institution—Paul E. Garber Fellowship

National Air and Space Museum
3341, MRC 313
Washington, DC 20560

Field of Study: Physical sciences, atmospheric/space studies

Purpose of Fellowship: To support scientific pre- and postdoctoral research at the Center for Earth and Planetary Studies and Laboratory for Astrophysics.

Criteria: Predoctoral applicants should have completed preliminary coursework and examinations and be engaged in dissertation research. Postdoctoral requirements are unspecified.

Financial Award: Unspecified

Deadline: Mid-January

Smithsonian Institution—Predoctoral Fellowships

955 L'Enfant Plaza, Suite 7000
MRC 902, Desk P
Washington, DC 20560
Phone: (202) 287-3691
E-mail: siofg@ofg.si.edu

Field of Study: Sciences

Purpose of Fellowship: To provide doctoral candidates an opportunity to conduct dissertation research at the Smithsonian Institution for a period of 3 to 12 months.

Criteria: Open to Ph.D. students. Candidates must have completed predissertation requirements at the time of appointment.

Financial Award: $15,000 per year plus allowances

Deadline: Mid-January

Smithsonian Institution—Summer and Fall Internship Positions

Beth Nalker
2123 Ripley Center
Washington, DC 20560

Field of Study: Environmental studies or environmental education

Purpose of Fellowship: To assist with the development of Ocean Planet, a traveling museum exhibition on ocean conservation, and to provide administrative support for the program.

Criteria: Applicants must be full-time students or recent college graduates. Undergraduate and graduate students are invited to apply.

Financial Award: Stipend of $1,000–$1,250 per month

Deadline: Call committee

Smithsonian Marine Station at Link Port Fellowships

5612 Old Dixie Highway
Fort Pierce, FL 34946
Phone: (407) 465-6630
E-mail: mnhfp003@simnh.si.edu

Field of Study: Marine sciences

Purpose of Fellowship: To support graduate and postdoctoral level research in marine sciences.

Criteria: Unspecified

Financial Award: Unspecified

Deadline: Mid-February

Society for the Psychological Study of Social Issues

SPSSI Central Office
P.O. Box 1248
Ann Arbor, MI 48106-1248

Field of Study: Psychology, social sciences, or related discipline

Purpose of Fellowship: To recognize social issues researchers who have made substantial contributions to the field.

Criteria: Senior researchers over the age of 60 who have retired from a previous research or teaching position in psychology, social sciences, or related disciplne; investigators who have made substantial contributions to social issues research within five years of receiving graduate degrees and who have demonstrated the potential to continue such contributions.

Financial Award: Up to $2,000 to pay for project costs

Deadline: Call committee

Society of Exploration Geophysicists (SEG)—Foundation Scholarship Program

P.O. Box 702740
Tulsa, OK 74170-2740
Phone: (918) 497-5530
Fax: (918) 497-5558

Field of Study: Geophysics or a closely related field

Purpose of Fellowship: To encourage students pursuing studies in geophysics.

Criteria: Graduate students in geophysics or a closely related field, whose studies are directed toward a career in exploration geophysics in operations, teaching, or research.

Financial Award: $500–$3,000 per year

Deadline: Early March

Sudden Infant Death Syndrome Reseach—Student Training Fellowships

10500 Little Patuxent Parkway, Suite 420
Columbia, MD 21044
Phone: (800) 221-SIDS

Field of Study: Medicine, health sciences, and related professions

Purpose of Fellowship: To give competent research-oriented students exposure to SIDS research for an 8–12 week period supervised by a specialist knowledgeable about the disease. The ultimate goal is to encourage students to pursue SIDS research as part of their professional careers.

Criteria: Graduate students who have completed at least two years of graduate study and wish to conduct a specific research study on SIDS.

Financial Award: $2,000

Deadline: March 15

Thesis Parts Program

Argonne National Laboratory
9700 South Cass Avenue
Argonne, IL 60439-4845
Phone: (708) 252-4579

Field of Study: Sciences

Purpose of Fellowship: To provide students with an opportunity to utilize Argonne National Laboratory facilities or capabilities during the course of their thesis research.

Criteria: Full-time graduate students at U.S. universities.

Financial Award: Living expenses and transportation

Deadline: Rolling

Welder Wildlife Foundation Scholarships

Director
Rob & Bessie Welder Wildlife Foundation
P.O. Drawer 1400
Sinton, TX 78387
Phone: (512) 364-2643
Fax: (512) 364-2650

Field of Study: Biological and environmental sciences

Purpose of Fellowship: To support field research in wildlife and wildlife-related problems.

Criteria: M.S. or Ph.D. candidates conducting research in wildlife. Priority given to studies already in progress or studies to be initiated at the Welder Wildlife Foundation.

Financial Award: $850–$900 per month for up to one year, plue $1,200 per year for travel

Deadline: Rolling

Woodrow Wilson National Fellowship Foundation—Dissertation Grants in Women's Health

Department WS
Woodrow Wilson National Fellowship Foundation
CN 5281
Princeton, NJ 08543-5281
Fax: (609) 452-0066
E-mail: charlotte@woodrow.org

Field of Study: Fields related to women's health

Purpose of Fellowship: To encourage original and significant research on issues related to women's health.

Criteria: Students in doctoral programs who have completed all predissertation requirements in any field of study at graduate schools in the United States.

Financial Award: $2,000 for expenses

Deadline: Mid-October

10 Engineering

If you've browsed through the past few chapters, you've probably noticed that in the "Field of Study" section, engineering pops up all over the place. Indeed, the engineering profession allows its members an incredible amount of leeway in terms of their specializations and courses of study. For this reason, it's not so surprising that you'll find engineering fellowships that focus on everything from the sciences to the media and public policy.

So what makes a successful candidate in the field of engineering? Probably a combination of a number of factors, which include grades, extracurricular activities, and work experiences. But what truly distinguishes those who win fellowships from those who fail is the way successful candidates package themselves during their college years. The key to earning an award in engineering is to demonstrate that you have gained specialized skills that will impress fellowship committees.

What's Out There for Engineers?

Engineers who are interested in fellowships and grants will find a wide range of fields from which they can choose. These include:

- Aerospace engineering
- Agricultural engineering
- Biological/biomedical engineering
- Chemical engineering

- Electrical engineering
- Industrial engineering
- Mechanical engineering
- Applied science

Most opportunities, however, are not specific to a particular field of engineering. What this means, then, is that candidates must provide a compelling case for their particular area of interest in both their application form and written proposal.

One area in which engineering students have a distinct advantage over others in their search for fellowships and grants is in their ability to secure jobs outside of the classroom. In particular, there is an abundance of paid summer internships in the fields of engineering and technology. Hence earning an internship is much easier for engineers than it is for those in most other fields.

So one important step you can take toward strengthening your fellowship application is to take advantage of the internship opportunities available. Many government research labs have summer programs, giving you access to some of the latest and greatest technology in science and engineering. Take some time at your institution's career services office to look over the various internships available—many schools have ties to major high-technology firms and have developed a feeder system for their students to pick up summer jobs and internships. Remember, think specialization. The more you can show fellowship committees that you've gained a wealth of experience in a particular field, the more impressed they will be with your application.

Abel Wolman Graduate Fellowship Program

3400 North Charles Street
Baltimore, MD 21218

Field of Study: Sciences and engineering

Purpose of Fellowship: To encourage doctoral candidates to pursue advanced study in an engineering field, especially training and research in water supply and treatment.

Criteria: All Ph.D. applicants to Johns Hopkins Whiting School of Engineering are eligible for consideration. Applicants submit no special forms; the graduate application is all that is required.

Financial Award: Stipends exceed standard graduate support, plus full tuition payment.

Deadline: Varies

Associated Western Universities, Inc.—Graduate Fellowships at National Laboratories and Cooperating Facilities

4190 S. Highland Drive
Suite 211
Salt Lake City, UT 84124-2600
Phone: (801) 277-5632
E-mail: info@sl.awu.org
Web site:
http://online.awu.org/

Field of Study: Engineering

Purpose of Fellowship: To provide qualified master's and doctoral degree candidates in engineering the opportunity to conduct research toward their theses or dissertations, in whole or in part, at one of over 50 cooperating facilities.

Criteria: This program is open to master's and doctoral degree candidates who have an established thesis research program. Institutional affiliation and citizenship restrictions may apply for some awards or facilities.

Financial Award: Stipends of at least $1,300 per month, tuition assistance, and travel allowance

Deadline: Mid-February

Environmental Fellows Program

American Association for Advancement of Science
1333 H Street NW
Washington, DC 20005
Phone: (202) 326-6600
Fax: (202) 289-4950
Web site:
science_policy@aaas.org

Field of Study: Engineering

Purpose of Fellowship: To provide fellows with the opportunity to spend ten weeks during the summer working at special research consultants with the Office of Research and Development of the U.S. Environmental Protection Agency (EPA) in Washington, DC.

Criteria: Candidates must be U.S. residents. Prospective fellows must demonstrate exceptional competence and have a strong interest and/or some experience in applying knowledge toward the solution of societal problems.

Financial Award: $950 per week

Deadline: Early November

Environmental Protection Agency Fellowships

U.S. Environmental Protection Agency, Region II
290 Broadway
New York, NY 10007
Fax: (212) 637-3591
E-mail: hoang.kim-chi@epamail.epa.gov
Web site:
http://www.epa.gov/docs/oer/rfa

Field of Study: Engineering, social sciences

Purpose of Fellowship: To support graduate students in environmentally related fields of study.

Criteria: Masters or Ph.D. candidates in environmental sciences and technology.

Financial Award: Up to $34,000 per year for a maximum of three years

Deadline: February

Graduate Research Award Program—Public Sector Aviation Issues

2101 Constitution Avenue, N.W.
Room GR-326E
Washington, DC 20418
Phone: (800) 424-9818,
ext. 3206

Field of Study: Mathematics, political science, economics, engineering

Purpose of Fellowship: To stimulate thought, discussion, and research on public-sector aviation issues by those who may become the future managers and policy makers in aviation.

Criteria: U.S. citizens or permanent residents currently enrolled in a graduate program in an accredited institution of higher learning in a graduate course leading to a master's or doctoral degree.

Financial Award: $6,000 stipend

Deadline: Late October

Los Alamos National Laboratory—Graduate Research Assistant Program

Los Alamos National Laboratory
Mail Stop P282
Los Alamos, NM 87545
Phone: (505) 667-8622

Field of Study: Engineering

Purpose of Fellowship: To allow students to gain paid relevant work experience while pursuing a graduate degree.

Criteria: Applicants with a cumulative GPA of at least 2.5 who have completed a bachelor's degree by date-of-hire and who intend to continue with graduate studies.

Financial Award: Salaries awarded based on experience and education

Deadline: Not specified

Mass Media Fellows Program

American Association for Advancement of Science
1333 H Street, N.W.
Washington, DC 20005
Phone: (202) 326-6600
Fax: (202) 289-4950
E-mail: science_policy@aaas.org

Field of Study: Natural and social sciences, engineering, media

Purpose of Fellowship: To strengthen the relationship between science and technology and the media, and to enhance coverage of science-related issues in the media in order to improve public understanding and appreciation of science and technology.

Criteria: Priority will be given to graduate students in the natural and social sciences and engineering.

Financial Award: Weekly stipend plus travel expenses for a 10-week summer appointment

Deadline: Mid-January

Miccioli Scholars Program

Manager, Technical Training,
Raytheon Company
141 Spring Street
Lexington, MA 02173

Field of Study: Physical sciences and engineering

Purpose of Fellowship: To support and assist full-time graduate studies in science and engineering leading to the masters or doctoral degrees.

Criteria: Recent college graduates in engineering or the physical sciences who are applying for a full-time position with Raytheon Corporation and Raytheon engineers and scientists. Candidates must meet all admissions requirements of the institutions they wish to attend.

Financial Award: Stipend, tuition, and most fees for one academic year plus work at Raytheon Corporation

Deadline: December

National Aeronautics and Space Administration (NASA)—Space Grant Fellowships

Sue Chamberlain
NASA New York Space Grant Office
517 Space Sciences Building
Cornell University
Ithaca, NY 14853
Phone: (607) 255-2710

Field of Study: Electrical engineering

Purpose of Fellowship: To attract highly qualified students in space-related fields.

Criteria: Candidates must be U.S. citizens.

Financial Award: Tuition and stipend for one academic year

Deadline: Call committee

National Research Council Young Investigator Programs on Russia

2101 Constitution Avenue, N.W.
FO 2014
Washington, DC 20418
Phone: (202) 334-2658
E-mail: sdeets@nas.edu

Field of Study: Agricultural economics and engineering, environmental studies

Purpose of Fellowship: To assist scholars in making professional contributions during the early stages of their careers.

Criteria: Must be a U.S. citizen, green card holder, or permanent resident. Must be engaged in teaching and/or research careers or planning such a career. Must have earned the Ph.D. degree or achieved equivalent accomplishments.

Financial Award: All travel expenses including airfare, food, and lodging, and transportation within Russia

Deadline: Late February

National Research Service Awards (NSRA)

6701 Rockledge Drive
Room 1040
National Institutes of Health
Bethesda, MD 20892
Phone: (301) 435-0714

Field of Study: Engineering

Purpose of Fellowship: To increase the capability of the institutes of the National Institutes of Health (NIH) and the Alcohol, Drug Abuse, and Mental Health Administration (ADAMHA) to carry out their responsibility of maintaining a superior national program of research into physical and mental diseases.

Criteria: Demonstrated interest and relevant background in health services research.

Financial Award: Stipends vary with level of experience

Deadline: Call committee

National Science Foundation Graduate Fellowships

ORAU
P.O. Box 3010
Oak Ridge, TN 37831-3010
Phone: (423) 241-4300
Fax: (423) 241-4513
E-mail: nsfgrfp@orau.gov

Field of Study: Science, mathematics, engineering, history, and philosophy

Purpose of Fellowship: To improve the human resource base of science, mathematics, and engineering in the United States and to reinforce its diversity.

Criteria: U.S. citizens, nationals, or permanent resident aliens who are near the beginning of graduate study.

Financial Award: $14,000 stipend for one year, plus tuition

Deadline: Early November

National Science Foundation Grants for Improving Doctoral Dissertation Research

Data Support Services Section
National Science Foundation
Washington, DC 20550

Field of Study: Biological, physical, and social sciences and engineering

Purpose of Fellowship: To provide funds not normally available from the student's university or other sources for items required by a student who is at the point of initiating dissertation research.

Criteria: Candidates must be graduate students.

Financial Award: Varies

Deadline: Rolling

National Science Foundation/National Institutes of Health—Summer Institute in Japan

Division of International Programs, NSF
4201 Wilson Blvd.
Arlington, VA 22230
Phone: (703) 306-1701
Fax: (703) 306-0474
E-mail: NSFJinfo@nsf.gov

Field of Study: Science and engineering

Purpose of Fellowship: To provide U.S. graduate students with first-hand experience in a Japanese research environment, intensive Japanese language training, and an introduction to the science and science-policy infrastructure of Japan.

Criteria: Applicants must be U.S. citizens or permanent residents, be enrolled at a U.S. institution in a relevant Ph.D., M.D., or M.S. program of which at least one year has been completed, and be pursuing studies in fields of science or engineering that are supported by the NSF or NIH.

Financial Award: Travel costs to and from Japan and an allowance of $2,000

Deadline: Early December

Natural Sciences and Engineering Research Council of Canada Visiting Fellowships in Canadian Government Laboratories

Natural Sciences and Engineering Research Council of Canada
350 Albert Street
Ottawa, Ontario
Canada
Phone: (613) 996-4363
Fax: (613) 992-5337

Field of Study: Biological and physical sciences, engineering, computer science

Purpose of Fellowship: To provide promising young scientists and engineers with the opportunity to work with research groups or leaders in Canadian government laboratories and research institutions.

Criteria: Candidates must have received a doctoral degree in the natural sciences or engineering from a recognized university within the past five years.

Financial Award: $35,184 stipend for one year plus travel expenses for fellow, spouse, and children

Deadline: Call committee

Nuclear Engineering Institute

Argonne National Laboratory
Argonne, IL 60439-4845
Phone: (708) 252-4759

Field of Study: Engineering and computer science

Purpose of Fellowship: To provide an opportunity to participate in a broad range of engineering activities directed toward the development of the liquid-metal reactor at Argonne's Idaho site.

Criteria: U.S. citizens or permanent resident aliens of junior, senior, or graduate standing who are full-time engineering or computer science students.

Financial Award: $225 per week, plus housing allowance and round-trip travel for distances greater than 100 miles

Deadline: Early February

Oak Ridge Institute for Science and Education—Applied Health Physics Fellowship

Oak Ridge Institute for Science and Education
P.O. Box 117
Oak Ridge, TN 37831-0117
Phone: (423) 576-2600

Field of Study: Sciences and engineering

Purpose of Fellowship: To support highly capable students interested in pursuing an M.S. in applied health physics and a Ph.D. in health physics at Department of Energy-designated participating universities.

Criteria: U.S. citizens and permanent resident aliens who hold a B.S. degree in physical sciences, engineering, or mathematics and have not completed more than one academic term of graduate studies.

Financial Award: $1,200–$1,400 monthly stipend, tuition and fees, relocation allowance, travel allowance

Deadline: Call committee

Oak Ridge Institute for Science and Education—Industrial Hygiene Graduate Fellowship

Oak Ridge Institute for Science and Education
P.O. Box 117
Oak Ridge, TN 37831-0117
Phone: (423) 576-7009

Field of Study: Sciences and engineering

Purpose of Fellowship: To support graduate education and research in industrial hygiene and to strengthen professional ties between the academic community and Department of Energy facilities.

Criteria: U.S. citizens who hold a B.S. degree in physical sciences, life or health sciences, environmental sciences, or engineering. Applicants who are entering or first-year graduate students are preferred.

Financial Award: $1,200–$1,400 monthly stipend, tuition and fees, dislocation allowance, travel allowance

Deadline: Call committee

Oak Ridge Institute for Science and Education—Magnetic Fusion Science and Magnetic Fusion Energy Technology Fellowships

Oak Ridge Institute for Science and Education
P.O. Box 117
Oak Ridge, TN 37831-0117
Phone: (423) 576-2600

Field of Study: Sciences and engineering

Purpose of Fellowship: To support highly capable students interested in pursuing doctoral study in fusion sciences or engineering at participating universities.

Criteria: U.S. citizens and permanent resident aliens who hold a B.S. degree in physical sciences, engineering, or mathematics and are entering or first-year graduate students.

Financial Award:
$1,200–$1,400 monthly stipend, tuition and fees, relocation allowance, travel allowance

Deadline: Call committee

Oak Ridge Institute for Science and Education—Nuclear Engineering Graduate Fellowship

Oak Ridge Institute for Science and Education
P.O. Box 117
Oak Ridge, TN 37831-0117
Phone: (423) 576-2600

Field of Study: Sciences and engineering

Purpose of Fellowship: To support nuclear engineering education.

Criteria: U.S. citizens and permanent resident aliens who hold a B.S. degree in physical sciences, engineering, or mathematics, and have not completed more than one academic term of graduate studies.

Financial Award:
$1,200–$1,400 monthly stipend, tuition and fees, relocation allowance, travel allowance

Deadline: Call committee

Oak Ridge Institute for Science and Education—U.S. Nuclear Regulatory Commission Graduate Fellowship

Oak Ridge Institute for Science and Education
P.O. Box 117
Oak Ridge, TN 37831-0117
Phone: (423) 576-9279
E-mail: coxre@orau.gov

Field of Study: Sciences and engineering

Purpose of Fellowship: To support highly capable students interested in pursuing a career in nuclear power regulation, or master's study in health physics, nuclear engineering, criticality engineering, electrical engineering, or probabilistic risk assessment.

Criteria: U.S. citizens who hold a B.S. degree in life or physical sciences, engineering or mathematics, and are entering or have completed up to one year of graduate study. A minimum nine-month, paid prefellowship orientation period is required prior to beginning graduate studies.

Financial Award: $1,800 monthly stipend plus full payment of tuition and fees; following completion of master's degree, fellows must return to NRC employment to complete four years of obligatory service

Deadline: Late January

Technology Policy Fellows Program

American Association for the Advancement of Science
Fellowship Programs
1333 H St., N.W.
Washington, DC 20005
Phone: (202) 326-6600
Fax: (202) 289-4950
E-mail: science_policy@aaas.org

Field of Study: Physical, biological, or social sciences and engineering

Purpose of Fellowship: To offer fellows the opportunity to work in the White House Office of Science and Technology Policy and provide expertise in industrial research and development, technology transfer, international competitiveness, etcetera.

Criteria: Candidates must have a minimum of five years of experience. Prospective fellows must demonstrate exceptional competence and have a strong interest and/or some experience in applying knowledge toward the solution of societal problems.

Financial Award: Varies

Deadline: Mid-January

Fellowships and Grants for Minorities

11

Since the Civil Rights movement of the 1960s, fellowship organizations across the country have made concerted efforts to increase the opportunities available to minority students. At first, the grand majority of these prizes were reserved solely for African Americans. But today, there are fellowships and grants available to students from all walks of life.

If you are a member of at least one of the following ethnic groups, you are eligible for many of the 80-plus minority fellowships and grants listed in this chapter:

- African American
- Hispanic
- Asian
- Native American
- Native Alaskan
- Native Pacific Islander

Minority fellowships cover just about any field of study you could imagine. In addition, they are among the best-paying awards, with prizes of up to $55,000 per year. Of course, this means that the competition for most of these fellowships and grants is fierce. But if you look through the awards listed in the following pages, you'll probably agree that the prizes are well worth the effort.

Choosing Between Minority Awards and National Awards

If you are a minority candidate, one important question you must ask yourself before beginning the applications process is whether you want to apply to minority awards, national awards, or both. There is no correct response to this question, because the answer must ultimately be decided on an individual basis.

In general, minority fellowships and grants offer bigger prizes than national ones, and this may be the deciding factor for you. On the other hand, many minority awards place larger restrictions upon the candidate in terms of where he can study, what he can study, and for how long he can study. In addition, many minority fellowships are set up so that recipients end up working solely with members of their ethnic groups. This appeals to some and bothers others.

Ultimately, the fellowships or grants you choose will depend upon your priorities as an applicant. Write down all the factors that you will use to help make your final decision and list them in order of importance. Then see whether those factors are applicable to minority awards, national awards, or both. This should help you reach a final conclusion.

The following are some questions you might want to ask yourself if stuck between accepting a national award and a minority award:

- Which award best suits my skills?
- Does either award limit my abilities to successfully complete my project?
- Which award offers the type of money that will suit my project's needs?
- Which award's location appeals most to me?
- Does the work environment between the awards differ significantly, and if so, which appeals most?
- Which award will best help me get me to my ultimate goal?

If you find that either type of award would suit you, a suggested course of action is to look at awards from a color-blind point of view. Determine which opportunities appeal most to your career plans and long-term goals, and go from there. While minority awards have their advantages and disadvantages as compared with their national counterparts, there are certain to be opportunities on both sides of the fence that have a great deal to offer you. Choose the ones that will help you get to your ultimate destination, and apply to those, whether or not they are minority awards.

American Economic Association/Federal Reserve System Minority Graduate Fellowships in Economics

1090 Vermont Avenue, N.W.
Suite 1100
Washington, DC 20005-4961
Phone: (202) 789-3523

Field of Study: Economics and related fields

Purpose of Fellowship: To support minority students who are enrolled in an accredited graduate program in economics in the United States.

Criteria: U.S. citizens who are black, Hispanic, or Native American and are enrolled in an accredited graduate program in economics in the United States. Students must be nominated by the director of graduate studies or chairman of their economics department.

Financial Award: Monthly stipend of $900 during the academic year

Deadline: Early March

American Indian Graduate Center Fellowships

4520 Montgomery Boulevard, N.E.
Suite 1-B
Albuquerque, NM 87109-1291
Phone: (505) 881-4584
Fax: (505) 884-0427

Field of Study: Business, education, engineering, health, law

Purpose of Fellowship: To support Native American and Native Alaskan college graduates continuing graduate work.

Criteria: Candidate must be an enrolled member of a federally recognized Native American tribe or Native Alaskan group, or possess one-fourth degree Native American blood; must be pursuing master's or doctorate degree full time at accredited U.S. graduate school; must apply for campus-based aid through the general financial aid process.

Financial Award: Varies

Deadline: Call committee

American Institute of Certified Public Accountants Fellowships for Minority Doctoral Students

1211 Avenue of the Americas
New York, NY 10036-8775
Phone: (212) 596-6200
Fax: (800) 362-5066

Field of Study: Accounting

Purpose of Fellowship: To allow more minorities to enter or move ahead in the accounting profession.

Criteria: U.S. citizens from the following groups: African American, Native American, Pacific Islander, or Hispanic. Applicants must be pursuing a Ph.D. and must hold a master's degree or three years of full-time experience in accounting practice.

Financial Award: $12,000 per year

Deadline: Early April

American Planning Association Planning Fellowships/Transportation Planning Division Scholarship

1776 Massachussetts Avenue, N.W.
Washington, DC 20036
Fax: (800) 800-1589

Field of Study: Urban planning

Purpose of Fellowship: Planning: to foster increased minority interest in the study of urban planning. Transportation: to provide financial assistance to a minority student specializing in transportation planning.

Criteria: Applicants for the planning fellowship must be first- or second-year graduate students; transportation fellowship applicants must have transportation planning specialization. All applicants must be U.S. citizens and of either African, Hispanic, Asian, or Native American descent.

Financial Award: Planning: $2,000–$5,000; Transportation: $2,500

Deadline: Mid-May

American Political Science Association Ph.D. Fellowships for Minority Students

1527 New Hampshire Avenue, N.W.
Washington, DC 20036
Phone: (202) 483-2512
Fax: (202) 483-2657

Field of Study: Political science

Purpose of Fellowship: To identify, encourage, and aid prospective African American, Native American, and Latino/a political science graduate students.

Criteria: African American, Native American, and Latino/a graduate students in political science who are enrolled in doctoral programs. Must be U.S. citizens.

Financial Award: Unspecified

Deadline: December 1

American Psychological Association Minority Fellowship in HIV/AIDS Research Training

APA Minority Fellowship Program
750 First St., NE
Washington, DC 20002-4242
Phone: (202) 335-6027
Fax: (202) 336-6012
E-mail: mfp@apa.org

Field of Study: Psychology with a specialty in HIV/AIDS research

Purpose of Fellowship: To increase the number of ethnic minority research scientists studying HIV/AIDS issues among ethnic minority populations; to increase the availability and quality of ethnic minority research training; and to increase the knowledge of issues related to ethnic minority HIV/AIDS prevention and treatment.

Criteria: Candidates should be U.S. citizens or permanent residents who are members of an ethnic minority group and/or demonstrate commitment to a career in psychology with a specialty in HIV/AIDS research related to ethnic minorities. They must be enrolled in a full-time, APA-approved doctoral

Continued

Continued

program by the time the fellowship is awarded.

Financial Award: Up to $958 per month

Deadline: January 15

American Psychological Association Minority Fellowship on Aging Training

APA Minority Fellowship Program
750 First St., N.E.
Washington, DC 20002-4242
Phone: (202) 336-6027
Fax: (202) 336-6012
E-mail: mfp@apa.org

Field of Study: Psychology, with a specialty in gerontology and ethnic studies

Purpose of Fellowship: To support members of ethnic and racial minorities who will complete doctoral degrees in psychology involving research related to aging and ethnic minority health.

Criteria: U.S. citizens or permanent residents who are members of an ethnic minority group and/or demonstrate commitment to research careers related to ethnic minority gerontology. Must be enrolled in a full-time, APA-approved doctoral program by the time the fellowship is awarded.

Financial Award: Up to $10,000 per year

Deadline: January 15

American Psychological Association Minority Fellowship Program and Substance Abuse Mental Health Services Administration Fellowship in Clinical Training

APA Minority Fellowship Program
750 First St., N.E.
Washington, DC 20002-4242
Phone: (202) 336-6027
Fax: (202) 336-6012
E-mail: mfp@apa.org

Field of Study: Psychology (clinical, school, and counseling)

Purpose of Fellowship: To support doctoral training in psychological practice, to increase the number of clinicians and researchers skilled in the prevention, treatment, and study of problems affecting ethnic minority populations; to increase the availability and quality of clinical and research training of ethnic minorities.

Criteria: U.S. citizens or permanent residents who are members of an ethnic minority group and/or demonstrate a committment to careers in psychology related to ethnic minority mental health. Must be enrolled in a full-time, APA-approved doctoral program by the time the fellowship is awarded.

Financial Award: Up to $958 per month

Deadline: January 15

American Psychological Association Minority Fellowship Program in Research Training

APA Minority Fellowship Program
750 First Street, N.E.
Washington, DC 20002-4242
Phone: (202) 336-6027
Fax: (202) 336-6012
E-mail: mfp@apa.org

Field of Study: Psychology, specializing in research fields

Purpose of Fellowship: To support doctoral training in psychological practice, to increase the number of ethnic minority research scientists, and to increase the availability and quality of ethnic minority research training.

Criteria: U.S. citizens or permanent residents who are members of an ethnic minority group and/or demonstrate commitment to a career in psychology related to ethnic minority mental health. Must be enrolled in a full-time, APA-approved doctoral program by the time the fellowship is awarded.

Financial Award: Up to $958 per month

Deadline: January 15

American Society for Microbiology—Graduate Fellowships

1325 Massachussetts Avenue, N.W.
Washington, DC 20005-4171
E-mail:
fellowships-careerinformation@asmusa.org
Web site:
http://www.asmusa.org/mbrsrc/mbr14.htm

Field of Study: Microbiological sciences

Purpose of Fellowship: To support underrepresented minority students who wish to conduct research in the microbiological sciences.

Criteria: Graduate students from underrepresented minorities who are members of the American Society for Microbiology and have completed their coursework.

Financial Award: Unspecified

Deadline: Early May

American Sociological Association Minority Fellowship Program

ASA Minority Affairs
Program/MFP
1722 N St., NW
Washington, DC 20036
Phone: (202) 833-3410,
ext. 322
E-mail:
minority.affairs@asanet.org

Field of Study: Sociology

Purpose of Fellowship: To support the development and training of minority sociologists in mental health.

Criteria: U.S. citizens, noncitizen nationals, or permanent residents of minority background that have been accepted and/or enrolled in a full-time sociology doctoral program in the United States.

Financial Award: $10,000 stipend; arrangements for payment of tuition will be made with the university or department

Deadline: Late December

American Water Works Association—Holly A. Cornell Scholarship

Scholarship Coordinator, AWWA
6666 W. Quincy Ave.
Denver, CO 80235
Phone: (303) 794-7711,
ext. 6194
Web site: http://www.awwa.org

Field of Study: Sciences and engineering related to water supply industry

Purpose of Fellowship: To encourage and support outstanding female and/or minority students wishing to pursue advanced training in the field of water supply and treatment.

Criteria: Female and/or minority students who are currently master's students, and will complete requirements for a master's degree in engineering no sooner than December 1.

Financial Award: $5,000

Deadline: Mid-December

Budget Fellowship Program

Budget Fellowship Program
New York State Division of the Budget
State Capital
Albany, NY 12224
Phone: (518) 474-8616

Field of Study: Open

Purpose of Fellowship: To create an opportunity for the division to employ people with unique skills and backgrounds not generally available through traditional civil service mechanisms.

Criteria: Postbaccalaureate students; applications from women, minorities, and Vietnam era veterans and the disabled are encouraged.

Financial Award: Salaries ranging from $25,039 to $33,221, varying with education and appointment level

Deadline: Early April

Builder Grant

Altrusa International Foundation, Inc.
332 South Michigan Avenue
Suite 1123
Chicago, IL 60603
Phone: (312) 427-4410

Field of Study: Open

Purpose of Fellowship: To offer financial assistance for those trying to improve their literacy level or that of other individuals.

Criteria: U.S. citizens or internationals who reside in an area, or are pursuing a program of study, in a country where an Altrusa Club exists; must be enrolled or engaged in a field of study related to improving their own literacy level or that of other individuals; must re-enter the job force within one year of receiving the award.

Financial Award: Unspecified

Deadline: Call committee

Cesar E. Chavez Dissertation Fellowship for U.S. Latina/o Scholars

6062 Wentworth, Room 305
Dartmouth College
Hanover, NH 03755-3526
Phone: (603) 646-2107

Field of Study: Open

Purpose of Fellowship: To increase the number of U.S. Latina/o faculty in higher education by supporting U.S. Latina/o scholars for a year-long residency at Dartmouth College.

Criteria: U.S. Latina/o Ph.D. candidates who have completed all requirements but dissertation. The fellow will be expected to complete the dissertation during the tenure of the fellowship and to participate in selected activities with undergraduate students.

Financial Award: $25,000 stipend, $2,500 research assistance fund

Deadline: Mid-February

Chancellor's Graduate Fellowship Program

Campus Box 1187
One Brookings Drive
St. Louis, MO 63130-4899
Phone: (314) 935-6821

Field of Study: Open

Purpose of Fellowship: To facilitate training for African Americans interested in becoming college or university professors.

Criteria: African Americans who are admissible into any of Washington University's Ph.D. or D.Sc. programs in arts and sciences, business, engineering, or social work. Also eligible are African Americans admissible to other Washington University programs providing final disciplinary training for prospective college professors.

Financial Award: $16,000 plus full tuition

Deadline: Mid-January

Charles A. Eastman Dissertation Fellowship for Native American Scholars

6062 Wentworth, Room 305
Dartmouth College
Hanover, NH 03755-3526
Phone: (603) 646-2107

Field of Study: Open

Purpose of Fellowship: To increase the number of Native American faculty members in American higher education by supporting Native American scholars in completing their dissertations, through a year-long residency at Dartmouth College.

Criteria: Native American scholars who have completed all Ph.D. requirements except the dissertation.

Financial Award: Stipend of $25,000 plus $2,500 research assistance fund

Deadline: Mid-March

College of William and Mary—Multicultural Teaching Fellows Program

College of William and Mary
P.O. Box 8795
Williamsburg, VA 23187-8795
Phone: (804) 221-2615
Fax: (804) 221-2614

Field of Study: Anthropology, biology, economics, government, music

Purpose of Fellowship: To provide minority undergraduate students the opportunity to teach during summer sessions at the college, allow faculty to evaluate the fellows for future employment at William and Mary, and to enhance the educational experience of William and Mary students.

Criteria: Students entering the final year of terminal degree programs or who have received terminal degrees and are preparing to be college faculty.

Financial Award: $3,500

Deadline: Call committee

College of William and Mary—Multicultural Teaching Fellows Program

Multicultural Teaching Fellows Program
P.O. Box 8795
Williamsburg, VA 23187-8795
Phone: (804) 221-2615
Fax: (804) 221-2614

Field of Study: Open

Purpose of Fellowship: To provide minority undergraduate students the opportunity to teach during summer sessions at the College of William and Mary, allow faculty to evaluate the fellows for future employment at the institution, and to enhance the educational experience of William and Mary students.

Criteria: Students must be entering the final year of terminal degree programs or have received terminal degrees and are preparing to be college faculty. Fellows teach one course during a five- or six-week term.

Financial Award: $3,500

Deadline: Call committee

Community Service Society Research Internships for Minority Graduate Students

105 East 22nd Street
New York, NY 10010

Field of Study: Open

Purpose of Fellowship: To assist minority graduate students to prepare for careers in research on poverty and related public policies.

Criteria: U.S. citizens or permanent residents who are African American, Hispanic, Native American, or Asian.

Financial Award: $12,500 for early years of graduate study; $20,000 for doctoral candidates with an approved dissertation topic

Deadline: Late January

Compact for Faculty Diversity

New England Board of Higher Education
45 Temple Place
Boston, MA 02111
Phone: (617) 357-9620

Field of Study: Science, engineering, mathematics

Purpose of Fellowship: To promote faculty diversity among college leaders.

Criteria: African American, Hispanic, and Native American U.S. citizens who plan to begin their doctoral studies in September at participating New England colleges.

Financial Award: $12,500 for each scholar's first year, tuition and fees for five years, graduate assistantships for year two and beyond

Deadline: Call committee

Congressional Black Caucus Foundation, Inc.—Congressional Fellows Program

1004 Pennsylvania Avenue, S.E.
Washington, DC 20003
Phone: (202) 675-6730
Fax: (202) 547-3806

Field of Study: All fields

Purpose of Fellowship: To offer talented young men and women the opportunity to work on congressional committees and learn all aspects of the legislative process; and to provide scholarly research on critical issues before Congress.

Criteria: Full-time graduate or law students, professionals with five or more years of experience who are pursuing part-time graduate studies, or college faculty members who have an interest in the legislative policy-making process. Applicants must be U.S. citizens.

Financial Award: $15,000

Deadline: Late April

Consortium for Graduate Study in Management—Merit-Based Minority Fellowships

200 S. Hanley Road
Suite 1102
St. Louis, MO 63105-3415
Phone: (314) 935-6364
Fax: (314) 935-5014
E-mail: cgsm@wuolin.wustl.edu
Web site: http://www.cgsm.wustl.edu:8010

Field of Study: Business administration

Purpose of Fellowship: To provide management education opportunities to African Americans, Hispanic Americans, and Native Americans seeking careers in business, government, or nonprofit organizations.

Criteria: College seniors or bachelor's degree holders who are U.S. citizens and African American, Hispanic American, or Native American.

Financial Award: Full tuition and fees for two years of study at university in which student has enrolled

Deadline: Early February

Doctoral Fellowships in Sociology

Minority Fellowship Program
American Sociological Association
1722 N St., N.W.
Washington, DC 20036

Field of Study: Sociology

Purpose of Fellowship: To encourage graduate students, especially members of a minority group, to approach mental health issues relating to minorities from an indigenous perspective.

Criteria: U.S. citizens who are engaged in graduate study and show an interest in teaching, research, or service careers on the sociological aspects of mental health issues of ethnic and racial minorities.

Financial Award: $8,500 stipend; arrangements for the payment of tuition will be made with the university or department

Deadline: Mid-December

Five College Fellowship Program for Minority Scholars

Five Colleges, Inc.
97 Spring Street
Amherst, MA 01002-2324
Phone: (413) 256-8316

Field of Study: All fields

Purpose of Fellowship: To enable fellows to complete their dissertations, to encourage their interest in college teaching, and to acquaint them with the five colleges. Each fellow is hosted within an appropriate department or program at one of the five colleges.

Criteria: Minority graduate students who have completed all requirements except their dissertation.

Financial Award: $25,000 plus office space, housing assistance, and library privileges

Deadline: Mid-January

Ford Foundation—Postdoctoral Fellowships for Minorities

Fellowship Office
2102 Constitution Avenue
Washington, DC 20418
Phone: (202) 334-2872
E-mail: infofell@nas.edu
Web site:
http://fellowships.nas.edu

Field of Study: Behavioral and social sciences, humanities, engineering

Purpose of Fellowship: To increase the presence of underrepresented minorities in teaching and research careers on the nation's college and university faculties.

Criteria: Must have held advanced degree for not more than seven years. U.S. citizens or nationals who are Native American, Alaskan Native (Eskimo or Aleut), African American, Mexican American/Chicano, Native Pacific Islander (Polynesian or Micronesian), or Puerto Rican.

Financial Award: $25,000 plus travel and relocation allowance of $3,000 and $2,000 research allowance

Deadline: Early January

Ford Foundation—Predoctoral and Dissertation Fellowships for Minorities

Fellowship Office
National Research Council
2101 Constitution Avenue
Washington, DC 20418
Phone: (202) 334-2872
E-mail: infofell@nas.edu

Field of Study: Behavioral and social sciences, humanities, engineering

Purpose of Fellowship: To increase the presence of under-represented minorities on the national's college and university faculties.

Criteria: U.S. citizens from the following minority groups: Native American, Alaskan Native (Eskimo or Aleut), African American, Mexican American/Chicano, Native Pacific Islander (Polynesian or Micronesian), and Puerto Rican. Predoctoral: near the beginning of graduate study. Dissertation: all requirements.

Financial Award: $14,000 for each of the three years of fellowship tenure; annual grand total of $7,500 for institution in lieu of tuition and fees

Deadline: Mid-November

Forgivable Loan/Doctoral Incentive Program

400 Golden Shore
Suite 422
Long Beach, CA 90802-4275

Field of Study: Natural sciences, mathematics, computer science, engineering

Purpose of Fellowship: To increase the number of California State University faculty members who are minorities, women, and persons with disabilities.

Criteria: Full-time students enrolled or accepted into doctoral programs at accredited universities in the United States. Not required to have attended CSU. Applicants should be interested in filling instructional faculty positions at campuses of the California State University.

Financial Award: $10,000 per year up to a total of $30,000. For each year of full-time postdoctoral teaching in the CSU, 20 percent of the loan is forgiven.

Deadline: Mid-February

Geological Society of America Research Grants

Geological Society of America
P.O. Box 9140
Boulder, CA 80301
Phone: (303) 447-2020
Fax: (303) 447-1133

Field of Study: Open

Purpose of Fellowship: To provide partial support for master's and doctoral thesis research for graduate students at universities in the United States, Canada, Mexico, and Central America.

Criteria: GSA strongly encourages women, minorities, and people with disabilities to apply.

Financial Award: Up to $2,500

Deadline: Mid-February

Getty Center for the History of Art and the Humanities Research Support Grants

The Getty Center for the History of Art and the Humanities
401 Wilshire Blvd
Santa Monica, CA 90401

Field of Study: Humanities

Purpose of Fellowship: To assist scholars and advanced students who are unaffiliated with the Getty Center to pursue short-term research projects using the resources of the Center's resource collections.

Criteria: Must show the ability to demonstrate a compelling need to use Center materials that are not available to students in other libraries and archives.

Financial Award: Varies

Deadline: Rolling

Graduate Fellowships for Minority Students

1527 New Hampshire Avenue, N.W.
Washington, DC 20036

Field of Study: Political science

Purpose of Fellowship: To identify, encourage, and aid prospective African American, Chicano, and Latino political science graduate students.

Criteria: African American, Chicano, and Latino graduate students in political science who are enrolled in doctoral programs. Must be U.S. citizens. Potential for success in graduate studies and financial needs will be given major consideration.

Financial Award: $6,000 per year

Deadline: December 1

Holly A. Cornell Scholarship

American Water Works Association
6666 W. Quincy Avenue
Denver, CO 80235
Phone: (303) 794-7711, ext. 6206

Field of Study: Sciences and engineering related to water supply industry

Purpose of Fellowship: To encourage and support outstanding female and/or minority students wishing to pursue advanced training in the field of water supply and treatment.

Criteria: Female and/or minority students who are currently master's students, and will complete requirements for a master's degree in engineering.

Financial Award: $5,000

Deadline: Mid-December

Indian Fellowship Program

400 Maryland Avenue, S.W.
Room 2177
Washington, DC 20202-6335
Phone: (202) 401-6335

Field of Study: Open

Purpose of Fellowship: To help Native Americans and Native Alaskans pursue postbaccalaureate degrees.

Criteria: Native Americans and Native Alaskans who are U.S. citizens and full-time degree candidates at accredited institutions. Applicants must not have obtained a terminal postbaccalaureate degree.

Financial Award: $2,500–$39,300

Deadline: Mid-January

Institute for the Study of World Politics—Doctoral Dissertation Fellowships/ Dorothy Danforth Compton Fellowships

1775 Massachussetts Avenue, N.W.
Washington, DC 20036

Field of Study: History, economics, political science, international relations

Purpose of Fellowship: To promote scholarly examination of political, economic, and social issues that affect the security, well-being, and dignity of the people of the world. Fellowships support work that will develop knowledge and understanding essential to the resolution of fundamental international issues.

Criteria: Doctoral candidates who have completed course work and are conducting dissertation research. Candidates for the Dorothy Danforth Compton Fellowship must be African American, Hispanic American, or Native American graduate students preparing for careers in world affairs.

Financial Award: Varies

Deadline: Mid-February

Institute for the Study of World Politics—Doctoral Dissertation Fellowships/ Dorothy Danforth Compton Fellowships

1755 Massachussetts Avenue, N.W.
Washington, DC 20036

Field of Study: Social sciences

Purpose of Fellowship: To promote scholarly examination of political, economic, and social issues that affect the security, well-being and dignity of the peoples of the world. Fellowships support work which will develop knowledge and understanding essential to the resolution of fundamental international issues.

Criteria: Doctoral candidates who have completed coursework and are conducting dissertation research. The Institute's special Dorothy Danforth Compton Fellowship is awarded to African American, Hispanic American, and Native American graduate students preparing for careers in world affairs.

Financial Award: Varies according to fellows' needs and resources

Deadline: Mid-February

Knight Foundation—Minority Predoctoral Fellowships

Office of the Provost
Macalester College
1600 Grand Avenue
Saint Paul, MN 55105

Field of Study: All liberal arts

Purpose of Fellowship: To provide academic support for Ph.D. candidates as they complete requirements for that degree, to encourage minority scholars to consider teaching careers in the liberal arts, and to enrich the college's curriculum.

Criteria: Must have completed all the preliminary requirements for the Ph.D. and be in the final stages of writing dissertation; must be U.S. citizen.

Financial Award: Stipends of $18,000, plus $500 moving expenses and $500 support for travel and research

Deadline: Mid-February

Millender Fellowship

Wayne State University
Administration Building
4116 Faculty
Detroit, MI 48202
Phone: (313) 577-2280

Field of Study: Open

Purpose of Fellowship: To assist minorities in achieving distinguished accomplishment in public service-oriented careers. Fellows are assigned to high-level responsibilities with top executives in Detroit area organizations in public, private, and nonprofit areas.

Criteria: Applicants must demonstrate a record of successful accomplishment in some graduate educational program and/or through equivalent experience, broadly related to a public service career.

Financial Award: $18,000 stipend for nine months, plus fringe benefits

Deadline: Late March

Minority Cooperative Education Program

Stop #156
Division of Personnel
Washington, DC 20551
Phone: (202) 452-3850

Field of Study: Accounting, data processing/information systems

Purpose of Fellowship: To provide professional work experience to ethnic minority undergraduate and graduate students.

Criteria: U.S. citizens and members of ethnic minority groups.

Financial Award: Positions only awarded during the semester or during the summer

Deadline: Call committee

Minority Fellowship Program—Aging Training

American Psychological Association
Minority Fellowship Program
750 First Street, N.E.
Washington, DC 20002-4242
Phone: (202) 336-6027
Fax: (202) 336-6012
E-mail: mfp@apa.org

Field of Study: Psychology

Purpose of Fellowship: To support members of ethnic and racial minorities who complete doctoral degrees in psychology involving research related to aging and ethnic minority mental health.

Criteria: U.S. citizens or permanent residents who are members of an ethnic minority group and/or demonstrate a commitment to research careers related to ethnic minority gerontology. Must be enrolled in a full-time, APA-approved doctoral program by the time the fellowship is awarded.

Financial Award: Varies

Deadline: Late November

Minority Fellowship Program—Clinical Training

The American Psychological Association
Minority Fellowship Program
750 First Street, N.E.
Washington, DC 20002-4242
Phone: (202) 336-6027
Fax: (202) 336-6012
E-mail: mfp@apa.org

Field of Study: Psychology

Purpose of Fellowship: To support doctoral training in psychological practice, to increase the number of clinicians and researchers skilled in the prevention, treatment, and study of problems affecting ethnic minority populations; to increase the availability and quality of clinical and research training of ethnic minorities.

Criteria: U.S. citizens or permanent residents who are members of an ethnic minority group and/or demonstrate a commitment to careers in psychology related to ethnic minority mental health. Must be enrolled in a full-time, APA-approved doctoral program when fellowship is awarded.

Financial Award: Varies

Deadline: January 15

Minority Fellowship Program—Research Training

The American Psychological Association
Minority Fellowship Program
750 First Street, N.E.
Washington, DC 20002-4242
Phone: (202) 336-6027
Fax: (202) 336-6012
E-mail: mfp@apa.org

Field of Study: Psychology

Purpose of Fellowship: To support doctoral training in psychological practice, to increase the number of ethnic minority research scientists, and to increase the availability and quality of ethnic minority research training.

Criteria: U.S. citizens or permanent residents who are members of an ethnic minority group and/or demonstrate a commitment to careers in psychology related to ethnic minority mental health. Must be enrolled in a full-time, APA-approved doctoral program by the time the fellowship is awarded.

Financial Award: Varies

Deadline: January 15

Minority Graduate Fellows Program

Margaret Kent Bass
St. Lawrence University
Canton, NY 13617

Field of Study: Open

Purpose of Fellowship: To address the issue of faculty/staff diversity at St. Lawrence University. Fellows will teach one course and present a research-based paper each semester in a department commensurate with research interests.

Criteria: All graduate students from such underrepresented groups as African Americans, Hispanics, Native Americans, and Asians who have completed coursework and preliminary examinations for the Ph.D.

Financial Award: Stipend of $20,000 per year with possibility of additional funds for travel to conferences and professional meetings; office space, personal computer

Deadline: Early March

Minority Graduate Fellowship for Dissertation Research and Writing

George Washington University
Office of Fellowships and Graduate Student Support
2013 G Street, N.W.
Washington, DC 20052
Phone: (202) 994-6822

Field of Study: Arts and sciences, international affairs, engineering

Purpose of Fellowship: To support a minority student in the last phase of doctoral work.

Criteria: Candidates should have all course work completed and be at the dissertation stage of the Ph.D. degree.

Financial Award: $20,000 for the academic year

Deadline: Late December

Minority Teaching Fellowships

309 Administrative Services Building
St. Cloud State University
720 S. 4th Ave
St. Cloud, MN 53601-4498
Phone: (612) 255-3143

Field of Study: Business, education, fine arts, humanities, sciences

Purpose of Fellowship: To support minority graduate students who are preparing to be college teachers.

Criteria: Minority graduate students entering the final year of terminal degree academic programs and preparing to be college teachers.

Financial Award: $3,500 stipend for teaching one course during a five-week summer session

Deadline: Mid-November

Munson Institute—Paul Cuffe Memorial Fellowship

75 Greenmanville Avenue
Box 6000
Mystic, CT 06355-0990
Phone: (203) 572-5359
Fax: (203) 572-5329
E-mail: annamsm@aol.com

Field of Study: History and related studies

Purpose of Fellowship: To support research, using the scholarly resources of southeastern New England, on the participation of Native Americans and African Americans in maritime activities.

Criteria: Open

Financial Award: $2,400

Deadline: Mid-June

National Aeronautics and Space Administration—Graduate Student Researchers Program/ Underrepresented Minority Focus Component

Office Of Human Resources and Education
Code FEH
NASA Headquarters
Washington, DC 20546
Phone: (202) 358-1531
Fax: (202) 358-3048

Field of Study: Engineering, physics, mathematics, computer science

Purpose of Fellowship: To increase the number of underrepresented minority graduate students whose research interests are compatible with NASA's programs in space science and aerospace technology.

Criteria: U.S. citizens who are black, Hispanic, Native American, Pacific Islander, or individuals with a disability that limits major life activity. Must be enrolled in a full-time graduate program at an accredited U.S. college or university.

Financial Award: Up to $22,000 per year

Deadline: Early February

National Consortium for Graduate Degrees for Minorities in Engineering Fellowship

Box 537
Notre Dame, IN 46556
Phone: (219) 239-7183

Field of Study: Engineering

Purpose of Fellowship: To encourage minority students to pursue careers in engineering.

Criteria: American citizens belonging to a minority group underrepresented in engineering; minimum academic status of junior year enrollment in an accredited engineering school.

Financial Award: Tuition, fees, and a stipend of $5,000 per graduate academic year, plus a paid summer internship

Deadline: December 1

National Hispanic Scholarship Fund

Selection Committee
National Hispanic Scholarship Fund
P.O. Box 728
Novato, CA 94948

Field of Study: Open

Purpose of Fellowship: To assist Hispanic American students in completing their higher education.

Criteria: U.S. citizen or permanent resident of Hispanic parentage. Graduate students must be carrying a minimum of six units. Must be enrolled as full-time daytime students at accredited U.S. college or university.

Financial Award: $500–$1,000

Deadline: Mid-August

National Physical Science Consortium Fellowship

Attn: L. Nan Snow
Box 30001, Department 3NPS
Las Cruces, NM 99003-8001
Phone: (800) 952-4118

Field of Study: Astronomy, chemistry, computer science, geology, mathematics

Purpose of Fellowship: To support minority students pursuing or intending to pursue graduate study in the physical sciences.

Criteria: U.S. citizens from particular minorities who are returning undergraduate students or entering graduate students. Students must be enrolled at an NPSC institution. Students currently enrolled in a master's or Ph.D. program are not eligible. Minimum GPA: 3.0.

Financial Award: Tuition, fees, and nine-months' stipend of $12,500 for the first four years and $15,000 for years five and six

Deadline: Mid-November

National Science Foundation Graduate and Minority Graduate Fellowships

NSF Graduate Research Fellowship Program, ORAU
P.O. Box 3010
Oak Ridge, TN 37831-3010
Phone: (615) 241-4300
Fax: (615) 241-4513
E-mail: nsfgrf@orau.gov

Field of Study: Sciences, mathematics, engineering

Purpose of Fellowship: To improve the human resource base of science, mathematics, and engineering in the United States and to reinforce the diversity of that human resource base.

Criteria: U.S. citizens, nationals, or permanent resident aliens who are near the beginning of graduate study. Students from minority groups and women in engineering are particularly encouraged.

Financial Award: $14,400 stipend for one year, plus tuition

Deadline: Early November

Native American Community Scholar's Awards

955 L'Enfant Plaza
Suite 7000
Washington, DC 20560
Phone: (202) 297-3271
E-mail: siofg@sivm.si.edu

Field of Study: Open

Purpose of Fellowship: To support Native Americans who wish to undertake individually designed research projects related to Native American topics and using Native American resources at the Smithsonian.

Criteria: Native Americans formally or informally related to a Native American community.

Financial Award: Unspecified

Deadline: Call committee

New York State Regents Health Care Scholarships in Medicine and Dentistry

Bureau of College, School, and Community Collaboration
Cultural Education Center
Room 5C64
Albany, NY 12230

Field of Study: Medicine or dentistry

Purpose of Fellowship: To provide financial assistance to students enrolled in approved medical and dental schools in New York State.

Criteria: Applicants must be economically disadvantaged and a member of a minority group historically underrepresented in medicine or dentistry, or must be a graduate of a New York State-sponsored EOP, HEOP, SEEK, or College Discovery opportunity program.

Financial Award: $1,000–$10,000 per year for up to four years for educational expenses

Deadline: Early November

New York State Regents Professional Opportunity Scholarships

Bureau of College, School, and Community Collaboration
Cultural Education Center
Room 5C64
Albany, NY 12230

Field of Study: Architecture, landscape architecture, law, psychology

Purpose of Fellowship: To increase the number of professionals, particularly minorities and disadvantaged students, practicing in New York State.

Criteria: Applicants must be economically disadvantaged and a member of a minority historically underrepresented in the licensed professions, or enrolled in or a graduate of EOP, HEOP, SEEK, or College Discovery program.

Financial Award: $1,000–$5,000 per year

Deadline: Early March

New York Telephone/NYNEX Minority Teaching Fellowships

Empire State College
One Union Avenue
Saratoga Springs, NY
12866-4391

Field of Study: Open

Purpose of Fellowship: To offer an outstanding professional opportunity for minority doctoral candidates interested in college teaching, adult learning, and innovative higher education.

Criteria: Doctoral candidates with all degree requirements except the dissertation completed.

Financial Award: 12-month appointment including a $30,000 stipend plus fringe benefits

Deadline: Mid-November

President's Graduate Fellowship

President's Graduate Fellowship Program
Old Dominion University
Norfolk, VA 23508-9989
Phone: (804) 683-3460

Field of Study: Open

Purpose of Fellowship: To increase the pool of minority and women faculty members who hold the Ph.D. degree at Old Dominion.

Criteria: May be undergraduate or master's-level students, or may be specifically recruited for this program. Must be enrolled in or accepted into a graduate program leading to a terminal degree, and nominated by the graduate program director. Must be a U.S. citizen.

Financial Award: Varies

Deadline: Early March

Residential Fellowships

University of Rochester
302 Morey Hall
Rochester, NY 14627
Phone: (716) 275-7235

Field of Study: Open

Purpose of Fellowship: For predoctoral students to complete the dissertation.

Criteria: Must be engaged in writing their dissertations. Fellows will work with the director of the Frederick Douglass Institute for African and African American Studies and organize a colloquium.

Financial Award: $10,000 stipend for one year plus possibility of summer funding

Deadline: Late January

Resources for the Future—Joseph L. Fisher Dissertation Awards

Resources for the Future
1616 P Street, NW
Washington, DC 20036
Phone: (202) 328-5067

Field of Study: Economics, environmental and natural sciences

Purpose of Fellowship: To support doctoral dissertation research in economics on issues related to the environment, natural resources, or energy.

Criteria: Graduate students in the final year of their dissertation research, especially members of minority groups and women.

Financial Award: $12,000 stipend

Deadline: Late April

Social Science Research Council—Urban Underclass Program

Social Science Research Council
605 Third Avenue
New York, NY 10158
Phone: (212) 661-0280

Field of Study: Social sciences, genetics, nutrition, neurobiology

Purpose of Fellowship: To provide training in research design and analysis (qualitative and/or quantitative) and to assist students in developing a research interest or idea into a dissertation proposal.

Criteria: Minority graduate students who are completing at least their second year of graduate study but who have not yet started the actual writing of the dissertation.

Financial Award: Seminar fees, transportation, room and board, plus an additional $750 for those who complete the workshop

Deadline: Early December

State University of New York—Underrepresented Graduate Fellowship Program

Assistant Vice Chancellor
Diversity and Affermative Action
SUNY Plaza
Albany, NY 12246
Phone: (518) 443-5676
Fax: (518) 443-5103

Field of Study: Open

Purpose of Fellowship: To provide underrepresented graduate students access to outstanding programs in the state university system.

Criteria: Full-time students who are U.S. citizens or permanent residents from the following groups: African American, Hispanic American, or Native American.

Financial Award: $7,500–$10,000

Deadline: Call committee

Summer Multicultural Teaching Fellows Program

Bendetson Hall, Tufts University
Medford, MA 02155
Phone: (617) 627-3298
Fax: (617) 627-3150

Field of Study: Social sciences, arts, humanities, science, engineering

Purpose of Fellowship: To assist the development of a diverse and representative faculty, enhance the education experience of students, and better prepare them for the increasingly diverse United States and world of the 21st century.

Criteria: Underrepresented graduate students who are entering the final year of a terminal degree program or have already received terminal degrees and are preparing to be college faculty. Applicants must be U.S. citizens.

Financial Award: $3,500 for summer term plus on-campus housing

Deadline: Early November

Thurgood Marshall Dissertation Fellowships for African American Scholars

6062 Wentworth, Room 305
Dissertation Fellowship Committee
Dartmouth College
Hanover, NH 03755-3526
Phone: (603) 646-2107

Field of Study: Any discipline in the Dartmouth undergraduate arts

Purpose of Fellowship: To increase the number of African American faculty in American higher education by supporting African American scholars in completing the dissertation. Fellows are awarded a year-long residency at Dartmouth College.

Criteria: African American scholars who have completed all Ph.D. requirements except the dissertation.

Financial Award: $25,000 stipend plus $2,500 research assistance fund

Deadline: Mid-January

Tuskegee University and the International Foundation for Education and Self-Help—International Fellows Program

Office of International Programs
Tuskegee University
Tuskegee, AL 36088
Phone: (205) 727-8953

Field of Study: Social sciences and physical sciences

Purpose of Fellowship: A nine-month project supporting the participation of African American graduate students and others in technical and educational transfer of expertise to areas of need in Africa and other Third World countries.

Criteria: Graduate students or graduating seniors planning to enroll in a graduate program.

Financial Award: Unspecified

Deadline: Early February

United Negro College Fund/Merck Graduate Science Research Dissertation Fellowships

8260 Willow Oaks Corporate Drive
P.O. Box 10444
Fairfax, VA 22031-4511
Phone: (703) 205-3538

Field of Study: Biological and physical sciences

Purpose of Fellowship: To increase the number of African Americans in biomedical science education and research.

Criteria: Must be African American; enrolled full time in a doctoral program in the life or physical sciences; a third- or fourth-year graduate student; a U.S. citizen or permanent resident.

Financial Award: Fellowship stipend up to $25,000; institutional grant up to $15,000

Deadline: Late February

United Negro College Fund/Merck Postdoctoral Science Research Fellowships

8260 Willow Oaks Corporate Drive
P.O. Box 10444
Fairfax, VA 22031-4511
Phone: (703) 205-3538

Field of Study: Biological and physical sciences

Purpose of Fellowship: To increase the number of African Americans in the pipeline of biomedical science education and research.

Criteria: Candidates must be African American; appointed as postdoctoral fellows at an academic or nonacademic institution such as NIH or Centers for Disease Control; committed to conduct research at a Merck research facility for a minimum of three months; a U.S. citizen or permanent resident.

Financial Award: $40,000 stipend, $15,000 institutional grant

Deadline: Late February

University of California—President's Postdoctoral Fellowship Program

300 Lakeside Drive, 18th Floor
Oakland, CA 94612-3550
Phone: (510) 987-9500

Field of Study: Open

Purpose of Fellowship: To encourage outstanding minority and women Ph.D. recipients to pursue academic careers by offering postdoctoral research experiences that will help make them strong candidates for appointment at the University of California.

Criteria: U.S. citizens and permanent residents. Preference is given to minority and women candidates from historically underrepresented groups.

Financial Award:
$27,000–$29,000 stipend, health benefits, and up to $4,000 for supplemental and research-related expenses

Deadline: Early December

University of California/Berkeley—Chancellor's Postdoctoral Fellowship Program for Academic Diversity

University of California/Berkeley
Office of the Chancellor
200 California Hall
Berkeley, CA 94720-1500
Phone: (510) 642-1935

Field of Study: Open

Purpose of Fellowship: To provide funding, mentoring, and guidance in preparation for an academic career to members of minority groups committed to careers in university research and teaching. The program is intended to increase ethnic minority representation of the Univeristy of California/Berkeley faculty.

Criteria: Applicants must be U.S. citizens or permanent residents who are members of minority groups that are underrepresented in American universities, and must have received a doctorate within two years of the start of the appointment.

Financial Award: $31,000 stipend; moving costs up to

Continued

Continued

$2,000; $1,000 for health insurance; $500 for supplies and expenses; $1,000 for research-related expenses

Deadline: Early December

University of California/Los Angeles Graduate Fellowships—Eugene V. Cota Robles Fellowhip

1252 Murphy Hall
Box 951419
Los Angeles, CA 90095-1419
Phone: (310) 825-3521

Field of Study: Open

Purpose of Fellowship: To provide four years of funding for doctoral students from underrepresented groups who wish to pursue a career in university teaching and research.

Criteria: Candidates must apply to a UCLA graduate program. Students must be Native American, Native Alaskan, Native Hawaiian, African American, Hispanic, Filipino, or Puerto Rican. Asian American students in the humanities or social sciences are also eligible. Applicants must be U.S. citizens.

Financial Award: $12,500 per year plus registration fees

Deadline: Mid-December

University of California/Los Angeles Graduate Fellowships—Project 88 Graduate Support Program

1252 Murphy Hall
Box 951419
Los Angeles, CA 90095-1419
Phone: (310) 825-3521

Field of Study: Open

Purpose of Fellowship: To provide four years of funding for doctoral students from underrepresented groups.

Criteria: Candidates must apply to a UCLA graduate program. Students must be Native American, Native Alaskan, Native Hawaiian, African American, Hispanic, Filipino, or Puerto Rican. Asian American students in the humanities or social sciences are also eligible. Applicants must be U.S. citizens.

Financial Award: $12,000 stipend plus registration fees during first and fourth years of school; assistantship is awarded during second and third years

Deadline: Mid-December

University of California/ Santa Barbara Center for Black Studies Predoctoral Fellowships

Center for Black Studies
University of California/Santa Barbara
4603 South Hall
Santa Barbara, CA 93106-3140
Phone: (805) 893-3914

Field of Study: Open

Purpose of Fellowship: To increase the number of African American scholars in higher education.

Criteria: Candidates must have advanced to candidacy and have completed all requirements for the Ph.D. except the dissertation at an accredited university. Reasonable assurance of completion of the dissertation during the nine-month period of residency must be provided.

Financial Award: $18,000 stipend, office space, and library privileges. Up to $500 for expenses related to the dissertation preparation

Deadline: Late March

University of Colorado/ Boulder—Chancellor's Postdoctoral Fellowship Program for Academic Diversity

Box 26, University of Colorado
Boulder, CO 80309-0026
Phone: (303) 492-5773
E-mail:
barbara.kraus@colorado.edu

Field of Study: All disciplines represented at University of Colorado/Boulder

Purpose of Fellowship: To provide scholars with postdoctoral opportunities in all disciplines represented at University of Colorado/Boulder, plus mentoring and guidance in preparation for an academic career.

Criteria: Ph.D. within two years of the start of the appointment; U.S. citizen or permanent resident who is a member of an underrepresented group in higher education, or women in engineering, computer science, mathematics, and physical science fields.

Financial Award: $31,000 plus benefits and up to $2,000 for moving expenses.

Deadline: Early December

University of Maryland/College Park—Postdoctoral Fellowship Program for African American Scholars

Room 2126
Lee Building
College Park, MD 20742
Phone: (301) 405-4207
Fax: (301) 314-9305

Field of Study: Open

Purpose of Fellowship: To support the research projects of outstanding African American scholars in any discipline. Scholars will be expected to be in residence during the tenure of the award (a one- or two-year appointment).

Criteria: African Americans (U.S. citizens or permanent resident aliens) who have completed the Ph.D. degree from an accredited university or who will receive the degree by the year they begin the fellowship.

Financial Award: $34,000–$36,000 stipend, plus $3,000 for travel or research-related expenses

Deadline: Late January

University of Missouri/Columbia—Chancellor's Gus T. Ridgel Fellowship for Minority Americans

University of Missouri/Columbia
Graduate School
210 Jesse Hall
Columbia, MO 65211
Phone: (800) 877-6312

Field of Study: Open

Purpose of Fellowship: To support minority American graduate students enrolled in programs at the University of Missouri/Columbia who demonstrate superior academic achievement.

Criteria: Minority students enrolled in master's or doctoral programs at the University of Missouri.

Financial Award: $12,000 stipend

Deadline: Call committee

University of Southern California—All-University Predoctoral Diversity Fellowships

3601 Watt Way, GFS315
Los Angeles, CA 90089-1695

Field of Study: University of Southern California fields that offer a Ph.D.

Purpose of Fellowship: To offer diversity fellowships for students aiming toward the Ph.D. at U.S.C. and planning a career in university teaching and research.

Criteria: Seniors or graduates who present evidence of achievement and promise as scholars and are members of a group underrepresented as doctoral students in U.S. universities and are first-generation college students. Underrepresented groups include Native Americans, Native Alaskans, African Americans, Latinos, Mexican Americans, and Native Pacific Islanders.

Financial Award: $14,000 plus tuition and mandatory fees

Deadline: Early February

The Village Voice

The Village Voice
Editorial Department
Intern Program
36 Cooper Square
New York, NY 10003
Phone: (212) 475-3300

Field of Study: Journalism

Purpose of Fellowship: To provide a fellowship opportunity in journalism.

Criteria: Minorities only may apply.

Financial Award: Small weekly stipend

Deadline: Varies with internship period; contact Editorial Dept. for details

Washington University in St. Louis—Fellowships for Minority Graduate Students

Campus Box 1187
One Brookings Drive
St. Louis, MO 63130-4899

Field of Study: Open

Purpose of Fellowship: To support minority graduate students in a broad spectrum of traditional and interdisciplinary majors.

Criteria: U.S. citizens or nationals who are members of an ethnic or racial minority group.

Financial Award: Stipends of at least $9,500 plus tuition

Deadline: Mid-January

William B. Ruggles Right to Work Scholarship

8001 Braddock Road
Suite 500
Springfield, VA 22160
Phone: (800) 325-7892

Field of Study: Journalism, communications

Purpose of Fellowship: To support a student who exemplifies dedication to principle and high journalistic standards.

Criteria: Graduates or undergraduates in journalism programs in U.S. universities. Members of the National Right to Work Committee are not eligible.

Financial Award: $2,000

Deadline: Late March

Williams College—Gaius Charles Bolin Fellowships for Minority Graduate Students

David L. Smith, Dean of Faculty
Hopkins Hall
Williams College
Williamstown, MA 01267

Field of Study: Humanities, natural sciences, social sciences

Purpose of Fellowship: To encourage minority students to pursue careers in college teaching and to devote the bulk of their time during the academic year to the completion of dissertation work.

Criteria: Applicants must be U.S. citizens and have completed all doctoral work except the dissertation by the end of the current academic year. During the year of residence at Williams, the Bolin Fellows will be assigned faculty advisors and will be expected to teach a one-semester course.

Financial Award: $25,000 stipend, plus housing support and an allowance of up to $2,500 for expenses

Deadline: Early January

Woodrow Wilson National Fellowship Foundation—Rural Policy Fellowships

Woodrow Wilson National
Fellowship Foundation
P.O. Box 410
Princeton, NJ 08542

Field of Study: Open

Purpose of Fellowship: To encourage research that will expand current understanding of rural economies and communities in the United States.

Criteria: Candidates for a Ph.D. or Ed.D. degree in a graduate school in the United States, who are U.S. citizens.

Financial Award: $15,000 for one year, plus up to $3,500 for field research and a graduate school subvention of $2,000 in lieu of tuition

Deadline: Late December

Fellowships and Grants for Women

12

If you look through the list of fellowships at the end of this chapter, you'll see the names of some of the most influential women in American history. Indeed, the demand for women's fellowships has reflected the growing role of women in American society over the course of the century, and it is only fitting that these opportunities are as wide ranging and well endowed as any you will find in this book.

You may think there are distinct similarities between fellowships for women and for minorities, and in many ways, this is true. The clearest link between the two types of fellowships is that both place restrictions upon the types of people that can apply, and as such, the applicant pool is both smaller and less heterogeneous.

But the similarities go much deeper than just that. Like minority fellowships, women's fellowships cover a wide array of fields, leading to careers in nearly every area available. And they provide opportunities for a group that has long suffered from the effects of the "glass ceiling." What the organizations listed in this chapter are saying is this: It's high time that women earned the respect and opportunities in the working world they have always deserved.

The Pros and Cons of Women's Fellowships

Unfortunately, as has historically been the case, the grand hypocrisy is that the majority of fellowships for women simply do not offer as large an award as national prizes. Most organizations offer less than $10,000 per year for their fellows, and it is extremely rare that you will find a women's fellowship that pays more than $20,000. For this reason, if you're looking for an award that will keep you financially stable for an entire year, you should probably consider looking toward either national or minority fellowships.

That said, what makes these opportunities so rewarding is the range of fields they cover. In particular, individuals interested in women's studies, gender equity, and professional development will find a bevy of potential fellowships. What it all comes down to, then, is determining whether the fellowships designed specifically for women have more to offer you, with your particular field of interest than national or minority fellowships. For those of you looking to study women's issues or work for and among members of your own sex, it's a safe bet you've found the right chapter!

AT&T Bell Laboratories—Graduate Research Program for Women

Crawfords Corner Road
Room 1E-209
Holmdel, NH 07733-1988

Field of Study: Chemistry, chemical engineering, communications science

Purpose of Fellowship: To identify and develop research ability in women and to increase their representation in science and engineering. Participation is to begin at the outset of the candidate's graduate education.

Criteria: Women who are U.S. citizens or holders of immigrant visas, and who are admitted to full-time study in a doctoral program agreed to by AT&T Bell Laboratories.

Financial Award: $16,800 plus tuition

Deadline: Mid-January

Agnes Fay Morgan Research Award

Dr. Jeanne M. Buccigross
College of Mt. Joseph
5701 Delhi Road
Cincinnati, OH 45233-1670
Phone: (513) 244-4376

Field of Study: Chemistry or biochemistry

Purpose of Fellowship: To recognize research achievements by a woman chemist.

Criteria: Women chemists or biochemists must be 40 years of age or younger at the time of nomination. The nominee may be, but need not be, a member of Iota Sigma Pi.

Financial Award: $400

Deadline: Early December

Altrussa International Foundation, Inc.— Grant-in-Aid

332 South Michigan Avenue
Suite 1123
Chicago, IL 60603
Phone: (312) 427-4410

Field of Study: Open

Purpose of Fellowship: To offer financial assistance to women who have much to give to their own countries and the world.

Criteria: Those eligible may be female, full-time graduate students in countries other than their own or citizens of countries in Latin America, Asia, the Middle East, Africa, Polynesia, or Melanesia. Candidates must have satisfactorily completed of at least half of their programs, and must return to their home countries within three months of completion of their programs and enter employment there within one year.

Financial Award: Varies

Deadline: Late March

American Association of University Women (AAUW)— American Fellowships for Dissertation Work

AAUW Educational Foundation
Department 51
2201 N. Dodge St.
Iowa City, IA 52243-4030
Phone: (319) 337-1716, ext. 60

Field of Study: All fields of study except engineering

Purpose of Fellowship: To support women who will complete the writing of their dissertations between July 1, 1998 and June 30, 1999. Applicants are expected to receive a doctoral degree at the end of the fellowship year.

Criteria: Women who are U.S. citizens or permanent residents. Applicants must have completed all predissertation requirements and have their dissertation research proposal approved by mid-November. Students holding a dissertation writing fellowship for the year prior to the AAUW fellowship are not eligible.

Financial Award: $14,500

Deadline: Mid-November

American Association of University Women (AAUW)—American Fellowships for Postdoctoral Work

AAUW Educational Foundation
Department 51
2201 N. Dodge St.
Iowa City, IA 52243-4030
Phone: (319) 337-1716, ext. 60

Field of Study: Arts and humanities, social sciences

Purpose of Fellowship: Ten fellowships for women who have received the doctorate degree by mid-November.

Criteria: Women who are U.S. citizens or permanent residents.

Financial Award: $27,000

Deadline: Mid-November

American Association of University Women (AAUW)—Career Development Grants

AAUW Educational Foundation
Department 51
2201 N. Dodge St.
Iowa City, IA 52243-4030
Phone: (319) 337-1716, ext. 60

Field of Study: All fields

Purpose of Fellowship: To support women who are preparing to re-enter the work force, change careers, or advance their current careers. Candidates must be in the early stages of their programs.

Criteria: Women who are U.S. citizens or permanent residents, who hold a bachelor's degree, and who have received their last degree on or before June 30, 1993. Ph.D. candidates may only apply for funding for course work, not for researching or writing their dissertations.

Financial Award: $1,000–$5,000

Deadline: Mid-December

American Association of University Women—Charles and June Ross International Fellowships

AAUW Educational Foundation
1111 16th Street, N.W.
Washington, DC 20036-4873

Field of Study: Sciences

Purpose of Fellowship: To provide Australian women scientists with an opportunity for full-time graduate or postgraduate study or research in the United States.

Criteria: Women scientists who are Australian citizens.

Financial Award: $14,000

Deadline: Unspecified

American Association of University Women (AAUW)—Community Action Grants

AAUW Educational Foundation
Department 51
2201 N. Dodge St.
Iowa City, IA 55243-4030
Phone: (319) 337-1716, ext. 60

Field of Study: Community service

Purpose of Fellowship: To provide seed money to AAUW branches, states, or individual women for nondegree research projects that promote education and equity for women and girls.

Criteria: Applicants must be U.S. citizens or permanent residents and hold a bachelor's degree. Applicants may apply no more than twice for the same proposed grant.

Financial Award: $500–$5,000

Deadline: Call committee

American Association of University Women (AAUW)—International Fellowships

AAUW Educational Foundation
Department 51
2201 N. Dodge St.
Iowa City, IA 52243-4030
Phone: (319) 337-1716, ext. 60

Field of Study: All fields

Purpose of Fellowship: To allow women of outstanding academic ability, who are not citizens or permanent residents, to conduct postgraduate study or research in the United States.

Criteria: Women who are not U.S. citizens or permanent residents, who hold the equivalent of a U.S. bachelor's degree before early December. Upon completion of their studies, fellowship recipients must return to their home countries to pursue a professional career. Judged on professional potential and importance of projects.

Financial Award: $15,160

Deadline: Early December

American Association of University Women (AAUW)—Intern Program

1111 16th Street, NW
Washington, DC 22036-4873
Phone: (202) 785-7795

Field of Study: Open

Purpose of Fellowship: To work on special projects for the Development and Program Staff. Interns are given the opportunity to tailor their experiences to their own academic or professional needs.

Criteria: Not specified

Financial Award: $500–$1,000

Deadline: Call committee

American Association of University Women (AAUW)—Selected Professions Fellowships

AAUW Educational Foundation
Department 51
2201 N. Dodge St.
Iowa City, IA 52243-4030
Phone: (319) 337-1716, ext. 60

Field of Study: Focus group professions; science and technology

Purpose of Fellowship: To support women in fields where female participation has traditionally been low; special consideration given to applicants who demonstrate professional promise in innovative or neglected areas and/or practice in public interest concerns.

Criteria: Women who are U.S. citizens or permanent residents. Applicants for the focus professions must be entering their final year of study in September. Science and technology group fellowships are available for the final year of a master's degree (including one-year programs) and for engineering dissertations.

Financial Award: $5,000–$12,000

Deadline: Early January

American Fellowship for Dissertation Work

AAUW Educational Foundation
Department 51
2201 N. Dodge Street
Iowa City, IA 52243-4030

Field of Study: All fields of study except engineering

Purpose of Fellowship: To support women who will complete the writing of their dissertations in the course of one year. Applicants are expected to receive a doctoral degree at the end of the fellowship year.

Criteria: Women who are U.S. citizens or permanent residents. Applicants must have completed all predissertation requirments and have their dissertation research proposal approved. Students holding a dissertation writing fellowship for the year prior to the AAUW fellowship are not eligible. Special consideration is given to qualified AAUW members, minorities, women pursuing their first terminal degrees, and women pursuing degrees in nontraditional fields.

Financial Award: $14,500

Deadline: Mid-November

American Fellowship for Postdoctoral Work

AAUW Educational Fundation
Department 51
2201 N. Dodge Street
Iowa City, IA 52243-4030
Phone: (319) 337-1716

Field of Study: All fields of study

Purpose of Fellowship: Nine fellowships for women who have received the doctorate degree.

Criteria: Women who are U.S. citizens or permanent residents. Applicants must have achieved a doctorate by mid-November of the previous year.

Financial Award:
$20,000–$25,000

Deadline: Mid-November

Avon Fundation for Women in Business Studies

2012 Massachussetts Avenue, N.W.
Washington, DC 20036

Field of Study: Business-related fields, including management and administration

Purpose of Fellowship: To provide the support necessary for women to complete their education and develop successful and productive careers in business.

Criteria: Women who are U.S. citizens, 30 years of age or older, and graduating within 12–24 months from date of grants. Applicants must demonstrate critical need for financial assistance (i.e., gross income for family of four must be $25,000 or less). Does not cover study at the doctoral level.

Financial Award: $500–$1000

Deadline: Mid-April

Berkshire Summer Fellowship

Berkshire Summer Fellowship Program
34 Concord Avenue
Cambridge, MA 02138
Phone: (617) 495-8212
Fax: (617) 495-8136

Field of Study: History

Purpose of Fellowship: To support women historians, particularly junior scholars, who normally do not have access to Boston-area resources.

Criteria: Women historians at the postdoctoral level working in any field of history.

Financial Award: $3,000

Deadline: Mid-January

Budget Fellowship Program

Budget Fellowship Program
New York State Division of the Budget
State Capital
Albany, NY 12224
Phone: (518) 474-8616

Field of Study: Not specified

Purpose of Fellowship: To create an opportunity for the Division to employ persons with unique skills and backgrounds not generally available through traditional civil service mechanisms.

Criteria: Post-baccaulaureate; applications from women, minorities, Vietnam-era veterans, and the disabled are encouraged.

Financial Award: Salaries range from $25,039–$33,221, varying with education and appointment level

Deadline: Early April

Bunting Fellowship Program

The Bunting Institute of
Radciffe College
Fellowships Office
34 Concord Avenue
Cambridge, MA 02138
Phone: (617) 495-8212
Fax: (617) 459-8136

Field of Study: Arts, classics, music, theatre arts

Purpose of Fellowship: The support of women of exceptional promise and demonstrated accomplishment.

Criteria: Women scholars, researchers, creative writers, visual and performing artists. Scholars must have held Ph.D. or relevant terminal degree for at least 2 years prior to appointment. Need to have record of significant accomplishment. Artists must have had solo or group shows; writers, published works.

Financial Award: $33,000

Deadline: Mid-October

The Bunting Institute of Radcliffe College—Biomedical Research Fellowship Program

The Bunting Institute of
Radcliffe College
Fellowships Office
34 Concord Avenue
Cambridge, MA 02138
Phone: (617) 495-8212
Fax: (617) 495-8136

Field of Study: All fields of biomedical research

Purpose of Fellowship: To cover research expenses.

Criteria: Women scientists; U.S. citizens or permanent residents; must have held doctorate for two years prior to appointment.

Financial Award: $34,000, plus $3,000 in research expenses for a one-year appointment

Deadline: Mid-October

The Bunting Institute of Radcliffe College—Peace Fellowship

The Bunting Institute of
Radcliffe College
Fellowships Office
34 Concord Ave.
Cambridge, MA 02138
Phone: (617) 495-8212
Fax: (617) 495-8136

Field of Study: Open

Purpose of Fellowship: To support women actively involved in fostering peaceful solutions to conflict among groups or nations.

Criteria: Women committed to international or domestic policy studies that promote cooperative security, peace, and conflict resolution.

Financial Award: $30,000 for one year

Deadline: Mid-January

Career Advancement Scholarship Program

2012 Massachussetts Avenue, N.W.
Washington, DC 20036

Field of Study: Computer science, teacher preparation, paralegal studies

Purpose of Fellowship: To assist women seeking the education necessary for entry or re-entry into the work force, or advancement within a career field.

Criteria: Women who are U.S. citizens, 30 years of age or older, graduating within 12–24 months of date of grants. Applicants must demonstrate critical need for financial assistance (i.e., gross income for family of four must be $25,000 or less). Does not cover study at the doctoral level.

Financial Award: $500–$1,000

Deadline: Mid-April

Children's Hospital/Radcliffe College—Joint Fellowship on Family Violence (sponsored by NIMH)

The Bunting Institute of
Radcliffe College
Fellowships Office
34 Concord Avenue
Cambridge, MA 02138
Phone: (617) 495-8212
Fax: (617) 495-8136

Field of Study: Sociology, psychology, anthropology

Purpose of Fellowship: To bridge research and practice in the family violence field by offering opportunities for scholars to collaborate with clinicians and researchers on issues affecting the treatment of abused children and battered women.

Criteria: Doctoral degree in the above fields or in medicine, social work, or nursing; candidates must conduct research on issues related to family violence. Level of stipend is based on seven or more years of postdoctoral experience, according to a schedule established by NIMH.

Financial Award: $18,000–32,300

Deadline: Mid-January

Fellowship on Women and Public Policy

Michelle Forbes
Draper Hall, Room 302
Albany, NY 12222
Phone: (518) 442-3900

Field of Study: Open

Purpose of Fellowship: To encourage greater participation of women in the public policy process, develop public policy leaders, and encourage the formulation of state policy which recognizes and responds to the needs of women.

Criteria: Matriculated graduate students in New York state program. Applicant must have completed 12 credits of graduate work by May of the year prior to the application, with degree completion scheduled for the year of application or later. Background in research, employment, or volunteer activities designed to improve status of women.

Financial Award: $9,000 for seven-month period

Deadline: Late May

Forgivable Loan/Doctoral Incentive Program

CSU Office of the Chancellor
Forgivable Loan
400 Golden Shore, Suite 222
Long Beach, CA 90802-4275

Field of Study: Natural sciences, mathematics, computer science

Purpose of Fellowship: To increase the number of California State University faculty members who are minorities, women, and persons with disabilities.

Criteria: Full-time students enrolled or accepted into doctoral programs at accredited universities in the United States. Not required to have attended CSU. Applicants should be interested in filling instructional faculty positions at campuses of the California State University.

Financial Award: $10,000 per year, up to a total of $30,000

Deadline: Mid-February

Frances C. Allen Fellowships

Committee on Awards
The Newberry Library
60 W. Walton St.
Chicago, IL 60610-3310
Phone: (313) 943-9090, ext. 267

Field of Study: Open

Purpose of Fellowship: To assist women of Native American heritage in pursuing an academic program beyond the undergraduate degree.

Criteria: Candidates should be women of Native American heritage. Candidates may be working in any graduate or preprofessional field, but particularly in the humanities or social sciences.

Financial Award: Residency at McNickle Center for one month to a year; monthly stipend varies

Deadline: Early February

Geological Society of America Research Grants

Geological Society of America
P.O. Box 9140
Boulder, CA 80301
Phone: (303) 447-2020
Fax: (303) 447-1133

Field of Study: Open

Purpose of Fellowship: To provide partial support for master's and doctoral thesis research for graduate students at universities in the United States, Canada, Mexico, and Central America.

Criteria: GSA strongly encourages women, minorities, and people with disabilities to apply.

Financial Award: Up to $2,500

Deadline: Mid-February

Gertrude Fogelson Cultural Program in Creative Arts Awards

Alice Miller
American Mothers Inc.
1296 East 21st Street
Brooklyn, NY 1120
Phone: (718) 253-5676

Field of Study: All fields

Purpose of Fellowship: To encourage and honor mothers in artistic pursuits.

Criteria: Mothers demonstrating talents in visual arts, creative writing, and vocal music.

Financial Award: Up to $1,000

Deadline: Early January

Grace Legendre Fellowships

212 Mayro Building
239 Genesee St.
Utica, NY 13501

Field of Study: Open

Purpose of Fellowship: To support women in advanced graduate study at an accredited New York state college or university.

Criteria: Women who are residents of New York State and U.S. citizens, and who are within two years of completing an advanced graduate degree program at an accredited New York State college or university.

Financial Award: $1,000

Deadline: Late February

Henry A. Murray Research Center of Radcliffe College—Jeanne Humphrey Block Dissertation Award Program

Henry A. Murray Research
Center of Radcliffe College
10 Garden St.
Cambridge, MA 02138

Field of Study: Social and behavioral sciences; psychology

Purpose of Fellowship: To support graduate study of girls' or women's psychological development.

Criteria: Women doctoral students; proposals should focus on sex and gender differences or some developmental issue of particular concern to girls or women.

Financial Award: Up to $2,500 to cover research costs

Deadline: Early April

Holly A. Cornell Scholarship

Scholarship Coordinator
American Water Works Association
6666 W. Quincy Avenue
Denver, CO 80235
Phone: (303) 794-7711, ext. 6206

Field of Study: Sciences and engineering related to water supply industry

Purpose of Fellowship: To encourage and support outstanding female and/or minority students wishing to pursue advanced training in the field of water supply and treatment.

Criteria: Female and/or minority students who are currently master's students.

Financial Award: $5,000

Deadline: Mid-December

International Federation of University Women Fellowships and Grants Competition

37 Quai Wilson
CH-1201
Geneva, Switzerland
Phone: (41) (22) 731-2380
Fax: (41) (22) 738-0440

Field of Study: Open

Purpose of Fellowship: To support university women who wish to undertake research, study, or training in a country other than that in which the applicant received her education or in which she habitually resides.

Criteria: Applicants must be either a member of one of IFUW's 59 national federations or, in the case of women graduates living in countries where there is not yet a national affiliate, an independent member of IFUW.

Financial Award: Varies

Deadline: September

Joseph L. Fisher Dissertation Awards

1616 P Street, N.W.
Washington, DC 20036
Phone: (202) 328-5067

Field of Study: Economics; environmental and natural sciences

Purpose of Fellowship: To support doctoral dissertation research in economics on issues related to the environment, natural resources, or energy.

Criteria: Graduate students in the final year of their dissertation research. Fellowship candidates must have completed the preliminary examinations for the doctorate. Women and minorities are especially encouraged to apply.

Financial Award: $12,000

Deadline: Late April

Karla Scherer Foundation Scholarships

100 Renaissance Center
Suite 1680
Detroit, MI 48243
Phone: (313) 259-4520

Field of Study: Business, economics, finance

Purpose of Fellowship: To provide scholarships for women wishing to pursue business careers.

Criteria: Candidates must be women.

Financial Award: Unspecified

Deadline: Rolling

Lena Lake Forrest Fellowships

2012 Massachussetts Avenue, N.W.
Washington, DC 20036
Phone: (202) 293-1100

Field of Study: Humanities and social sciences

Purpose of Fellowship: To fund students engaged in contemporary and historical research in the U.S. on economic issues of importance to today's working women.

Criteria: Postdoctoral scholars or doctoral candidates who have completed all coursework and qualifying exams and are American citizens.

Financial Award: $500–$3,000

Deadline: January 1

Margaret McNamara Memorial Fund

1818 H Street, N.W.
Room G-1000
Washington, DC 20433
Phone: (202) 473-8751
Fax: (202) 676-0419

Field of Study: Open

Purpose of Fellowship: To strengthen the roles of women from developing countries.

Criteria: Women from developing countries with a record of service to women and/or children. Applicants must be planning to return to their countries within approximately two years of the grant date.

Financial Award: Up to $6,000

Deadline: Early February

Marian Cabot Putnam Fellowship

The Bunting Institute of
Radcliffe College
Fellowships Office
34 Concord Avenue
Cambridge, MA 02138
Phone: (617) 495-8212
Fax: (617) 495-8136

Field of Study: Human development and family studies, human services

Purpose of Fellowship: To aid in the research of infant and child development.

Criteria: Professional women in the field of infant and child development, conducting research within the framework of, or contributing to, psychoanalysis.

Financial Award: $33,000 for one year

Deadline: Mid-January

Mary Isabel Sibley Fellowship

The Phi Beta Kappa Society
1811 Q St., N.W.
Washington, DC 20009

Field of Study: French or Greek language, literature, or history

Purpose of Fellowship: To support dissertation or postgraduate research in the study of French or Greek language and literature (French in even years, Greek in odd years).

Criteria: Unmarried women between the ages of 25 and 35 who have fulfilled predissertation requirements for the Ph.D. or hold a doctorate and plan full-time research during the fellowship year. Not restricted to Phi Beta Kappa members.

Financial Award: $10,000

Deadline: Mid-January

Mary McEwen Schimke Scholarship

Career Center
Wellesley College
106 Central St.
Wellesley, MA 02181-8260

Field of Study: Open

Purpose of Fellowship: To provide a supplemental award to afford relief from household and child care while pursuing graduate study.

Criteria: Award made on basis of scholarly expectation and identified need.

Financial Award: Up to $1,000

Deadline: Mid-December

Monticello College Foundation Fellowship for Women

Committee on Awards
The Newberry Library
60 W. Walton St.
Chicago, IL 60610-3380

Field of Study: Any field appropriate to the Newberry Library's collections

Purpose of Fellowship: To assist women in the early stages in their professional careers whose work gives clear promise of scholarly productivity and whose careers would be significantly enhanced by six months of research and writing.

Criteria: Women possessing the Ph.D. who are U.S. citizens or permanent residents.

Financial Award: $12,500 for six months

Deadline: Mid-January

National Council of Administrative Women in Education—Women and Leadership Research Grant

Dr. Regina T. White
Committee 46
Woodledge Court
Rockaway, NJ 07866

Field of Study: Open

Purpose of Fellowship: Doctoral research addressing issues pertaining to either women in educational administration or the development of leadership skills among female students.

Criteria: Research must be completed and approved within one year prior to submission date.

Financial Award: $500 plus airfare to the annual NCAWE Conference

Deadline: Mid-January

National Federation of Press Women—Helen Miller Malloch Scholarship

National Federation of Press
Women Scholarships
Box 99
Blue Springs, MO 64013

Field of Study: Communications

Purpose of Fellowship: To support studies toward degrees or advancement in careers.

Criteria: Female juniors, seniors, or graduate students in communications. Recipients chosen on the basis of academic performance, career potential, and financial need.

Financial Award: $1,000

Deadline: Early May

Old Dominion University—President's Graduate Fellowship

Research and Graduate Studies
Old Dominion University
Norfolk, VA 23508-9989
Phone: (804) 683-3460

Field of Study: Open

Purpose of Fellowship: To increase the pool of women and minority faculty members who hold the Ph.D. degree at Old Dominion University.

Criteria: May be undergraduate or Master's level students and U.S. citizens; must be enrolled in or accepted into a graduate program leading to a terminal degree and nominated by the graduate program director.

Financial Award: Varies

Deadline: Early March

P.E.O. Sisterhood—International Peace Scholarship Fund

P.E.O. Executive Office
3700 Grand Ave.
Des Moines, IA 50312

Field of Study: Open

Purpose of Fellowship: To provide grants-in-aid for selected women from other countries for graduate study in the United States and Canada. Applicants must return to their own country upon completion of their degree programs.

Criteria: Applicants must be women qualified to admission to full-time graduate study, working toward graduate degrees in the United States or Canada. Citizens of the United States or Canada and doctoral students who have completed course work are ineligible.

Financial Award: Up to $5,000 for one year

Deadline: Late January

Science Scholars Fellowship Program

The Bunting Institute of
Radcliffe College
Fellowships Office
34 Concord Ave.
Cambridge, MA 02138
Phone: (617) 495-8212

Field of Study: Sciences, mathematics, engineering

Purpose of Fellowship: To cover research expenses for one year.

Criteria: Female U.S. citizens who have held a Ph.D. for two years prior to appointment.

Financial Award: $34,000 plus $3,000 in research expenses for one year

Deadline: Mid-October

Selected Professions Fellowships

AAUW Educational Foundation
Department 51
2201 N. Dodge St.
Iowa City, IA 52243-4030
Phone: (319) 337-1716, ext. 51

Field of Study: Business administration, law, medicine, architecture

Purpose of Fellowship: To support women in designated fields in which female participation has traditionally been low.

Criteria: Women who are U.S. citizens or permanent residents. Applicants in business administration, law, or medicine must be entering their final year of study. Applicants in architecture, sciences, engineering, or math must be in the final year of their master's degree.

Financial Award: $5,000–$9,000 stipend

Deadline: Call committee

Spencer T. Olin Fellowships for Women in Graduate Study

Graduate School of Arts
and Sciences
Washington University
Campus Box 1187
St. Louis, MO 63130-4899
Phone: (314) 935-6848

Field of Study: Open

Purpose of Fellowship: To encourage young women of exeptional promise to prepare for careers in higher education and the professions.

Criteria: Any female graduate or prospective graduate of a baccalaureate institution in the United States who plans to prepare for a career in higher education or the professions is eligible, provided she seeks to obtain the highest degree available in her chosen field through full-time study at Washington University.

Financial Award:
$20,000–$33,000

Deadline: Early February

University of California—President's Postdoctoral Fellowship Program

300 Lakeside Drive, 18th Floor
Oakland, CA 94612-3550
Phone: (510) 987-9500

Field of Study: Open

Purpose of Fellowship: To encourage outstanding minority and women Ph.D. recipients to pursue academic careers by offering postdoctoral research experiences that will help make them strong candidates for appointment at the University of California.

Criteria: U.S. citizens and permanent residents. Preference is given to minority and women candidates from historically underrepresented groups.

Financial Award:
$27,000–$29,000 stipend, health benefits, and up to $4,000 for supplemental and research-related expenses

Deadline: Early December

University of Colorado/ Boulder—Chancellor's Postdoctoral Fellowship Program for Academic Diversity

Box 26, University of Colorado
Boulder, CO 80309-0026
Phone: (303) 492-5773
E-mail:
barbara.kraus@colorado.edu

Field of Study: All disciplines represented at University of Colorado/Boulder

Purpose of Fellowship: To provide scholars with postdoctoral opportunities in all disciplines represented at University of Colorado/Boulder, plus mentoring and guidance in preparation for an academic career.

Criteria: Ph.D. within two years of the start of the appointment; U.S. citizen or permanent resident who is a member of an underrepresented group in higher education, or women in engineering, computer science, mathematics, and physical science fields.

Financial Award: $31,000 plus benefits and up to $2,000 for moving expenses

Deadline: Early December

William B. Ruggles Right to Work Scholarship

8001 Braddock Road
Suite 500
Springfield, VA 22160
Phone: (800) 325-7892

Field of Study: Journalism, communications, and related fields

Purpose of Fellowship: To support a student who exemplifies a dedication to principle and journalistic standards.

Criteria: Graduates or undergraduates in journalism programs in U.S. universities. Members of the National Right to Work Committee are not eligible.

Financial Award: $2,000

Deadline: Late March

Woodrow Wilson Women's Studies Research Grants for Doctoral Candidates

Department WS
CN 5281
Princeton, NJ 08543-5281
E-mail: maryh@wwnff.org

Field of Study: Open

Purpose of Fellowship: To encourage significant research about women.

Criteria: Students in doctoral programs who have completed all predissertation requirements at a graduate school in the United States.

Financial Award: $1,500 to be used for research expenses

Deadline: Late October

Study Abroad

13

One of the best reasons to consider applying for fellowships and grants is that if you choose the right one, you may earn yourself a ticket out of the United States. Certainly, leaving the friendly confines of home is not for everyone. But more students apply for fellowships and grants abroad than any other type available, and for good reason: The money is good, the awards span a wide range of fields, and the chance to learn about a whole new culture often proves too good an opportunity to pass up.

There are over 100 awards for study abroad that send recipients to literally dozens of country across the globe. Some of these opportunities offer students their choice of countries, but the majority are specific to one particular location. The Fulbright Award, for example, allows recipients to study in almost any country in the world, whereas a prize such as the Flemish Community Research Fellowship requires that students study in Flanders, Belgium.

Any number of fields are covered by these types of awards. If you are familiar with the Rhodes Scholarship, you know that recipients have the latitude to study anything from chemistry to Chaucer once they make it to Oxford. However, the majority of opportunities focus on:

- Language study
- Area studies (including culture, history, economics, and government)
- International relations

How to Prepare

The grand majority of the fellowships and grants listed in this chapter send recipients to foreign countries whose official language is not English. This proves to be the point when many potential applicants realize that applying for study abroad fellowships isn't their cup of tea. It also means that if you're applying for an award in one of these countries, you'd better know a good deal about its language, culture, and customs.

Of course, there's no better way to gain this experience than to have traveled to the country before. But for many students, such an excursion is a financial impossibility. This is not to say, however, that all is lost for individuals in this boat. Regardless of whether you've been to the country before or not, what fellowship committees really want to see is that you'll be able to fend for yourself once you step off the plane and have that first conversation in a foreign tongue.

The unique thing about applying for most foreign fellowships and grants is that unlike almost all others, candidates don't have to have their whole life planned out before they're ready to fill out the form. This gives students the chance to really sit down with the list of awards and really pick and choose.

However, this doesn't mean that any old Joe can win the award of his choice. Most successful applicants have studied the languages of their target countries for prolonged periods of time and have come up with project proposals that are applicable to these countries. It would probably be a mistake, for example, to submit a plan to study the history of salsa dancing in Sweden. Knowing your target country's traditions and heritage—even if you've never been there—is the best way to impress award committees.

American Institute of Indian Studies Advanced Language Programs in India

American Institute of Indian Studies
1130 East 59th Street
Chicago, IL 60637
Phone: (312) 702-8638

Field of Study: Languages

Purpose of Fellowship: To support language instruction in Hindi, Tamil, and Bengali for 9 months during the academic year or 10 weeks during the summer.

Criteria: Students at U.S. universities with at least two years of study in the language are eligible, except that students with one year of language may apply for the summer programs in Bengali and Tamil only.

Financial Award: Round-trip airfare, tuition, stipend to cover living expenses

Deadline: Late December

American Research Center in Egypt—Egyptian Graduate Student Fellowships

The American Research Center in Egypt
50 Washington Square South
New York, NY 10012
Phone: (212) 998-8890
Fax: (212) 995-4144

Field of Study: Economics, development studies, health, education

Purpose of Fellowship: Awards given to doctoral dissertation proposals that have direct relevance to the economic and social development of Egypt or that prompt thinking on current policy issues relating to development.

Criteria: Graduate students who have completed all requirements for the doctoral degree except the dissertation. Must be currently enrolled in a graduate program in the United States or Canada and have J1 or F1 student visas.

Financial Award: International airfare, living stipend, allowance for research expenses

Deadline: Early November

American School for Classical Studies at Athens—Samuel H. Kress Joint Athens/Jerusalem Fellowship

993 Lenox Drive, Suite 101
Lawrenceville, NJ 08648
Phone: (609) 844-7577
Fax: (609) 844-7524

Field of Study: Archaeology, art history, architecture, classical cultures

Purpose of Fellowship: To enable doctoral students to do research in Greece and Israel in the same academic year in order to promote a better understanding of the interrelationships between ancient cultures of the Aegean and the Near East.

Criteria: Open to U.S. citizens who are doctoral candidates in the above fields. The fellowship period should be continuous without frequent trips outside Greece or Israel.

Financial Award: $5,500 stipend

Deadline: Mid-November

Awards for Study in Scandinavia

American-Scandinavian Foundation
725 Park Avenue
New York, NY 10012
Phone: (212) 879-9779
Fax: (212) 249-3444

Field of Study: Open

Purpose of Fellowship: To encourage ties between the United States and Scandinavia by assisting individuals to pursue research or study in one or more Scandinavian countires for up to one year.

Criteria: U.S. citizens or permanent residents who have completed their undergraduate education prior to starting their projects in Scandinavia. Proposals should consist of a well-defined research or study project that makes a stay in Scandinavia essential.

Financial Award: $3,000–$15,000

Deadline: Early November

Berkeley Professional Studies Program in India—M.A./Ph. D. Internships

Linnea Soderlund
University of California/Berkeley
160 Stephens Hall
Berkeley, CA 94720
Phone: (510) 642-1356
E-mail:
eapucb@uclink.berkeley.edu

Field of Study: Open

Purpose of Fellowship: To provide nine months of interdisciplinary study in India for graduate students in professional programs.

Criteria: U.S. citizens or permanent residents with professional interests who are enrolled in graduate programs and have completed at least one year of graduate work.

Financial Award: Living allowance for nine months, health insurance, project-related travel within India, language tutoring and orientation

Deadline: Late January

Bundeskanzler Scholarships for Germany

1350 Connecticut Avenue, N.W.
Suite 903
Washington, DC 20036
Phone: (202) 296-2990
Fax: (202) 833-8514

Field of Study: Germanic studies, history, economics, government

Purpose of Fellowship: To provide the opportunity to continue or follow up studies and/or research, and to gain substantial insight into the political, economic, social, and cultural life of Germany.

Criteria: U.S. citizens who are undergraduate, graduate, or postgraduate students, or young professionals who are generally 30 years old or less.

Financial Award: Monthly allowance for housing and living expenses between 2,500–5,500 deutschmarks, travel expenses, and language courses

Deadline: Late October

Canada Mortgage and Housing Corporation University Scholarship

Canada Mortgage and Housing Corporation
700 Montreal Road
Ottawa, ONT K1A OP7
Phone: (613) 748-2249
Fax: (613) 748-2402

Field of Study: Open

Purpose of Fellowship: To encourage highly capable and promising Canadians to specialize in the fields of housing and community planning. Scholarships are for full-time graduate study at Canadian or other universities.

Criteria: Candidates must be Canadian citizens or must have obtained permanent resident status in Canada and be full-time graduate students seeking a master's degree during the time they hold the scholarship.

Financial Award: Up to $14,154

Deadline: Late March

Chiang Ching-kuo Foundation Grants for Chinese Studies

Office of Fellowships and Grants
American Council of Learned Societies
228 E. 45th Street
New York, NY 1001-3398
Fax: (212) 949-8058

Field of Study: Chinese culture or society

Purpose of Fellowship: Dissertation research in any country outside the United States with the exception of the People's Republic of China. The dissertation must be related to China, although it may be comparative in nature.

Criteria: Candidates must be full-time doctoral candidates, enrolled in U.S. institutions.

Financial Award: $15,000 stipend for one year

Deadline: Call committee

Council for European Studies—Predissertation Fellowships

1509 International Affairs
Building
Columbia University
New York, NY 10027

Field of Study: Anthropology, economics, history, geography, political science

Purpose of Fellowship: To enable graduate students to pursue short-term, exploratory research in Western or Southern Europe in order to determine the viability and to better define the scope of their proposed dissertations.

Criteria: U.S. or Canadian citizens or permanent residents enrolled in a doctoral program; must have completed two years of full-time graduate study (or its equivalent) prior to beginning research.

Financial Award: $2,500 for travel and living expenses

Deadline: February

Delft University of Technology Research Fellowship

College van Dekanen
Delft University of Technology
Julianalaan 134
2628 BL Delft
The Netherlands
Phone: (31) 15 784631
Fax: (31) 15 783100

Field of Study: Mathematics, architecture, sciences

Purpose of Fellowship: To encourage international scientific contacts by offering a limited number of research fellowships to young scientists and graduate students at the Delft University of Technology.

Criteria: Applicants must have completed their Ph.D. work or must possess a Master's degree in engineering or science and have at least one additional year of experience in research.

Financial Award: 3,000 Dfl. per month

Deadline: Late January

Dumbarton Oaks Prize Fellowships

Assistant Director
Dumbarton Oaks Library
1703 32nd Street, N.W.
Washington, DC 20007

Field of Study: Byzantine studies

Purpose of Fellowship: To support one year of research abroad.

Criteria: Candidates must wish to spend one year deepening their knowledge and understanding of Byzantine culture; not intended to support dissertation research or writing.

Financial Award: $15,000

Deadline: Early November

East-West Center Graduate Fellowships

Room 2066
1777 East-West Rd
Honolulu, HI 96848
Phone: (808) 944-7735
Fax: (808) 944-7730

Field of Study: Open

Purpose of Fellowship: To promote better relations and understanding between the United States and the nations of Asia and the Pacific through cooperative study, training, and research.

Criteria: Students who are at the Ph.D. dissertation stage. Awards are available for two years. After an initial period of residency at the Center in Honolulu, the fellow may spend up to one year of research in the field.

Financial Award: Unspecified

Deadline: Early November

East-West Center Joint-Doctoral Research Fellowships

Room 2066
1777 East-West Rd
Honolulu, HI 96848
Phone: (808) 944-7735
Fax: (808) 944-7730

Field of Study: Open

Purpose of Fellowship: To promote better relations and understanding between the United States and the nations of Asia and the Pacific through cooperative study, training, and research.

Criteria: Students who are at the Ph.D. dissertation stage. Awards are available for two years. After an initial period of residency at the Center in Honolulu, the fellow may spend up to one year of research in the field.

Financial Award: Round-trip airfare to Honolulu, monthly stipend, shared office space, health insurance, housing

Deadline: Early December

European Space Agency Fellowship Programme

European Space Agency
8, 10, rue Mario Nikis
75738 Paris
Cedex 15, France

Field of Study: Space sciences, mathematics

Purpose of Fellowship: To provide opportunities for experienced research scientists and engineers to undertake research in space sciences, space applications, or spacecraft technology. Fellowships are granted for European research groups active in the ESA or national space programs, and at ESA establishments.

Criteria: ESA fellowships are open to nationals of ESA member states (Austria, Belgium, Denmark, France, Germany, Ireland, Italy, Netherlands, Norway, Spain, Sweden, Switzerland, and United Kingdom); may not be used in candidate's own country.

Financial Award: Unspecified fixed stipend plus travel expenses and partial insurance coverage

Deadline: Late September

Fellowship in Landscape Architecture at the American Academy in Rome

American Academy in Rome
7 E. 60th Street
New York, NY 10022-1001
Phone: (212) 751-7200
Fax: (212) 751-7220

Field of Study: Landscape architecture

Purpose of Fellowship: To provide American landscape architects with the opportunity for advanced study, travel, and association with fellows and professors at the American Academy in Rome.

Criteria: Candidates must be American landscape architects.

Financial Award: Unspecified

Deadline: Mid-November

Flemish Community Graduate Fellowships

3330 Garfield Street, N.W.
Belgian Embassy
Washington, DC 20008
Phone: (202) 333-6900
Fax: (202) 342-8346

Field of Study: Open

Purpose of Fellowship: To support students with a record of academic excellence who want to study in Flanders for an entire academic year.

Criteria: Candidates must be U.S. citizens under 35 and hold a bachelor's or master's degree. Fellowship recipients cannot have other Belgian sources of income.

Financial Award: Monthly stipend of 23,000 Belgian francs; tuition up to 17,000 BF; a one-time 25,000 BF stipend

Deadline: Early March

Flemish Community Research Fellowships

3330 Garfield Street, N.W.
Belgian Embassy
Washington, DC 20008
Phone: (202) 333-6900
Fax: (202) 342-8346

Field of Study: Open

Purpose of Fellowship: To support students with a record of academic excellence who want to pursue short-term research in Flanders.

Criteria: Candidates must hold a master's or doctorate degree. Fellowship recipients cannot have other Belgian sources of income.

Financial Award: Monthly stipend of 22,000 Belgian francs; 5,000 BF to cover installation costs for grantees staying in Flanders for one month or more

Deadline: Early March

Fondation Des Etats-Unis—Harriet Hale Woolley Scholarships

The Director, Harriet Hale
Woolley Scholarships
Fondation des Etats-Unis
15 Blvd. Jourdan
75 690 Paris
Cedex 14 France

Field of Study: Art and music

Purpose of Fellowship: To support the study of art and music in Paris.

Criteria: Applicants must be U.S. citizens 21–29 years old who demonstrate artistic or musical accomplishment, good moral character, personality, adaptability, physical health, and emotional stability. Project must be approved by the Fondation director and should include enrollment in a recognized school or private instruction.

Financial Award: 8,500 French francs for one academic year

Deadline: Late January

Fulbright Fellowships

Institute of International
Education
809 United Nations Plaza
New York, NY 10017-3580
Phone: (212) 883-8200

Field of Study: Open

Purpose of Fellowship: To foster mutual understanding among nations through educational and cultural exchanges. The program enables U.S. students to benefit from unique resources and gain international competence in an increasingly interdependent world. Recipients are sent to over 100 countries around the world. The Institute of International Education works with the U.S. government.

Criteria: Candidates may be U.S. citizens or citizens of other nations. Graduating seniors, young professionals, artists, and graduate students are eligible. Preference will be given to applicants who have completed most of their education in the United States. Applicants must hold a B.A. or the equivalent before the beginning date of the grant. Applicants may not hold a doctoral degree at the time of application.

Students enrolled in a U.S. institution at the time of application must apply through the Fulbright Program Adviser on their campus. Others should contact the Institute of International Education.

There is a single application for for all types of grants. When reviewing application materials, the Fulbright National Screening Committee pays particular attention to the Statement of Proposed Study, the Curriculum Vitae essay, and the future career plans of the candidate.

Financial Award: Varies with award and country

Deadline: October 23

Fulbright Scholar Program—Lecture and Research Award Openings

3007 Tilden Street, N.W.
Suite 5M
Box UPD
Washington, DC 20008-3009

Field of Study: Varies with award

Purpose of Fellowship: To promote international exchange of scholars in various disciplines.

Criteria: American citizens with appropriate qualifications for specific awards or teaching assignments.

Financial Award: Unspecified monthly stipend and round-trip travel

Deadline: Varies

Garden Club of America—Awards in Tropical Botany

World Wildlife Fund
1250 24th St. N.W.
Washington, DC 20037-1175
Phone: (202) 778-9714
Fax: (202) 293-9211

Field of Study: Tropical botany

Purpose of Fellowship: To promote the preservation of tropical forests by enlarging the body of botanists with field expertise.

Criteria: Ph.D. students at American universities, conducting field research in tropical botany.

Financial Award: $5,500

Deadline: December 31

Geological Society of America Research Grants

Geological Society of America
P.O. Box 9140
Boulder, CA 80301
Phone: (303) 447-2020
Fax: (303) 447-1133

Field of Study: Open

Purpose of Fellowship: To provide partial support for master's and doctoral thesis research for graduate students at universities in the United States, Canada, Mexico, and Central America.

Criteria: GSA strongly encourages women, minorities, and people with disabilities to apply.

Financial Award: Up to $2,500

Deadline: Mid-February

Gilbert Chinard Fellowships

Institut Français de Washington,
Department of Romance Languages
CB #3170
Chapel Hill, NC 27599

Field of Study: French history, literature, art and music

Purpose of Fellowship: To support scholars undertaking research in France. Award supports maintenance (not travel) for periods of at least two months.

Criteria: Applicants must be in final stages of Ph.D. dissertations or have held the Ph.D. no longer than six years before application deadline. Upon return, the awardee will send a brief report to the Institut.

Financial Award: $1,000

Deadline: Mid-January

Institute for Advanced Studies in the Humanities—University of Edinburgh Fellowships on the European Enlightenment

University of Edinburgh
Hope Park Square
Edinburgh, Scotland
Phone: (44) (131) 650-4671
Fax: (44) (131) 668-2252
E-mail: IASH@ed.ac.uk

Field of Study: Open

Purpose of Fellowship: To encourage 100 leading scholars from any discipline whose work concerns the European enlightenment to pursue research at the Institute.

Criteria: Open to degree holders who wish to pursue research individually or collaboratively. The academic record and publications of all applicants will be considered.

Financial Award: No stipend

Deadline: Late December

Institute for Advanced Studies in the Humanities—University of Edinburgh Visiting Research Fellowships

University of Edinburgh
Hope Park Square
Edinburgh, Scotland
Phone: (44) (131) 650-4671
Fax: (44) (131) 668-2252
E-mail: IASH@ed.ac.uk

Field of Study: Humanities and social sciences

Purpose of Fellowship: To promote enquiry of the highest standards in the humanities. Emphasis placed on the issues of medical ethics, business ethics, and environmental ethics.

Criteria: Postgraduate students who demonstrate the need to pursue research in Edinburgh.

Financial Award: Up to 500 pounds

Deadline: Early December

Inter-American Foundation—Field Research Programs at the Doctoral and Master's Levels

901 N. Stuart Street, 10th Floor
Dept. 555
Arlington, VA 22203

Field of Study: Grassroots development topics

Purpose of Fellowship: To support field research in independent Latin American and Caribbean countries (except Cuba, Puerto Rico, the Virgin Islands, or the Netherlands Antilles) on grassroots development topics by graduate students enrolled in U.S. universities.

Criteria: Applicants must be enrolled in U.S. universities and write and speak the local language.

Financial Award: Doctoral awards: $14,000–$18,000 for 18 months; master's awards: $2,000–$3,000 for six months

Deadline: Call committee

Inter-American Press Association Scholarship

Inter-American Press Association
One Herald Plaza
Miami, FL 33132-1639
Phone: (305) 376-3522

Field of Study: Journalism

Purpose of Fellowship: To support young newspaper reporters who wish to study in and report from Latin America for a period of six to nine months.

Criteria: Candidates must be between 21 and 35 years old, citizens of Canada or the United States, hold a bachelor's degree, and be fluent in Spanish, Portuguese, or French.

Financial Award: $10,000

Deadline: Call committee

Interchange Fellowship in Horticulture and Landscape Design

Garden Club of America
598 Madison Avenue
New York, NY 10022
Phone: (212) 753-8287
Fax: (212) 753-0134

Field of Study: Horticulture, botany, landscape architecture

Purpose of Fellowship: To foster British-American relations through the interchange of scholars in fields related to horticulture. The scholarship allows an American student to undertake a work-study program in the United Kingdom.

Criteria: Applicants must live or attend school in either Connecticut, Maine, Massachussetts, New Hampshire, New York, Rhode Island, or Vermont.

Financial Award: Cost of tuition, travel expenses, board, lodging, and incidental college expenses, as well as an allowance for personal needs

Deadline: Mid-November

International Dissertation and Advanced Research Fellowships

Social Science Research Council
605 3rd Avenue
New York, NY 10158
Phone: (212) 557-9508

Field of Study: Social sciences and humanities

Purpose of Fellowship: To advance interdisciplinary social science research related to international issues. Scholarships are devoted to world area studies and issues of global concern.

Criteria: Doctoral or postdoctoral candidates who have completed all requirements for the Ph.D. except the dissertation. Some area programs restrict awards to U.S. citizens. For some awards, applicants must be enrolled or affiliated with a U.S. institution.

Financial Award: Two- to twelve-month stipend (varies with fellowships), which includes maintenance, transportation, and research-related expenses.

Deadline: Call committee

International Federation of University Women Fellowships and Grants Competition

IFUW Headquarters
8 rue de l'Ancien Port
CH-1201 Geneva
Switzerland
Phone: (41) (22) 731-2380
Fax: (41) (22) 738-0440

Field of Study: Open

Purpose of Fellowship: To support university women who wish to undertake research, study, or training in countries other than that in which they received their education or in which they habitually reside.

Criteria: Applicants must be either a member of one of IFUW's 59 national federations or associations or, in the case of women graduates living in countries where there is not yet a national affiliate, an independent member of IFUW.

Financial Award: Varies

Deadline: Early September

James Harrison Steedman Memorial Fellowship in Architecture

School of Architecture
Washington University
Campus Box 1079
One Brookings Dr.
St. Louis, MO 63130-4899

Field of Study: Architecture

Purpose of Fellowship: To assist well-qualified architectural graduates who wish to travel and study architecture in foreign countries.

Criteria: Open on equal terms to all graduates in architecture in accredited schools. Candidates must have at least one year of practical experience in the office of a practicing architect.

Financial Award: $20,000, not including travel and lodging expenses

Deadline: Early December

Japan Foundation Doctoral Fellowship

152 West 57th Street
39th Floor
New York, NY 10019
Phone: (212) 489-0299
Fax: (212) 489-0409

Field of Study: Humanities and social sciences

Purpose of Fellowship: To support dissertation research in Japan.

Criteria: Doctoral candidate who has completed all requirements except dissertation and who has the necessary Japanese language skills to undertake research in Japan.

Financial Award: 310,000 yen monthly stipend for 4–14 months, plus additional allowances

Deadline: Early November

Japan Foundation Research Fellowship

152 West 57th Street
39th Floor
New York, NY 10019
Phone: (212) 489-0299
Fax: (212) 489-0409

Field of Study: Humanities and social sciences

Purpose of Fellowship: To support scholars, researchers, and professionals who wish to conduct research in Japan for periods ranging from 2–12 months.

Criteria: Scholars should hold an academic position in a research institution and have substantial research, teaching, and writing experience in their respective fields of study. Applications from researchers or professionals with equivalent research or analytical experience are also eligible.

Financial Award: Two- to twelve-month award, 370,000–430,000 yen monthly stipend, plus additional allowances

Deadline: Early November

Jennings Randolph Program for International Peace

1550 M Street, N.W.
Suite 700
Washington, DC 20005-1708
Phone: (202) 457-1706
Fax: (202) 429-6063

Field of Study: Humanities and social sciences

Purpose of Fellowship: To increase understanding about international peace and conflict management.

Criteria: People from any country who have specific interest or experience in international peace and conflict management, and who have an undergraduate degree from a recognized university.

Financial Award: $13,000

Deadline: Mid-November

Kate Neal Kinley Memorial Fellowship

110 Architecture Building
University of Illinois
608 Taft Drive
Champaign, IL 61820

Field of Study: Architecture, fine art, music

Purpose of Fellowship: To defray expenses of advanced study of fine art in America or abroad.

Criteria: College graduates who have studied art, architecture, or music; preference is given to applicants under 25 years of age.

Financial Award: Up to $7,000

Deadline: Mid-February

Kenan T. Erim Award

Archaeological Institute of America
Boston University
656 Beacon St.
Boston, MA 02215-2010
Phone: (617) 353-6000
Fax: (617) 353-6000
E-mail: aia@bu.edu

Field of Study: Archaeology, art history

Purpose of Fellowship: To support research scholars working on Aphrodisial material.

Criteria: Open to American or international research scholars. If the project involves work at Aphrodisias, candidates must submit written approval from the field director with their applications.

Financial Award: $4,000

Deadline: Mid-November

Lady Davis Fellowship Trust

P.O. Box 1255
Jerusalem, Israel
Phone: (972) 2-663-848
Fax: (972) 2-663-848

Field of Study: All fields

Purpose of Fellowship: To support, study, research, and teaching in Israel at Hebrew University of Jerusalem or the Technion-Israel Institute of Technology—study at the graduate level, research at the postdoctoral level, and teaching at the professional level.

Criteria: Intended for students in a doctoral program abroad (preference given to Canadians) who wish to use library and research facilities in Israel. Postdoctoral candidates may apply no later than three years after completing dissertation.

Financial Award: Travel costs, tuition fees (where applicable), and a monthly stipend.

Deadline: November 30

Leo Baeck Institute—DAAD Fellowships

Leo Baeck Institute
129 East 73 Street
New York, NY 10021
Phone: (212) 744-6400

Field of Study: Social, communal, and intellectual history of Germany

Purpose of Fellowship: To assist doctoral students and recent Ph.D.'s in research that requires time in libraries, archives or research institutions in the Federal Republic of Germany.

Criteria: U.S. citizens. Ph.D. candidates not older than 32; recent Ph.D.'s not older than 35.

Financial Award: Funds for research; stipend of DM 1,490 per month; one-time sum of DM 1,000 for travel

Deadline: November 1

Luigi Einaudi Graduate Fellowships

The Institute for European Studies
120 Uris Hall
Cornell University
Ithaca, NY 14853
Phone: (607) 255-7592

Field of Study: Modern European government, history, economics

Purpose of Fellowship: To enable graduate students to conduct field and archival dissertation research in Europe for one year.

Criteria: Cornell graduate students who have completed the "A" exam, or have dates scheduled prior to departure, and have dissertation projects approved by their special committee.

Financial Award: Cost of in absentia fees, travel, and a stipend of $14,600

Deadline: March 1

Manon Michele Einaudi Summer Research Grant

The Institute for European Studies
120 Uris Hall
Cornell University
Ithaca, NY 14853
Phone: (607) 255-7592

Field of Study: Modern European art and architecture, art history

Purpose of Fellowship: To enable a graduate student to conduct European-based, exploratory, predissertation graduate research during the summer.

Criteria: Cornell graduate students who need to conduct research in Europe, and who have been recommended by their faculty committees.

Financial Award: Unspecified

Deadline: February 23

Mario Einaudi Fellowship

Institute for European Studies
120 Uris Hall
Cornell University
Ithaca, NY 14853
Phone: (607) 255-7592

Field of Study: Social sciences, history, or philosophy

Purpose of Fellowship: To support young American or Italian scholars whose research reflects Mario Einaudi's goal of interpreting the United States to Europe and Europe to the United States.

Criteria: American or Italian scholars, alternate years. Open to advanced graduate students and postdoctoral scholars who plan to spend an academic year in Europe, preferably but not necessarily in Italy.

Financial Award: $25,000 designed to cover a further semester for write-up of research results.

Deadline: January 15

Matsumae International Foundation Research Award

The Matsumae International Foundation
Ninth Floor
Shinjuku Tokai Building
3-27-4 Shinjuku
Tokyo, Japan
Phone: (81) (3) 5379-30610
Fax: (81) (3) 5379-3120

Field of Study: Natural sciences, engineering, medicine

Purpose of Fellowship: To invite non-Japanese researchers to conduct research in Japan for three to six months to promote peace throughout the world.

Criteria: Applicants must hold a degree similar to the Japanese doctorate or have 2 years experience after the master's; must be under 40 years of age; have conversational ability in English or Japanese; should not have been to Japan previously. Applicants from developing countries encouraged.

Financial Award: Travel to Japan; 300,000 yen upon arrival; a stipend of 200,000 yen monthly; accident and health insurance.

Deadline: July 31

Metropolitan Museum of Art—Theodore Rousseau Fellowships

Pia Quintano
Theodore Rousseau Fellowship
The Metropolitan Museum of Art
1000 Fifth Avenue
New York, NY 10028

Field of Study: Art history

Purpose of Fellowship: To train students whose goal is to enter museums as curators of painting. This award is intended to develop the skills of connoisseurship by supporting first-hand examination of paintings in major European collections, rather than by supporting library research.

Criteria: Applicants must have completed at least one year of an advanced degree program.

Financial Award: 3-month and 12-month fellowships to support study in Europe; stipend of $18,000 for 12 months and travel

Deadline: November 1

Michele Sicca Research Grants

Institute for European Studies
20 Uris Hall
Cornell University
Ithaca, NY 14853
Phone: (607) 255-7592

Field of Study: Social sciences and the humanities

Purpose of Fellowship: To support European-based research in either a comparative or historical framework focusing on economic, social, and political developments in modern Europe. Research in the humanities will also be considered.

Criteria: Candidates must be Cornell graduate students.

Financial Award: $900 to $1,500

Deadline: February 23

Monbusho Scholarship

Consulate General of Japan
in New York
299 Park Avenue
New York, NY 10171
Phone: (212) 371-8222

Field of Study: Humanities, social sciences, and natural sciences

Purpose of Fellowship: To support research on a broad range of research topics at the graduate level in Japanese universities and educational institutions.

Criteria: U.S. citizens under the age of 35 who have obtained a four-year degree and demonstrated proficiency in the Japanese language and potential to receive instruction.

Financial Award: Round-trip airfare, exemption from all school fees, arrival allowance of 25,000 yen, stipend of 180,500 yen per month

Deadline: Late August

National Endowment for the Humanities Fellowships for Research in Turkey

American Research Institute in Turkey
c/o University of Pennsylvania Museum
33rd and Spruce Streets
Philadelphia, PA 19104
Phone: (215) 898-3474
Fax: (215) 898-0657

Field of Study: Humanities

Purpose of Fellowship: To support up to one year of post-doctoral research in Turkey.

Criteria: Advanced graduate students or degree recipients engaged in research on Turkey in ancient medieval or modern times.

Financial Award: Stipends ranging from $10,000 to $30,000 are made available on the basis of individual proposals.

Deadline: November 15

Rome Prize Fellowship

American Academy in Rome
Programs Department
7 E. 60th Street
New York, NY 10022-1001
Phone: (212) 751-7200

Field of Study: Fine arts, classical studies, humanities

Purpose of Fellowship: To enable fellows to pursue artistic and intellectual endeavors at the Academy in Rome, Italy, and to foster interdisciplinary exchange.

Criteria: Open to U.S. citizens and permanent residents; up to 29 fellowships are awarded annually.

Financial Award: Stipends from $9,000 to $17,800, generally awarded over one-year period; residential accommodations; meals; studies or studios in which to pursue work

Deadline: November 15

Scuola Normale Superiore Doctoral Scholarships

Director, Scuola Normale
Superiore
Piazza dei Cavalieri
7, 56100
Pisa, Italy
Phone: (39) (50) 509237
Fax: (39) (50) 563513

Field of Study: Humanities, modern philology and linguistics, art

Purpose of Fellowship: To support non-Italians in the humanities who wish to enroll in a three-year, doctoral program at the Scuola Normale Superiore.

Criteria: Non-Italians who have graduated at most two years before applying and who are under 30 years of age.

Financial Award: Free board and lodging during the academic year, plus 11,460,000 lira annually

Deadline: Early November

Summer Fellowships and Grants

14

Contrary to popular belief, there is a difference between internships and summer fellowships. Whereas internships usually provide on-the-job training at a specific work site, summer fellowships can be thought of as "baby" fellowships. The money's not quite as much and the duration of payment is considerably shorter, but the overall goal is the same—to provide funding for academic projects or research.

The summer fellowships listed in this section cover virtually all the fields mentioned in the previous nine chapters. If you look closely enough, you'll probably find that there's something here for you.

Beating the Clock

The key difference between summer and year-long fellowships is the issue of time. It plays a role the whole way through, from the application process to the end of the fellowship's duration. For this reason, deadlines are crucial: Blink, and you may either have missed the due date for your application form or misjudged the amount of time you needed to complete your project in a timely fashion.

The majority of the applications for summer fellowships are due shortly after the New Year, but they span all the way from November of the year preceding the fellowship to March of the fellowship's year. Unlike year-long awards, which generally start in early fall, the window for a recipient to make his decision on a summer fellowship is extremely small. This means that organization is a must.

If you are set on landing a summer fellowship, make sure you prioritize the awards to which you have applied so that you can make a quick decision once you've heard from all of the fellowship-issuing organizations. There is a very short period between school's end and the beginning of your fellowship, especially if you are just completing an academic year. Make sure you give yourself enough time to adjust and settle in.

One of the pitfalls of making a rough adjustment is that you lose the precious time you need to complete your project. The majority of summer fellowships last no longer than eight weeks, which means that you have a great deal to do in a short period. So it's a good idea to have thoroughly mapped out your plan before beginning the project; this is best accomplished by writing a very detailed proposal for your application. Committees are looking for students who have demonstrated the ability to complete a substantive project in a short span of time. This puts the onus on the candidate to write a stellar proposal, and makes this the most important part of the entire application.

American Institute for Economic Research

Assistant to the Director
American Institute for Economic Research
Great Barrington, MA 01230
Phone: (413) 528-1216
Fax: (413) 528-0103

This fellowship has been temporarily discontinued for the year 1997–1998. Please contact the Institute for information on its availability in 1999 and subsequent years.

Field of Study: Economics and closely related fields

Purpose of Fellowship: To share with students of economics some view they may not otherwise encounter during their formal education and, in the process, to subject the ideas of the members of the American Institute for Economic Research to the criticisms of award recipients.

Criteria: Most summer fellows are graduate students who are enrolled in U.S. colleges and universities. They range in age from 20 to 35 years, and are working on graduate degrees in economics.

Students enrolled in foreign universities are ineligible for this award, although foreign students may participate if they are accepted by or enrolled in an American university.

Financial Award: The Institute finances an eight-week period of study with room and board at the Institute; $125 per week stipend

Deadline: Late March

American Institute of Indian Studies Advanced Languages Programs in India

American Institute of Indian Studies
1130 East 59th Street
Chicago, IL 60637
Phone: (312) 702-8638

Field of Study: Languages

Purpose of Fellowship: To support language instruction in Hindi, Tamil, and Bengali for 9 months during the academic year or 10 weeks during the summer.

Criteria: Students at U.S. universities with at least two years of study in the languages are eligible, except that students with one year of language may apply for the summer programs in Bengali and Tamil only.

Financial Award: Nine month program: round-trip airfare, tuition, stipend for living expenses; ten-week program: airfare plus tuition

Deadline: Late December

Berkshire Summer Fellowship

Berkshire Summer Fellowship Program
34 Concord Avenue
Cambridge, MA 02138
Phone: (617) 495-8212
Fax: (617) 495-8136

Field of Study: History

Purpose of Fellowship: To support women historians, particularly junior scholars, who normally do not have access to Boston-area resources.

Criteria: Women historians at the postdoctoral level working in any field of history.

Financial Award: $3,000

Deadline: Mid-January

College of William and Mary—Multicultural Teaching Fellows Program

Multicultural Teaching Fellows Program
P.O. Box 8795
Williamsburg, VA 23187-8795
Phone: (804) 221-2615
Fax: (804) 221-2614

Field of Study: Open

Purpose of Fellowship: To provide minority undergraduate students the opportunity to teach during summer sessions at the College of William and Mary, allow faculty to evaluate the fellows for future employment at the institution, and to enhance the educational experience of William and Mary students.

Criteria: Students must be entering the final year of terminal degree programs or have received terminal degrees and be preparing to be college faculty. Fellows teach one course during a five- or six-week term.

Financial Award: $3,500

Deadline: Call committee

DAAD—Summer Language Courses in Germany

950 Third Avenue
19th Floor
New York, NY 10022
Phone: (212) 758-3223
Fax: (212) 755-5780
E-mail: daadny@acf2.nyu.edu

Field of Study: Open

Purpose of Fellowship: To support German language study at 3-week, 6-week, and 8-week summer institutes.

Criteria: College juniors, seniors and graduate students enrolled as full-time students. Applicants must have completed three to four semesters of college-level German.

Financial Award: Course fees, living expenses, room, and partial board

Deadline: Late January

Dumbarton Oaks Summer Fellowships

Office of the Director
Dumbarton Oaks Library
1703 32nd Street N.W.
Washington, DC 20007

Field of Study: Byzantine studies, Precolombian studies

Purpose of Fellowship: To assist students in conducting important research in areas offered by the Library.

Criteria: Fellowship accepts students of any level.

Financial Award: $150 per week, plus housing and other expenses

Deadline: Early November

Edna Bailey Sussman Environmental Internships

For information, contact:
Joanne Bordonaro
Director of Graduate Fellowships and Financial Aid
143B Caldwell Hall
Cornell University
Ithaca, NY 14853
Phone: (607) 255-5819

Applications available through field offices.

Field of Study: Environmental studies

Purpose of Fellowship: To support summer research internships in environment-related fields.

Criteria: Students who have arranged a summer research internship with a host organization involving environmentally based research. The research should be of direct benefit to the environment.

Financial Award: $2,500–$4,000 for three months

Deadline: Early March

Environmental Fellows Program

American Association for
Advancement of Science
1333 H Street N.W.
Washington, DC 20005
Phone: (202) 326-6600
Fax: (202) 289-4950
Web site:
science_policy@aaas.org

Field of Study: Environmental sciences and engineering

Purpose of Fellowship: To provide fellows with the opportunity to spend ten weeks during the summer working at special research consultants with the Office of Research and Development of the U.S. Environmental Protection Agency (EPA) in Washington, DC.

Criteria: Candidates must be U.S. residents. Prospective fellows must demonstrate exceptional competence and have a strong interest and/or some experience in applying knowledge toward the solution of societal problems.

Financial Award: $950 per week

Deadline: Early November

Ford Foundation Summer Internship Program

The Ford Foundation
320 East 43rd Street
New York, NY 10017
Phone: (212) 573-4972

Field of Study: All fields

Purpose of Fellowship: To introduce graduate students to public interest work, encourage them to explore work in the public sector, give them experience in the field of philanthropy, and provide overseas experience for students of international development.

Criteria: Graduate students who are returning to school in the fall. Foreign students may not apply for positions in their home countries. Specific requirements vary by program.

Financial Award: $1,000 a month for overseas interns, from $2,000–$2,400 per month for New York-based interns; housing plus travel expenses

Deadline: Late November

Garden Club of America—Awards for Summer Environmental Studies

Mrs. Monica Freeman
598 Madison Avenue
New York, NY 10022
Phone: (212) 753-8287
Fax: (212) 753-0134

Field of Study: Ecology, environmental studies, and related fields

Purpose of Fellowship: To provide financial aid toward a summer course in environmental studies. The Garden Club encourages studies and careers in the environmental field with the specific intent of protecting the quality of the environment through conservation and education.

Criteria: Undergraduate and graduate students are eligible.

Financial Award: $1,500 toward a summer course

Deadline: Mid-February

Government Scholars Program

2 Washington Street, 15th Floor
New York, NY 10004
Phone: (212) 487-5698

Field of Study: Open

Purpose of Fellowship: A ten-month internship program that allows students to learn about New York City government. Through assignments in various professional fields and a weekly seminar program, Scholars gain an in-depth perspective of municipal government and acquire hands-on experience.

Criteria: Applicants must be undergraduates or recent graduates who are willing to commit to full-time employment during the course of the internship.

Financial Award: $2,500

Deadline: Late January

Graduate Student East European Travel Grants

American Council of Learned Societies
228 East 45th Street
New York, NY 10017-3398

Field of Study: Eastern European social sciences, humanities

Purpose of Fellowship: Predissertation travel grants for graduate students who are beginning to formulate a research program for a dissertation on Eastern Europe, but lack the necessary field experience. These grants are intended to help such students define and shape the dissertation proposal.

Criteria: U.S. citizens or permanent residents. Applicants must be accepted into a Ph.D. program and have completed at least one year of full-time graduate study.

Financial Award: Up to $5,000

Deadline: Early February

Grass Fellowships in Neurophysiology

Grass Foundation
77 Reservoir Road
Quincy, MA 02170

Field of Study: Neurophysiology

Purpose of Fellowship: To encourage independent research and to increase research opportunities for students trained for careers in neurophysiological investigation.

Criteria: Candidates in the late predoctoral or early postdoctoral category are eligible.

Financial Award: 14 weeks' support for summer residence at the Marine Biological Laboratory in Woods Hole, Massachusetts

Deadline: Early December

Health Sciences Student Fellowships

4351 Garden City Drive
Landover, MD 20785
Phone: (301) 459-3700

Field of Study: Health sciences

Purpose of Fellowship: To stimulate individuals to pursue careers in epilepsy in either research or practice settings.

Criteria: Predoctoral students in the health sciences. The project may be undertaken at a U.S. institution of the student's choice and carried out during any free period of the student's year.

Financial Award: $2,000

Deadline: Early March

Language Training Grants in East European Studies

American Council of Learned Societies
228 East 45th Street
New York, NY 10017-3398

Field of Study: Eastern European languages

Purpose of Fellowship: To support first- or second-year study of any Eastern European language in the United States or to support intermediate or advanced training in these languages in Eastern Europe.

Criteria: U.S. citizens or permanent residents. Applicants must hold a four-year degree at minimum; graduate students and postdoctoral students are also eligible. Awards are intended for people who will use the languages in their academic or professional careers.

Financial Award: $2,000–$2,500

Deadline: Early February

Library Company of Philadelphia and Historical Society of Pennsylvania Summer Research Fellowships in American History and Culture

Library Company of Philadelphia
1314 Locust St.
Philadelphia, PA 19107
Phone: (215) 546-3181

Field of Study: American history and culture

Purpose of Fellowship: To support summer research at the Library Company of Philadelphia.

Criteria: Candidates must be scholars possessing Ph.D. degrees or doing dissertation research.

Financial Award: $1,200 per month

Deadline: Early February

Library of Congress Junior Fellows Program

Michele Ostrow
Collections Services, LM 642
Library of Congress
Washington, DC 20540

Field of Study: American history and literature, geography, architecture

Purpose of Fellowship: To increase knowledge and use of the Library of Congress's collections throughout the nations. To help the Library inventory, chronicle, and make available previously unexplored materials. To give selected fellows an opportunity to explore the Library's collections. To expose fellows to career opportunities.

Criteria: Applicants must be either enrolled in an ongoing academic program at the junior or senior level, or have just completed their degree at an accredited college or university.

Financial Award: $1,200 per month

Deadline: Early March

Los Alamos National Laboratory—Graduate Research Assistant Program

Personnel Services Division
Mail Stop P282
Los Alamos National Laboratory
Los Alamos, NM 87545
Phone: (505) 667-8622

Field of Study: Sciences, economics

Purpose of Fellowship: To allow students to gain paid relevant work experience while pursuing a graduate degree.

Criteria: Applicants with a cumulative GPA of at least 2.5 who have completed a bachelor's degree by the date of hire and who intend to continue with graduate studies.

Financial Award: Varies

Deadline: Call committee

Masaryk Fellowship Program

The Foundation for a Civil Society
1270 Avenue of the Americas
Suite 609
New York, NY 10020

Field of Study: Open

Purpose of Fellowship: The Foundation for a Civil Society places fellows in locations throughout the Czech Republic and Slovakia to teach English language during the summer.

Criteria: U.S. or Canadian citizens interested in teaching English abroad.

Financial Award: $200 stipend

Deadline: Early March

Mass Media Fellows Program

American Association for Advancement of Science
1333 H Street, N.W.
Washington, DC 20005
Phone: (202) 326-6600
Fax: (202) 289-4950
E-mail: science_policy@aaas.org

Field of Study: Natural and social sciences, engineering, media

Purpose of Fellowship: To strengthen the relationship between science and technology and the media, and to enhance coverage of science-related issues in the media in order to improve public understanding and appreciation of science and technology.

Criteria: Priority will be given to graduate students in the natural and social sciences and engineering.

Financial Award: Weekly stipend plus travel expenses for a 10-week summer appointment

Deadline: Mid-January

Mathematica Policy Research Summer Fellowships

Patrick C. Mooney
P.O. Box 2392
Princeton, NJ 08543-2393

Field of Study: Social sciences

Purpose of Fellowship: To pursue independent research on a social policy issue of relevance to the economic and social problems of minority groups.

Criteria: Students must be enrolled in a master's or Ph.D. program.

Financial Award: $5,000

Deadline: Late March

National Research Council Young Investigator Programs on Russia

2101 Constitution Avenue, N.W.
FO 2014
Washington, DC 20418
Phone: (202) 334-2658
E-mail: sdeets@nas.edu

Field of Study: Agricultural economics and engineering, environmental studies

Purpose of Fellowship: To assist scholars in making professional contributions during the early stages of their careers.

Criteria: Must be a U.S. citizen, green card holder, or permanent resident. Must be engaged in teaching and/or research careers or planning such careers. Must have earned the Ph.D. degree or achieved equivalent accomplishments.

Financial Award: All travel expenses including airfare, food and lodging, and transportation within Russia

Deadline: Late February

National Science Foundation/National Institutes of Health—Summer Institute in Japan

Division of International Programs, NSF
4201 Wilson Blvd.
Arlington, VA 22230
Phone: (703) 306-1701
Fax: (703) 306-0474
E-mail: nsfjinfo@nsf.gov

Field of Study: Science and engineering

Purpose of Fellowship: To provide U.S. graduate students first-hand experience in a Japanese research environment, intensive Japanese language training, and an introduction to the science and science-policy infrastructure of Japan.

Criteria: Applicants must be U.S. citizens or permanent residents, be enrolled at a U.S. institution in a relevant Ph.D., M.D., or M.S. program of which at least one year has been completed, and be pursuing studies in fields of science or engineering which are supported by the NSF or NIH.

Financial Award: Travel costs to and from Japan and an allowance of $2,000

Deadline: Early December

New York City Summer Internship Program

Division of Citywide Personnel Services
2 Washington Street
New York, NY 10004
Phone: (212) 487-6100
Fax: (212) 487-6113

Field of Study: Open, particularly relevant to government and public policy

Purpose of Fellowship: To provide employment opportunities to students through internships that allow them to make important contributions to the City, while participating in a challenging and rewarding experience.

Criteria: Applicants must be currently enrolled or accepted into a graduate program.

Financial Award: Varies

Deadline: Varies

New York State Assembly Summer Internship

Assembly Intern Program
Legislative Office Building
Room 104A
Albany, NY 12248
Phone: (518) 455-4704
Fax: (518) 455-4705

Field of Study: Open

Purpose of Fellowship: To give students an opportunity to work for the Assembly for 10 weeks in the summer.

Criteria: Open

Financial Award: $3,000

Deadline: Mid-March

Nuclear Engineering Institute

Argonne National Laboratory
Argonne, IL 60439-4845
Phone: (708) 252-4759

Field of Study: Engineering and computer science

Purpose of Fellowship: To provide an opportunity to participate in a broad range of engineering activities directed toward the development of the liquid-metal reactor at Argonne's Idaho site.

Criteria: U.S. citizens or permanent resident aliens of junior, senior, or graduate standing who are full-time engineering or computer science students.

Financial Award: $225 per week, plus housing allowance and round-trip travel for distances greater than 100 miles

Deadline: Early February

Smithsonian Institution—Summer Internship

Environmental Awareness Program
Smithsonian Institution
2123 Ripley Center
Washington, DC 20560

Field of Study: Environmental studies or environmental education

Purpose of Fellowship: To provide administrative support for the Environmental Awareness Program.

Criteria: Applicants must be full-time students or recent college graduates.

Financial Award: $1,000–$1,250 stipend per month

Deadline: Early May

Smithsonian Institution—Summer and Fall Internships

Beth Nalker
Smithsonian Institution
2123 Ripley Center
Washington, DC 20560

Field of Study: Environmental studies or environmental education

Purpose of Fellowship: To assist with the development of Ocean Planet, a traveling museum exhibition on ocean conservation, and to provide administrative support for the program.

Criteria: Applicants must be full-time students or recent college graduates. Undergraduate and graduate students are invited to apply.

Financial Award: Stipend of $1,000–$1,250 per month

Deadline: Call committee

Student Research Participation

Argonne National Laboratory
Argonne, IL 60439-4845
Phone: (708) 252-4579

Field of Study: Physical and life sciences, mathematics, computer science

Purpose of Fellowship: To support basic research in coal conservation, environmental impact and technology, fission, and fusion energy.

Criteria: U.S. citizens or permanent resident aliens who are juniors, seniors, or in the first year of graduate study with a GPA of at least 3.0.

Financial Award: $225 per week stipend, plus free housing and round-trip travel for distances greater than 100 miles

Deadline: Early February

Summer Fellowship for Intensive Advanced Turkish Language Study

Washington University
Campus Box 1230
One Brookings Drive
St. Louis, MO 63130-4899

Field of Study: Open

Purpose of Fellowship: To provide intensive advanced Turkish instruction at Bosphorus University in Istanbul for eight weeks during the summer.

Criteria: Citizens or permanent residents of the United States; currently enrolled in a degree program; instructor of Turkish or related language and area studies; minimum B average if in degree program; minimum of two years of college-level, Turkish language study or equivalent.

Financial Award: One full academic-year course in advanced Turkish

Deadline: Mid-February

Summer Internships in Program Direction

Educational Testing Service
Mail Stop 16-T
Princeton, NJ 08541-0001
Phone: (609) 734-1806

Field of Study: Psychology, teaching/administration, business management

Purpose of Fellowship: To provide opportunities, especially for women and minority professionals, for a work/learning experience that allows them to explore career alternatives in the field of measurement and evaluation.

Criteria: Candidates must have completed a master's level graduate program; predoctoral students are especially welcome.

Financial Award: $2,500 with allowance for spouse or child at $350 and for spouse and children at $500, plus travel expenses

Deadline: Early February

Summer Program in Research for Graduate Students

Educational Testing Service
Mail Stop 16-T
Princeton, NJ 08541-0001
Phone: (609) 734-1806

Field of Study: Open

Purpose of Fellowship: To sponsor graduate students participating in ongoing research projects under the supervision of ETS staff for eight weeks during the summer. To increase the number of women and minority professionals in educational measurement and related fields.

Criteria: Graduate students who have completed 40 or more graduate credits in a doctoral program; a letter or recommendation from the advisor or committee chair; undergraduate and graduate transcripts.

Financial Award: $2,500 with a $350 supplemental living allowance for participants who bring their spouse and $500 for those who bring their children, plus travel expenses

Deadline: Early February

Tibor T. Polgar Fellowships for Hudson River Research

40 West 20th Street
9th Floor
New York, NY 10011

Field of Study: Physical, chemical, biological sciences; environmental studies; public policy

Purpose of Fellowship: To support research anywhere within the Hudson estuary; seeks to gather information that contributes to understanding the complex natural patterns, processes, and relationships that exist in the estuary, and to train students in estuarine studies.

Criteria: Undergraduate or graduate students sponsored by a major professor who is willing to commit sufficient time for supervision of the research and to review the studies; applicants must submit letters of interest from student and sponsor, a description of the project, a detailed timetable and budget, and a curriculum vitae.

Financial Award: $3,500, plus limited research funds; sponsoring professors receive a $250 stipend

Deadline: Early March

United Nations Institute for Training and Research—Fellowship on Climate Change

Gao Pronove, Programme Officer
UNITAR
Palais des Nations
CH-1211 Geneva
Switzerland
Phone: (41) (22) 798-5850, ext. 258
Fax: (41) (22) 733-1383

Field of Study: Environmental studies and policy, international relations

Purpose of Fellowship: To provide an opportunity for learning about current international developments, especially in the area of sustainable development and environmental change.

Criteria: Advanced graduate students in one of the fields listed above. Work experience in developing countries is an advantage, as is knowledge of French and excellent communication skills in English. Working ability with PC applications is required.

Financial Award: Unspecified

Deadline: Late April

William Randolph Hearst Foundation Fellowship

Hearst Fellowship Program
The Abigail Adams Smith Museum
421 E. 61st Street
New York, NY 10021

Field of Study: Humanities or social sciences

Purpose of Fellowship: To support an eight-week research period at the Abigail Adams Smith Museum in New York City in the summer.

Criteria: Graduate and undergraduate students conducting an independent research project on a topic relating to the museum's history, its collection, or the history of New York City.

Financial Award: Graduate students: $2,575; Undergraduate students: $2,325

Deadline: Mid-March

Young Scientists' Summer Program

American Academy of Arts
and Sciences
Norton's Woods
136 Irving Street
Cambridge, MA 02138-1996
Phone: (617) 576-5019
Fax: (617) 576-5050

Field of Study: Physical sciences

Purpose of Fellowship: To offer young people a challenging opportunity to take part in an international exchange of ideas on the development and application of systems analysis and related fields.

Criteria: Second- or third-year predoctoral candidates who expect to be awarded a Ph.D. or equivalent and whose interests correspond with ongoing research at AASAA.

Financial Award: Unspecified

Deadline: Early January

Other Fellowships and Grants

15

Don't ignore the fellowships and grants listed at the end of this chapter just because they don't quite fit into any of the other chapters. The majority of these opportunities allow for students to apply for any field they choose at any institution they choose, an example of a freedom that hardly any other type of award affords its students.

The fellowships listed in this chapter generally fall into one of the following categories:

- Open to all fields
- Communications
- Print/broadcast journalism
- Cultural studies

Organizations that provide open-ended fellowships and grants aren't looking for anything in particular from their applicants. What they are looking for, however, is a solid project submitted by a candidate with the experience and talent to pull it off. For this reason, there is no one part of the application on which candidates should preferentially concentrate.

If you are interested in an open fellowship or grant, the best plan is to take a look at your credentials before deciding what type of project you would like to propose. Naturally, choosing a project within your major or postgraduate field of study is the safest bet. But if you have a wealth of experience in another area and would like to continue your studies in that field, more power to you!

The types of fellowships and grants that you'll find in this chapter allow you to be truly creative with your application and proposal. Take advantage of their special nature, and don't be afraid to shoot for the moon!

American Physical Society—Mass Media Fellowship Program

529 14th Street, N.W.
Suite 1050
Washington, DC 20045

Field of Study: Physics and closely related fields

Purpose of Fellowship: To improve public understanding and appreciation of science and technology and to sharpen the ability of the fellows to communicate complex technical issues to nonspecialists.

Criteria: Priority will be given to graduate students in physics, or a closely related field, but outstanding undergraduate and postdoctoral researcher applicants will also be considered. Applicants should possess outstanding written and oral communication skills and a strong interest in learning about the media.

Financial Award: $4,000 plus a travel allowance of $1,000

Deadline: Mid-January

Broadcast Education Association—National Scholarships in Broadcasting

1771 N Street, N.W.
Washington, DC 20036
Phone: (202) 429-5354

Field of Study: Communication, media law or policy, and other related fields

Purpose of Fellowship: To honor broadcasters and the broadcast industry.

Criteria: Students who demonstrate superior academic performance.

Financial Award: Prizes up to $5,000

Deadline: Mid-January

Dolores Zohrab Liebmann Fund

Mr. T. E. Roepe
270 Park Avenue, 21st Floor
New York, NY 10017

Field of Study: Open

Purpose of Fellowship: To support graduate study by individuals with outstanding undergraduate records, who have demonstrated need for financial assistance and are enrolled in accredited colleges and universities in the United States.

Criteria: U.S. citizens who hold a baccalaureate degree, have an outstanding undergraduate record, and who demonstrate a need for financial assistance.

Financial Award: Covers cost of study, tuition, room, board, living expenses, and income taxes

Deadline: Late January

Frederick Douglass Institute for African and African American Studies Fellowships

University of Rochester
302 Morey Hall
Rochester, NY 14627
Phone: (716) 275-2121
ext. 7235

Field of Study: African and African American studies

Purpose of Fellowship: Predoctoral: to support fellows in writing their dissertations; postdoctoral: to support the completion of a research project; graduate: to support graduate study.

Criteria: Predoctoral: candidates must be writing their dissertations; postdoctoral: fellows, who will also have departmental affiliation, will teach one course and conduct a seminar during the year; graduate: candidates who are interested in the relevant fields.

Financial Award: Tuition plus academic year stipends ranging from $6,000 to $8,000 for all candidates; $10,500 stipend for one year for predoctoral candidates; $30,000 per year for postdoctoral students

Deadline: Late January

Golden Key Scholar Awards

1189 Ponce de Leon Avenue
Atlanta, GA 30306
Phone: (800) 377-2401

Field of Study: All fields

Purpose of Fellowship: To support Golden Key Society members' postbaccalaureate or professional study at accredited institutions of higher learning.

Criteria: Lifetime member of Golden Key, undergraduate or recent alumnus of institution with active chapter of Golden Key National Honor Society, baccalaureate degree, or equivalent by the time scholarship is assumed, and completed scholar award application packet.

Financial Award: $10,000

Deadline: Mid-February

Grant-in-Aid of Research

LBJ Foundation
2313 Red River Street
Austin, TX 78705
Phone: (512) 478-7829

Field of Study: Open

Purpose of Fellowship: To defray living, travel, and related expenses incurred while conducting research at the LBJ Lbrary.

Criteria: Prior to submitting a Grant-in-Aid proposal, applicants must contact the Archives at the LBJ Library at telephone number (512) 482-5137 to obtain information about material available in the library on the proposed research topic.

Financial Award: $75 per day plus travel costs

Deadline: Rolling

Hagley Museum and Library—Grants-in-Aid

Dr. Philip B. Scranton
Hagley Museum and Library
P.O. Box 3630
Wilmington, DE 19807
Phone: (302) 658-4200

Field of Study: All fields

Purpose of Fellowship: Short-term Grants-in-Aid to support visits to Hagley for scholarly research in the imprint, manuscript, pictorial, and artifact collections.

Criteria: Available to both degree candidates and senior scholars, as well as applicants without advanced degrees.

Financial Award: No more than $1,000 per month for a maximum of two months

Deadline: Call committee

Harvard Academy for International and Area Studies—Academy Scholars Program

The Academy Scholars Program
Center for International Affairs
1737 Cambridge Street
Cambridge, MA 02138
Phone: (617) 495-2137

Field of Study: Area studies

Purpose of Fellowship: To identify some of the brightest young scholars whose work combines disciplinary excellence in the social sciences with an in-depth grounding in particular countries of regions.

Criteria: Social scientists who show promise of becoming leading scholars at major universities.

Financial Award: $20,000–$25,000 for predoctoral students; $30,000–$35,000 for postdoctoral students

Deadline: Mid-October

Harvard University—Society of Fellows

78 Mount Auburn Street
Cambridge, MA 02138
Phone: (617) 495-2645
E-mail:
socfell@nucleus.harvard.edu

Field of Study: Open

Purpose of Fellowship: To give students at an early stage of their career an opportunity to pursue their studies in any department of Harvard University, free from formal requirements.

Criteria: A candidate must be at an early stage of his or her career. Although prospective junior fellows need not be working toward advanced degrees, most have recently received or are candidates for the Ph.D. Candidates must be nominated by the faculty member with whom they have studied.

Financial Award: $42,000 stipend for the academic year; three-year term of appointment

Deadline: September

Huewl D. Perkins Doctoral Fellowship Program

Lousiana State University
Graduate School
Baton Rouge, LA 70803
E-mail:
grdfern@lsuvm.sncc.lsu.edu

Field of Study: Open

Purpose of Fellowship: To recognize past academic excellence and potential for significant scholarly contributions.

Criteria: Fellows are chosen from candidates demonstrating extraordinary potential for success in a doctoral program. Preference is given to Louisiana residents.

Financial Award: $14,000 per year stipend for up to three years

Deadline: Mid-February

Joint Japan/World Bank Graduate Scholarship Program

700 18th Street, N.W.
Room M-4107
Washington, DC 20433
Phone: (202) 473-6849
Fax: (202) 676-0962

Field of Study: Development-related fields.

Purpose of Fellowship: To support graduate study in fields related to development.

Criteria: Candidates must be nationals of a World Bank member country; be under the age of 45, normally under 35; hold a bachelor's degree in a development-related field; have 2–5 years of related work experience; be in superior academic standing; and be in good health. Evidence of admission or application to two universities must be provided.

Financial Award: Tuition, airfare, subsistence stipend, basic medical expenses

Deadline: Early February

Morris Doctoral Fellowship Program

Southern Illinois University/
Carbondale
Mailcode 4176
Carbondale, IL 62901

Field of Study: Arts and sciences, business, communications, education

Purpose of Fellowship: To assist students in pursuing doctoral study in relevant fields.

Criteria: Outstanding college seniors or postbaccalaureate students are eligible.

Financial Award: $12,000 stipend per year plus a tuition waiver

Deadline: Early January

National Institute for Justice—John B. Pickett Fellowship in Criminal Justice Policy and Management

79 John F. Kennedy Street
Harvard University
Cambridge, MA 02138
Phone: (617) 495-1153

Field of Study: Public administration, law enforcement, correction

Purpose of Fellowship: To support mid-career professionals working in public service who seek to expand their knowledge of criminal justice policy and management.

Criteria: Mid-career professionals with at least seven years of experience in law enforcement, corrections, courts, or other criminal justice professions. Applicants must be enrolled in or admitted to the Kennedy School of Government.

Financial Award: Some or all of the tuition for a one-year master's degree in public administration at the John F. Kennedy School of Government at Harvard University

Deadline: Early May

New York State Senate—Richard J. Roth Journalism Fellowship

90 South Swan Street
Room 401
Albany, NY 12247
Phone: (518) 455-2611
Fax: (518) 432-5470

Field of Study: All fields, especially journalism and communications

Purpose of Fellowship: To expose students to one year of working as a full-time staff member in the Senate Press Office. The fellowship is for students who can demonstrate that they are pursuing careers in journalism or public relations.

Criteria: Candidates must be U.S. citizens who are New York state residents and graduate students, or residents of other states enrolled in a New York state graduate school; have completed or be about to complete at least two semesters of graduate study; and have not graduated more than 30 days prior to the deadline.

Financial Award: $22,575

Deadline: Early May

Organization of American States—PRA Fellowships

General Secretariat of the OAS
Department of Fellowships
and Training
Washington, DC 20006

Field of Study: All fields except medicine

Purpose of Fellowship: To further the economic, social, technical, and cultural development of the American peoples by supporting research in a member country of the Organization of American States (this country may not be the candidate's country of residence). The United States is a member of the OAS.

Criteria: Graduate students from the OAS (primarily West Indies, South and Central America, and the United States) are eligible.

Financial Award: Covers travel, tuition, and expenses in country of study for up to two years

Deadline: Early March

Smithsonian Institution—Ten-Week Graduate Student Fellowships

955 L'Enfant Plaza, Suite 7000
MRC 902
Washington, DC 20560
Phone: (202) 287-3271
Fax: (202) 287-3691
E-mail: siofg@ofg.si.edu

Field of Study: Open

Purpose of Fellowship: To allow students to conduct independent research under the guidance of Smithsonian staff members for 10 weeks.

Criteria: Graduate students who have completed at least one full-time semester or its equivalent before the appointment period, and must not yet have been advanced to candidacy if enrolled in a doctorate program. Students are expected to write and converse fluently in English.

Financial Award: $3,500

Deadline: Mid-January

William B. Ruggles Right to Work Scholarship

8001 Braddock Road
Suite 500
Springfield, VA 22160
Phone: (800) 325-7892

Field of Study: Journalism, communication, and related fields

Purpose of Fellowship: To support students who exemplify the dedication to principle and high journalistic standards of William B. Ruggles.

Criteria: Graduates or undergraduates in journalism programs in U.S. universities. Members of the National Right to Work Commitee are not eligible.

Financial Award: $2,000

Deadline: Late March

Yale Daily News

OLDEST COLLEGE DAILY FOUNDED JANUARY 28, 1878

After You Get Your Fellowship or Grant

Making the Most of Your Fellowship or Grant

16

It's funny how sometimes, just when we think the worst is finally over, a whole new set of problems jumps us from behind. Just when the emotionally taxing application process has ended and you finally get a chance to relax, new sources of stress surface as you receive your award. It is at this point that you must begin to concern yourself with making the most of your opportunity.

But if you've made it this far, take a second from your busy schedule to step back and realize what you've accomplished. You have put yourself through a rigorous, trying, and competitive process and lived to tell about it. So sit back, relax, and enjoy the view for a little while . . . you've got a lot to be proud of.

Once the initial afterglow wears off, it's time to get serious. You have committed yourself to a project whose final result will reflect the time, thought, and effort you put into it. So once you embark on your fellowship journey, stay focused, and never succumb to complacency. It's a long road you have ahead of you, but if you keep sight of your goals and dreams, you're in for a smooth ride.

Say Thanks

One of your initial moves should be to get in touch with everyone who has significantly helped you in the course of the application process. Talk to your college career counselors, your recommenders, and the career services office to let them know of your good fortune and—more importantly—to thank them. Then send a letter to your fellowship organization to delineate when you plan on starting your project (if applicable) and thanking them for the opportunity.

Managing Your Money

Anyone who's made it this far in the fellowship or grant application process knows there's lots of money out there waiting to be taken. How should you claim it? The answer depends largely on what you plan on doing with it.

Claiming Your Prize

The simplest way to claim your prize is by check. This usually applies to students who have received a fellowship or grant for some sort of independent research. When you get your cash is a whole other story, and it has a great deal to do with just how trusting your sponsoring organization is. Some simply choose to give you the whole boat right off the bat, sending you a check the instant you start your work. Others wait until they're sure they like what they see in you, paying in several installments. Sometimes, such organizations will not send the final payment until they have proof you've done your job, waiting to see a final report before shelling out the cash.

Getting your money is a little less complicated if you're planning on using it toward further study. Many organizations send their money straight to the university where you plan to study, regardless of whether you plan to actually spend time in a classroom or do some type of research under the supervision of a faculty member. If you're the bookworm type, the university will say "thank you," gobble up your award, and use it toward paying your tuition. If you're doing research, however, the money often goes straight to your research adviser to account for research costs.

Keeping Track of Your Award

Award-issuing organizations let you know what has been done with your money every step of the way, and usually do a wonderful job of keeping you abreast of how much they've given you and where the cash has gone. This makes it extremely difficult for research advisers or graduate school to practice sleight of hand and use your award for their own purposes.

That said, it is important that as a fellowship or grant recipient, you keep tabs on what is being done with your money by keeping in close contact with the organization that awarded you the prize. If you are involved in a research project, make sure you make a detailed chart of what needs to be paid for and how much needs to be allotted for each step. If you're short 100 test tubes, or if those lab rats haven't made their way into your research laboratory, something's rotten in Denmark. But before you go blaming your boss, check back with the organization and make sure you're on the same page as they.

The likelihood of a graduate school playing illegal games with your award is negligible, and for a good reason: It's pretty hard for an institution to take away your tuition money without your realizing it. As long as you keep track of your financial standing with the school and don't take for granted that the award-issuing organization has already taken care of everything for you, there should be no problem.

Lingering Financial Blues

One of the most common misconceptions people have about getting a fellowship or grant is that the money awarded is a panacea for the postgraduate financial blues. While areas such as the social and natural sciences certainly offer awards that will keep recipients happy for a few years, it's not all peaches and cream in the land of fellowships and grants.

A Necessary Evil

Very few fellows can survive on their award money alone. Most fellowship and grant prizes are simply not large enough to cover a normal person's living expenses. So what's a fellow to do? The most obvious solution: Get a job! This can often be difficult, considering that you will need to spend a great deal of your time completing your fellowship project. Unfortunately, working for a living is often a necessary evil of life as a fellow.

In particular, students are often surprised and disappointed to hear that the money to support their first few years of graduate school just isn't there. While there certainly are awards that provide such assistance (e.g., the Harry S. Truman Scholarship), they are the exception rather than the norm.

It is equally difficult for the family-minded individual to secure enough money through a fellowship to support a spouse, let alone the pitter-patter of little feet. While a prestigious award may reach well above $30,000 a year, most allot under $10,000 for living expenses. Unless you want to raise your kids in a cardboard box, that amount probably isn't going to cut it.

What you need to realize from the get-go is that whatever money you earn on top of research funds or tuition is not enough to live on for an extended period of time. Plain and simple, this means that unless you can grow money from a tree (or unless your parents are generous enough to pay for you), chances are you're going to have to find an alternate source of cash to keep your balance in the black.

Adapting to a New Method of Education

There's no doubt that fellowship recipients suffer through an initial period of culture shock when they first begin their project. In some cases, this "culture shock" is quite literal: Those of you who will be studying abroad for your award will have to get used to both new surroundings and a completely new way of thinking.

But in a broader sense, the type of culture shock that all fellows experience during the first few weeks of their projects is that of adapting to a new method of education. While many fellowships and grants provide funding for graduate study, the majority allow students to go off and do their own thing. Committees trust in their fellows to develop their own styles of learning and to figure out the best ways to successfully complete the stated objectives of their proposal. Unfortunately, this leniency can prove unnerving for students who are used to the safety net with which their professors and advisors have provided them in college and graduate school. If you aren't a self-starter or a completely independent thinker, these awards may not be your cup of tea at first.

So how do you get over the culture shock? Ultimately, the answer to this question will be different for everyone, but it certainly helps to figure out what works and what doesn't work for you early in your award term. Familiarize yourself with your surroundings and the people with whom you will interact. Fulfill all of the responsibilities you have set for yourself in a timely fashion, and when possible, look for even more to do. And most importantly, give yourself leisure time to separate yourself from your project's daily grind. Keep yourself busy enough to learn a routine, but allow yourself the opportunity to enjoy your surroundings.

Stay Focused!

You know you have to stay focused in order to achieve your objectives. But you also know this is easier said than done. So what's an award recipient to do?

One of the greatest hurdles you must overcome as a fellow is to keep sight of the goals you set for yourself in the application. This is an especially difficult proposition because not all awards have a clear finish line. While those that provide funding for graduate school result in degrees of some sort, many fellowships—often referred to as *working fellowships*—do not have as clear an ending point.

Changing Course

The best thing you can do if you find yourself losing focus during your term is to sit down and seriously consider why you took the opportunity in the first place. Look at your written proposal and your personal statement one more time for a glimpse at where you thought you were headed when you first applied. Hopefully, you will find that you're not as far off course as you might have thought. But if you feel that your course has changed, don't worry. Just take some time to figure out where you want your road to lead and start traveling that new road.

Entering the Work Force

If your goal is to enter the work force after completing your fellowship or grant term, it is in your best interests to either start making contacts or continue your communication with established contacts during your tenure as a fellow. Keep potential employers abreast of your studies and any positive strides you have made.

And for the first time since you completed your application, go through the process of packaging yourself once again. This time, your audience is a little different than before. Instead of catering to admissions committees, who take a hard look at your grades and extracurricular activities, among other things, you must tailor yourself to the needs of future advisers and employers. The best way to make a strong impression is through your work as an award recipient; it will show your commitment, experience, and talent in your particular field of study.

Going to Graduate School

Other fellows use their awards as a stepping stone to graduate school. Remember: Just because you did not apply to a program that pays for your postgraduate education doesn't mean that you will never be able to attend graduate school.

If further education is in the cards for you, make sure you give yourself ample time to complete the necessary applications and garner the requisite letters of recommendation during your time as a fellow. A good idea is to request letters from your fellowship or grant committee, which will be monitoring your progress throughout your term.

A Golden Pathway

Remember that your award is a golden pathway that can lead you toward your ultimate goals. It can take you anywhere, as long as you stay focused and keep your feet on the ground!

Yale Daily News

OLDEST COLLEGE DAILY — FOUNDED JANUARY 28, 1878

Indices

Alphabetical Index

Award Title	Chapter
American Water Works Association—Thomas R. Camp Scholarship	7
Andrew W. Mellon Student Research Grants	9
Arthur Boller Apple Research Grants	9
Associated Western Universities, Inc.—Graduate Fellowships at National Laboratories and Cooperating Facilities	9, 10
Atlantic Salmon Federation—Olin Fellowships	9
Avon Fundation for Women in Business Studies	12
Awards for Study in Scandinavia	13
Barry M. Goldwater Scholarship Program	4
Beinecke Brothers Memorial Scholarship Program	4
Berkeley Professional Studies Program in India—M.A./Ph. D. Internships	13
Berkshire Summer Fellowship	12, 14
Bibliographic Society of America	6
The British Marshall Scholarship	4
Broadcast Education Association—National Scholarships in Broadcasting	15
Broadcast Music, Inc. Awards to Student Composers	5
Brookings Institution—Research Fellowships in Economic Studies	7
Brookings Institution—Research Fellowships in Foreign Policy Studies	7
Brookings Institution—Research Fellowships in Governmental Studies	7
Budget Fellowship Program	7, 11, 12
Builder Grant	11
Bundeskanzler Scholarships for Germany	13
Bunting Fellowship Program	12
The Bunting Institute of Radcliffe College—Biomedical Research Fellowship Program	12
The Bunting Institute of Radcliffe College—Peace Fellowship	12
Byron Hanke Fellowship	7
California Executive Fellows Program	7
Canada Mortgage and Housing Corporation University Scholarship	13
Career Advancement Scholarship Program	12
Center for Plant Conservation—Catherine H. Beattie Fellowship for Conservation Horticulture	9
Cesar E. Chavez Dissertation Fellowship for U.S. Latina/o Scholars	11
Chancellor's Graduate Fellowship Program	11

Award Title	Chapter
Esther Boyer College of Music Doctoral Fellowships in Composition, Music Education, and Performance	5
European Space Agency Fellowship Programme	13
Fellowship in Landscape Architecture at the American Academy in Rome	13
Fellowship on Women and Public Policy	12
Five College Fellowship Program for Minority Scholars	11
Flemish Community Graduate Fellowships	13
Flemish Community Research Fellowships	13
Fondation Des Etats-Unis—Harriet Hale Woolley Scholarships	13
Ford Foundation—Postdoctoral Fellowships for Minorities	11
Ford Foundation—Predoctoral and Dissertation Fellowships for Minorities	11
Ford Foundation Program Assistantship	7
Ford Foundation Summer Internship Program	14
Forgivable Loan/Doctoral Incentive Program	11, 12
Frances C. Allen Fellowships	12
Frederick Douglass Institute for African and African American Studies Fellowships	15
Fulbright Awards	13
Fulbright Grants	4
Fulbright Scholar Program—Lecture and Research Award Openings	13
Fund for the Improvement of Postsecondary Education	6
Garden Club of America—Awards for Summer Environmental Studies	14
Garden Club of America—Awards in Tropical Botany	13
Garden Club of America—Frances M. Peacock Scholarship for Native Bird Habitat	9
Geological Society of America Research Grants	11, 12, 13
Gertrude Fogelson Cultural Program in Creative Arts Awards	12
Getty Center for the History of Art and the Humanities—Predoctoral Fellowships	5
Getty Center for the History of Art and the Humanities Research Support Grants	5, 11
Gilbert Chinard Fellowships	13
Golden Key Scholar Awards	15
Government Scholars Program	14
Grace Legendre Fellowships	12
Graduate Fellowships for Minority Students	11

Award Title	Chapter
Graduate Research Award Program—Public Sector Aviation Issues	7, 10
Graduate Student East European Travel Grants	14
Grant-in-Aid of Research	15
Grass Fellowships in Neurophysiology	14
Hagley Museum and Library—Grants-in-Aid	15
Hagley/Winterthur Fellowships in Arts and Industries	5
Harriet Pomerance Fellowship	6
Harry J. Loman Foundation Matching Funds Scholarship Program	8
Harry S. Truman Library Institute—Dissertation Year Fellowships	7
Harry S. Truman Library Institute—Research Grants	7
Harry S. Truman Scholarship Program	4
Harvard Academy for International and Area Studies—Academy Scholars Program	15
Harvard University—Society of Fellows	15
Health Care Financing Administration—Dissertation Fellowship Grants	6
Health Sciences Student Fellowships	14
Henry A. Murray Dissertation Award Program	6
Henry A. Murray Research Center of Radcliffe College—Jeanne Humphrey Block Dissertation Award Program	12
Henry Luce Foundation/ACLS Dissertation Fellowship Program in American Art	5
The Herb Society of America—Research and Education Grant	6
Herbert Scoville Jr. Peace Fellowship	7
Herman Kahn Fellowships	6
Hertz Foundation Fellowships	4
Holly A. Cornell Scholarship	12
Howard Hughes Medical Institute—Predoctoral Fellowships in Biological Sciences	9
Howard Hughes Medical Institute—Research Training Fellowships for Medical Students	9
Hubert H. Humphrey Fellowships in Arms Control and Disarmament	7
Hudson River Foundation for Science and Environmental Research—Hudson River Research Grants	9
Huewl D. Perkins Doctoral Fellowship Program	15
Huntington Library Fellowships	6
Indian Fellowship Program	11
Indiana University/Bloomington Chancellor's Fellowship	6

Award Title	Chapter
Institute for Advanced Studies in the Humanities—University of Edinburgh Fellowships on the European Enlightenment	13
Institute for Advanced Studies in the Humanities—University of Edinburgh Visiting Research Fellowships	13
Institute for Advanced Study—Mellon Fellowships for Assistant Professors	6
Institute for Humane Studies	6
Institute for the Study of World Politics—Doctoral Dissertation Fellowships/ Dorothy Danforth Compton Fellowships	7, 11
Institute of Living—Predoctoral Internships in Clinical Psychology	6
Inter-American Foundation—Field Research Programs at the Doctoral and Master's Levels	13
Inter-American Press Association Scholarship	13
Interchange Fellowship in Horticulture and Landscape Design	13
Intercollegiate Studies Institute—Salvatori Fellowship Program	6
International Dissertation and Advanced Research Fellowships	13
International Federation of University Women Fellowships and Grants Competition	12, 13
International Foundation of Employee Benefit Plans	8
International Lead Zinc Research Organization, Inc. (ILZRO) Fellowship Opportunities	9
International Research and Exchanges Board—Individual Advanced Research Opportunities	6
International Research and Exchanges Board—Library and Information Service	6
Internship Program at the Solomon R. Guggenheim Museum	5
J. Clawson Mills Art History Scholarships	5
J. Desmond Slattery Marketing Awards	8
Jacob K. Javits Fellowship	6
James Harrison Steedman Memorial Fellowship in Architecture	13
James Madison Fellowship Program	4, 6
James Renwick Fellowship in American Crafts	5
Jane and Morgan Whitney Art History Fellowships	5
Japan Foundation Doctoral Fellowship	13
Japan Foundation Research Fellowship	13
Jennings Randolph Program for International Peace	13
John Carter Brown Library—Short-Term and Long-Term Research Fellowships	6
John F. Kennedy Library Foundation—Archival Internships	7

Award Title	Chapter
John F. Kennedy Library Foundation—Hemingway Research Grants	6
John F. Kennedy Library Foundation—Kennedy Research Grants	7
John F. Kennedy School of Government, Harvard University/ Center for Science and International Affairs—Fellowships in Science and International Affairs	7
Joint Japan/World Bank Graduate Scholarship Program	15
Joseph L. Fisher Dissertation Awards	12
Josephine de Karman Fellowships	6
Kappa Omicron Nu Fellowships/Grants	8
Karla Scherer Foundation Scholarships	12
Kate Neal Kinley Memorial Fellowships	5, 13
Kenan T. Erim Award	6, 13
Kieckhefer Adirondack Fellowships	9
Knight Foundation Minority Predoctoral Fellowships	11
L. W. Frohlich Charitable Trust Fellowship in Conservation	5
Laboratory-Graduate Research	9
Lady Davis Fellowship Trust	13
Language Training Grants in East European Studies	14
Lena Lake Forrest Fellowships	12
Leo Baeck Institute/DAAD Fellowships	6, 13
Leo Baeck Institute—David Baumgardt Memorial Fellowship	6
Leo Baeck Institute—Fritz Halbers Fellowship	6
Library Company of Philadelphia—Research Fellowships in American History and Culture	6
Library Company of Philadelphia/Historical Society of Pennsylvania—Summer Research Fellowships in American History and Culture	14
Library of Congress Junior Fellows Program	14
Los Alamos National Laboratory—Graduate Research Assistant Program	9, 10, 14
Luce Scholars Program	4
Luigi Einaudi Graduate Fellowships	13
Manon Michele Einaudi Summer Research Grant	13
Margaret McNamara Memorial Fund	12
Marian Cabot Putnam Fellowship	12
Mario Einaudi Fellowship	13

Award Title	Chapter
National Research Service Awards (NSRA)	9, 10
National Scholarship Trust Fund of the Graphic Arts	9
National Science Foundation Graduate Fellowships	9
National Science Foundation Graduate and Minority Graduate Fellowships	4, 11
National Science Foundation Grants for Improving Doctoral Dissertation Research	9, 10
National Science Foundation/National Institutes of Health—Summer Institute in Japan	10, 14
National Security Education Program—Graduate International Fellowships	7
Native American Community Scholar's Awards	11
Natural Sciences and Engineering Research Council of Canada Visiting Fellowships in Canadian Government Laboratories	9, 10
New Focus Research Award	9
New Jersey School of Conservation, Montclair State University—Graduate Fellowships in Environmental Studies	9
New York City Summer Internship Program	7, 14
New York Sea Grant—Coastal Management Fellowship	9
New York Sea Grant—Dean John A. Knauss Marine Policy Fellowship	9
New York State Assembly Summer Internship	14
New York State Department of Health Primary Care Service Corps Scholarship Program	9
New York State—Public Management Internship Program	7
New York State Regents Health Care Scholarships in Medicine and Dentistry	11
New York State Regents Professional Opportunity Scholarships	11
New York State Senate—Richard J. Roth Journalism Fellowship	15
New York Telephone/NYNEX Minority Teaching Fellowships	11
Newberry Library—Herzog August Bibliothek Wolfenbuttel Fellowship	6
Newberry Library—Short-Term Fellowships in the History of Cartography	6
Newberry Library—Short-Term Resident Fellowships for Individual Research	6
Nuclear Engineering Institute	10, 14
Oak Ridge Institute for Science and Education—Applied Health Physics Fellowship	9, 10
Oak Ridge Institute for Science and Education—Environmental Management Participation Program	9
Oak Ridge Institute for Science and Education—Industrial Hygiene Graduate Fellowship	9, 10
Oak Ridge Institute for Science and Education—Magnetic Fusion Science and Magnetic Fusion Energy Technology Fellowships	9, 10

Award Title	Chapter
Oak Ridge Institute for Science and Education—Nuclear Engineering Graduate Fellowship	9, 10
Oak Ridge Institute for Science and Education—U.S. Nuclear Regulatory Commission Graduate Fellowship	9, 10
Old Dominion University—President's Graduate Fellowship	12
One Thousand Friends of Oregon—Paul Gerhardt Jr. Internship	7
Organization of American States—PRA Fellowships	15
P.E.O. Sisterhood—International Peace Scholarship Fund	12
Pharmaceutical Research and Manufacturers for America Foundation Fellowships for Advanced Predoctoral Training in Pharmaceutics and Clinical Pharmacology	9
President's Graduate Fellowship	11
Purina Mills Research Fellowship Awards Program	9
The Raoul Wallenberg Scholarships	4
Residential Fellowships	11
Resources for the Future—Joseph L. Fisher Dissertation Awards	11
Rhodes Scholarship	4
Richard C. Maguire Scholarship for Postgraduate Study in History	6
Richard D. Irwin Doctoral Fellowships	8
Richard M. Weaver Fellowships	6
Rome Prize Fellowships	13
Science Scholars Fellowship Program	12
Scuola Normale Superiore Doctoral Scholarships	13
Selected Professions Fellowships	12
Semiconductor Research Corporation Education Alliance Graduate Fellowships Program	9
Smithsonian Astrophysical Observatory Predoctoral Fellowships	9
Smithsonian Institution—Paul E. Garber Fellowship	9
Smithsonian Institution—Predoctoral Fellowships	9
Smithsonian Institution—Summer and Fall Internship Positions	9, 14
Smithsonian Institution—Summer Internship	14
Smithsonian Institution—Ten-Week Graduate Student Fellowships	15
Smithsonian Marine Station at Link Port Fellowships	9
Social Science Research Council—Berlin Program for Advanced German and European Studies	6
Social Science Research Council—Urban Underclass Program	11

Award Title	Chapter
Society for the Psychological Study of Social Issues	9
Society of Exploration Geophysicists (SEG)—Foundation Scholarship Program	9
Spencer Foundation Dissertation Fellowships for Research Related to Education	6
Spencer T. Olin Fellowships for Women in Graduate Study	12
State University of New York—Underrepresented Graduate Fellowship Program	11
Student Research Participation	14
Sudden Infant Death Syndrome Reseach—Student Training Fellowships	9
Summer Fellowship for Intensive Advanced Turkish Language Study	14
Summer Internships in Program Direction	14
Summer Multicultural Teaching Fellows Program	11
Summer Program in Research for Graduate Students	14
Technology Policy Fellows Program	10
Thesis Parts Program	9
Thurgood Marshall Dissertation Fellowships for African American Scholars	11
Tibor T. Polgar Fellowships for Hudson River Research	14
Tuskegee University and the International Foundation for Education and Self-Help—International Fellows Program	11
U.S. Army Center of Military History—Dissertation Fellowships	6
U.S. Deparment of Health and Human Services—National Center on Child Abuse and Neglect	7
United Nations Headquarters Internship Programme	7
United Nations Institute for Training And Research—Fellowship on Climate Change	14
United Negro College Fund/Merck Graduate Science Research Dissertation Fellowships	11
United Negro College Fund/Merck Postdoctoral Science Research Fellowships	11
University of California—President's Postdoctoral Fellowship Program	11, 12
University of California/Berkeley—Chancellor's Postdoctoral Fellowship Program for Academic Diversity	11
University of California/Los Angeles Graduate Fellowships—Eugene V. Cota Robles Fellowhip	11
University of California/Los Angeles Graduate Fellowships—Project 88 Graduate Support Program	11
University of California/Santa Barbara Center for Black Studies Predoctoral Fellowships	11
University of Colorado/Boulder—Chancellor's Postdoctoral Fellowship Program for Academic Diversity	11, 12
University of Delaware/Hagley Program—Fellowships in the History of Industrialization	8

Award Title	Chapter
University of Louisville—Grawemeyer Award in Education	6
University of Maryland/College Park—Postdoctoral Fellowship Program for African American Scholars	11
University of Missouri/Columbia—Chancellor's Gus T. Ridgel Fellowship for Minority Americans	11
University of Southern California—All-University Predoctoral Diversity Fellowships	11
Urban Fellows Program	7
The Village Voice	11
Warren W. Willingham Graduate Research Assistantships in Psychometrics Program	6
Washington University in St. Louis—Fellowships for Minority Graduate Students	11
Welder Wildlife Foundation Scholarships	9
Wharton School of University of Pennsylvania—S.S. Huebner Foundation Fellowships	8
White House Fellowships	7
Whitney Museum of American Art Independent Study Program—Curatorial and Critical Studies Program	6
William B. Ruggles Right to Work Scholarship	11, 12, 15
William Randolph Hearst Foundation Fellowship	14
William Schallek Memorial Graduate Fellowship Awards	6
Williams College—Gaius Charles Bolin Fellowships for Minority Graduate Students	11
The Winston Churchill Foundation Scholarship	4
Woodrow Wilson International Center for Scholars—Fellowships in the Humanities and Social Sciences	6
Woodrow Wilson National Fellowship Foundation—Charlotte W. Newcombe Doctoral Dissertation Fellowships	6
Woodrow Wilson National Fellowship Foundation—Dissertation Grants in Women's Health	9
Woodrow Wilson National Fellowship Foundation—Rural Policy Fellowships	11
Woodrow Wilson National Fellowship Foundation—The Woodrow Wilson Dissertation Grants in Women's Studies	6
Woodrow Wilson Women's Studies Research Grants for Doctoral Candidates	12
Young Scientists' Summer Program	14

Subject Index

Subject/Award Title — Chapter

Subject/Award Title — Chapter

Subject/Award Title	Chapter

Subject/Award Title — Chapter

Subject/Award Title — Chapter

Subject/Award Title | Chapter

Subject/Award Title | Chapter

Subject/Award Title — Chapter

Subject/Award Title — Chapter

Subject/Award Title | Chapter

Subject/Award Title — Chapter

Subject/Award Title — Chapter

Subject/Award Title — Chapter

Subject/Award Title — Chapter

Subject/Award Title | Chapter

Subject/Award Title — Chapter

Subject/Award Title — Chapter

Subject/Award Title — Chapter

Subject/Award Title — Chapter

Subject/Award Title — Chapter

Subject/Award Title — Chapter

Subject/Award Title	Chapter

Subject/Award Title | Chapter

Subject/Award Title — Chapter

Subject/Award Title — Chapter

Subject/Award Title — Chapter

Subject/Award Title | Chapter

Subject/Award Title — Chapter

Subject/Award Title — Chapter

About KAPLAN® Educational Centers

Kaplan Educational Centers is one of the nation's premier education companies, providing individuals with a full range of resources to achieve their educational and career goals. Kaplan, celebrating its 60th anniversary, is a wholly-owned subsidiary of The Washington Post Company.

TEST PREPARATION & ADMISSIONS

Kaplan's nationally-recognized test prep courses cover more than 20 standardized tests, including entrance exams for secondary school, college, and graduate school as well as foreign language and professional licensing exams. In addition, Kaplan offers private tutoring and comprehensive, one-to-one admissions and application advice for students applying to graduate school.

SCORE! EDUCATIONAL CENTERS

SCORE! after-school learning centers help students in grades K-8 build academic skills, confidence, and goal-setting skills in a motivating, sports-oriented environment. Kids use a cutting-edge, interactive curriculum that continually assesses and adapts to their academic needs and learning style. Enthusiastic Academic Coaches serve as positive role models, creating a high-energy atmosphere where learning is exciting and fun for kids. With nearly 40 centers today, SCORE! continues to open new centers nationwide.

KAPLAN LEARNING SERVICES

Kaplan Learning Services provides customized assessment, education, and training programs to K-12 schools, universities, and businesses to help students and employees reach their educational and career goals.

KAPLAN INTERNATIONAL

Kaplan serves international students and professionals in the U.S. through Access America, a series of intensive English language programs, and LCP International Institute, a leading provider of intensive English language programs at on-campus centers in California, Washington, and New York. Kaplan and LCP offer specialized services to sponsors including placement at top American universities, fellowship management, academic monitoring and reporting, and financial administration.

KAPLOAN

Students can get key information and advice about educational loans for college and graduate school through **KapLoan** (Kaplan Student Loan Information Program). Through an affiliation with one of the nation's largest student loan providers, **KapLoan** helps direct students and their families through the often bewildering financial aid process.

KAPLAN PUBLISHING

Kaplan Books, a joint imprint with Simon & Schuster, publishes books in test preparation, admissions, education, career development and life skills; Kaplan and *Newsweek* jointly publish the highly successful guides, **How to Get Into College** and **How to Choose a Career & Graduate School**. *SCORE!* and *Newsweek* have teamed up to publish **How to Help Your Child Suceed in School**.

Kaplan InterActive delivers award-winning, high quality educational products and services including Kaplan's best-selling **Higher Score** test-prep software and sites on the internet **(http://www.kaplan.com)** and America Online. Kaplan and Cendant Software are jointly developing, marketing and distributing educational software for the kindergarten through twelfth grade retail and school markets.

KAPLAN CAREER SERVICES

Kaplan helps students and graduates find jobs through Kaplan Career Services, the leading provider of career fairs in North America. The division includes **Crimson & Brown Associates**, the nation's leading diversity recruiting and publishing firm, and **The Lendman Group and Career Expo**, both of which help clients identify highly sought-after technical personnel and sales and marketing professionals.

COMMUNITY OUTREACH

Kaplan provides educational resources to thousands of financially disadvantaged students annually, working closely with educational institutions, not-for-profit groups, government agencies and other grass roots organizations on a variety of national and local support programs. Also, Kaplan centers enrich local communities by employing high school, college and graduate students, creating valuable work experiences for vast numbers of young people each year.

Pass Life's Other Tests

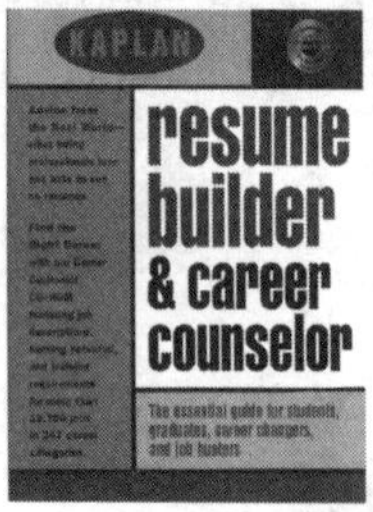

0-684-83692-0 $29.95

RESUME BUILDER WITH CAREER COUNSELOR CD-ROM

Writing powerful resumes made easy. Includes an award-winning multimedia program to match careers to individual skills and interests. A complete job-hunting package!

THE BUCK STARTS HERE: THE BEGINNER'S GUIDE TO SMART FINANCIAL CHOICES

The perfect tool to help begin managing financial life effectively. Features include painless budgeting tips, banking basics, credit cards, managing debt, and much more.

0-684-84172-X $12.00

GOING INDIE: SELF-EMPLOYMENT, FREELANCE, AND TEMPING OPPORTUNITIES

"Indies" are the savvy, self-employed workers of the 90's job market—freelancers, consultants, and other temporary employees. Combining a personalized plan for exploring self-employment options with practical tips on choosing, starting, and growing a business, this book is the essential guide to the growing "indie" phenomenon.

0-684-83756-0 $15.00

Kaplan Power Series

Whether students are preparing to take a standardized test, are polishing their communication or math skills, or just love to learn, this series provides a practical and engaging review of critical skills.

Grammar: 0-684-84157-6 $12.00
Math: 0-684-84155-X $12.00
Word: 0-684-84154-1 $12.00
Writing: 0-684-84156-8 $12.00

Make the Most of College

0-684-83757-9 $15.00

YALE DAILY NEWS GUIDE TO SUCCEEDING IN COLLEGE

The authoritative college handbook—written by students for students! Here are the vital tricks of the trade for everything from winning study tactics to surviving the social scene.

0-684-84388-9 $18.00

WHAT TO STUDY: 101 FIELDS IN A FLASH NEW!

The first comprehensive guide to help students select courses that will provide the knowledge and skills needed to meet their future goals. Includes information on over 100 fields of study, career prospects, helpful references, and more.

0-684-84170-3 $25.00

YALE DAILY NEWS GUIDE TO INTERNSHIPS 1999 NEW!

The definitive guide to finding and getting the internship that can help build a career after graduation. Includes information on over 15,000 internships at hundreds of top companies, real world insights, hot application tips, and more.

0-684-84169-X $10.00

THE "GOOD" STUDENT TRAP

A must-have resource to help college students do more than just take tests and write reports. This guide is packed with information on how to use college to plan a rewarding career when selecting courses, pursuing internships, finding mentors, and formulating career goals.

Feeling Left Out?

If your organization's fellowship or grant program wasn't listed here and you'd like it to appear in the next edition, please send the following information to the *Yale Daily News*:

- Award Title
- Organization address, phone and fax numbers, e-mail address, and Web site
- Field of Study
- Purpose of Fellowship
- Criteria
- Financial Award
- Deadline

Send by January 1, 1999 to:

Editor
Yale Daily News Guide to Fellowships and Grants
P.O. Box 209007
New Haven, CT 06520-9007
(203)432-2414/fax (203) 432-7425